In the Wake

IN THE WAKE

AN 80 DAY CANOE ODYSSEY
INTO CANADA'S NORTHERN WILDERNESS

James McNamara

In the Wake: An 80 Day Canoe
Odyssey into Canada's Northern Wilderness
© 2025 by James McNamara.

Published by Tumpline Books

ISBN: 979-8-218-38265-0

Cover design and typesetting by CoverKitchen

Contents

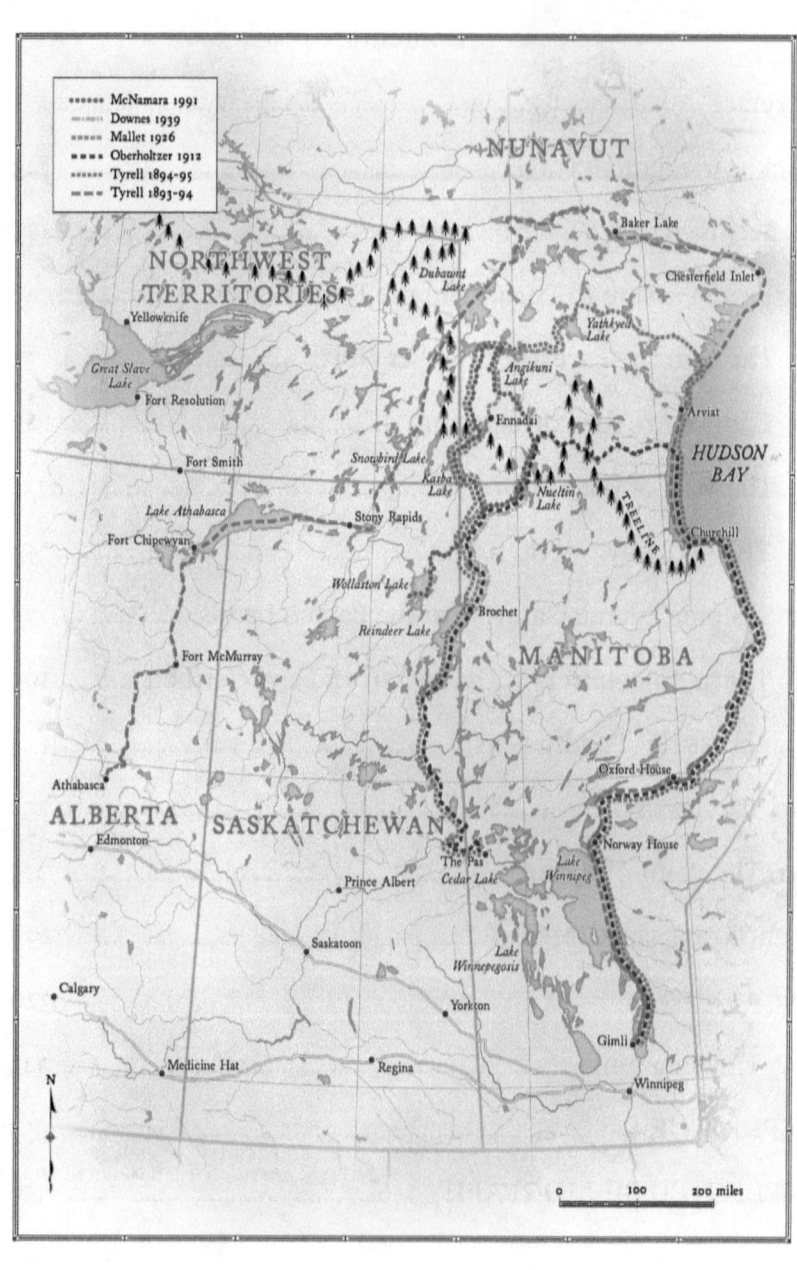

Legend:
- ●●●●● McNamara 1991
- ●●●●● Downes 1939
- ●●●●● Mallet 1926
- ■ ■ ■ Oberholtzer 1912
- ●●●●● Tyrell 1894-95
- ─ ■ ─ Tyrell 1893-94

NUNAVUT

NORTHWEST TERRITORIES

Yellowknife

Great Slave Lake

Fort Resolution

Fort Smith

Dubawnt Lake

Baker Lake

Chesterfield Inlet

Yathkyed Lake

Angikuni Lake

Ennadai

Arviat

HUDSON BAY

Snowbird Lake

Katba Lake

Nueltin Lake

Churchill

TREELINE

Lake Athabasca

Stony Rapids

Fort Chipewyan

Wollaston Lake

Reindeer Lake

Brochet

Fort McMurray

MANITOBA

Oxford House

Athabasca

ALBERTA

SASKATCHEWAN

Norway House

Edmonton

The Pas

Cedar Lake

Lake Winnipeg

Prince Albert

Saskatoon

Lake Winnepegosis

Calgary

Yorkton

Gimli

Medicine Hat

Regina

Winnipeg

N

0   100   200 miles

McNamara 1991

Dubawnt Lake

Tulemalu Lake

Yathyed Lake

Nowleye Lake

Kamilukuak Lake

Angikuni Lake

Kazan River

Nowleye River

Kazan River

NUNAVUT

North Henik Lake

NORTHWEST TERRITORIES

South Henik Lake

Hicks Lake

Ennadai

Tundra Gap

Snowbird Lake

Ennadai Lake

Thlewiaza River

Kasba Lake

Nueltin Lake

Forest Gap

Thlewiaza River

Kasmere Lake

SASKATCHEWAN

Charcoal Lake

MANITOBA

Wollaston Lake

N

Brochet

Reindeer Lake

0   50   100 miles

PREFACE

With so many people claiming to have been in the "middle of nowhere," one might suspect "nowhere" is a pretty crowded place. It's not. I've been there, and I didn't see anyone. I did talk to one person other than my wife, Laurie, during the six weeks it took us to get there, but nobody else during the six weeks it took us to get back. We met some fishermen in a cabin in our twelfth and final week. They fed us ice cream and informed us that the Soviet Union had dissolved a month or so earlier. Global politics had little impact on us where we were, hundreds of miles from the nearest road or coast with only one canoe and two and a half paddles.

On July 1, 1991, Laurie and I left our truck at the northern limit of roads in Saskatchewan, Canada, a province that stretches from the prairies along the US–Canada border to the edge of the northern forests where trees yield to tundra. We then spent eighty days paddling and portaging to the center and back of the largest roadless region in North America. When we got to our goal, we had lunch, took a photo, and then headed south in a race to return to the truck before winter. It was a challenging trip, in retrospect. We were rarely more than four-teen feet apart, the approximate distance between the seats in our canoe. We needed one another. There was no group dynamic to consider and no leader to follow when choices were tough. Nobody told us when the wind was too strong or the waves too big. There was nobody to hold us back, inspire us forward, or tell us when to move and when to rest. So we traveled every day for eighty days straight into the wind, rain, sun, or snow. There were a few days on big lakes when the wind was too strong to make any headway. So we paddled at night. We walked, too. We carried our canoe and gear around rapids and from one water body to another through forest homelands of the Dene and the tundra home of the Caribou Inuit, across trails forged by them and the traders, trappers, and explorers who came before us.

We took the trip when mobile phones were still carried in large cases with handles and global positioning systems were just emerging from purely military applications. I didn't know it then, but we were paddling into the end of an era, the time before the information revolution changed the world.

The core of this book I wrote from the perspective of a young man in 1991 when I put the first version to paper. I was longingly reflecting on a lost time in the past when the North Country wilderness hosted a community of travelers who paddled as a way of life. Today, I look at *our own trip* as one from a bygone era. We had no GPS, no phone, no outside communications at all. I now carry phones, locating devices, and electronic navigation tools on wilderness trips without apology. But I am thankful to have experienced traveling in deep wilderness before the world changed. This book is about our experience in those end times.

I wrote the first version of this book in the winter following the trip, sequestered with Laurie in a cabin buried in snow.

Mostly complete, the text sat in files on a floppy disk, an external hard disk, a server, and then the cloud, waiting for me to carve out time while Laurie and I built a family and pursued our careers. A few stories from that trip crept into the oral tradition of my life, retold over the years to illustrate adventure, perseverance, hardships, or joy. After each recollection, I wondered if I would ever finish the writing.

I came close after I spoke at the 2008 annual meeting of the Wilderness Canoe Association in Toronto, Canada. The organizer invited me when we met on an internet chat forum focused on wilderness canoe travel. I was delighted to learn that some members had heard of us from a brief mention in the introduction to the book, *Canoeing North into the Unknown* by Gwyneth Hoyle and Bruce Hodgins. I shared a stage with several authors whose books I had read and cherished. Inspiration from that event led to a new draft that circulated among those enthusiasts for a while before settling back into my digital archives to mature for another fifteen years.

The world changed between 1991 and 2024, as did my perspective. In this final version of *In the Wake*, the chronological narrative and trip details remain, but the history of the place and the context of the people who lived there, explored there, and paddled there before us became more important to the account as I discovered more about my own motivations to take the trip and to write this book. I explain this to help the reader understand why they may detect two different voices throughout the text: exuberance of youth and retrospective musings of age. I hope these voices merge well and reflect the evolution of the story and its writer.

While I'm at it, I must explain a few more things to guide the reader through this text:

The motivation. Many reasons converged to put me on the watery path north. There was the obsession to stand in remote places. The appeal of boundless wilderness that is wild by nature, not by law, mesmerized me. Indeed, the Canadian North rivals any wilderness on the planet. Then there was the compelling Indigenous history. The notion that subsistence societies overlapped in time with the new world while paddling was a way of life—this captured my imagination. I wanted to wander their camps and see their lives through the wilderness records. I also can't deny that the simple thrill of adventure drove me to go farther, travel harder than others, and match my skills against those who write books. And, of course, the pure joy of paddling a canoe on still waters, down swift creeks, and through frothing rapids filled my summer days and graced my winter dreams. But it was this last motivation that enabled all others—to be on the land and waterways that sustained so many for millennia. To paddle a canoe is the only way, short of flying, even to get a glimpse of the remote Canadian North. To paddle a canoe along the waterways of the Caribou Inuit, to drift the shores of the camps of the Dene, and to follow in the wake of the traders and trappers was my method to see and feel the community of occupants that called this wilderness home.

The route. Our thousand-mile route connected three significant lakes in three different watersheds—Wollaston Lake in the subarctic forests; Nueltin Lake straddling the forest–tundra transition; and Angikuni Lake solidly in the interior Arctic. This tundra–taiga triangle contains a compelling intersection of deep wilderness, canoe-country tradition, and Indigenous cultural history. The reader would be well served to review the geography of the region and pay attention to landmarks. Take a tour on a map. Find where the Cochrane River originates at Wollaston and follow its course to the bend where it turns south. Find Brochet on Reindeer Lake and then trace the Cochrane River back upstream to that same bend. Head straight north and locate Kasba Lake, then follow its blue lines to Baker Lake, Chesterfield Inlet, and Hudson Bay. Return to the north bend in the Cochrane River, then head northeast and locate Kasmere Lake, the Thlewiaza River, and Nueltin Lake. Last, find the line where forests transition to tundra, the treeless, frozen, and rocky plain near the Arctic Circle. This simple geographic awareness will help the reader understand our trip and the constellation of historical trips that create the foundation for this story.

The people. Although we were essentially alone, characters from the region's rich history were constant companions in my mind. I gained inspiration, confidence, and sometimes route descriptions through their stories. The title *In the Wake* honors those who created and lived that exciting past. The stories of people who lived and traveled throughout the region represent the typical progression of humans in wild landscapes, from the First Nations and early explorers to modern tourists. A few names from each stage in that progression inspired me throughout the trip and will accompany the reader throughout this story.

Let me introduce some of those characters:

Meet the geologist and explorer Joseph Tyrrell, the first outsider to travel the rivers of the interior Arctic by canoe. First explorers of wild places were typically commissioned by nations and their interests to discover lands in the New World. In the 1890s, the Geological Survey of Canada commissioned Tyrrell to locate what resources might exist in the vast, largely unexplored country between the northern forests and the Arctic coast.

Tyrrell and his crew explored the Dubawnt and Kazan rivers over two incredible years. Tyrrell identified their sources, speculated where they might empty along the coast, and headed north by canoe. His journey contained all the elements of a classic exploration story, with extreme conditions pushing the crew to the limits of human endurance in a forbidding landscape. As a fellow geoscientist and paddler, I was inspired by how his journey combined two passions—canoe travel and scientific fieldwork. His story was on my mind throughout the trip and is sprinkled throughout this book.

Meet the adventurer–explorer Ernest Oberholtzer. Adventurer-explorers are the intrepid travelers who may not have been sanctioned by nations but were inspired for their own reasons to follow in the wake of the first explorers. Ernest Oberholtzer epitomizes the spirit of the adventure–explorer. In 1912, at age twenty-six, he and one partner in one canoe set out to retrace Tyrrell's route down the Kazan and finish where Tyrrell left off (Tyrrell didn't make it to the mouth). He and his partner, Billy Magee, didn't make it to the mouth of the Kazan River either, but they did complete an astounding five-month, two thousand-mile canoe expedition through largely unknown and unmapped country along the southern margins of our route. Being a conservationist, Oberholtzer chose not to live off the land as was the norm then, but instead carried all his provisions. His story told me that an exploratory trip like the one we planned was possible for someone like me. We were the same age, had similar backgrounds, and shared a passion for the North Country and its history as seen from the canoe. If he could paddle an entire season with just one partner in one canoe, we could too.

Meet the businessman Captain Thierry Mallet. Commerce and scientific discovery typically overlapped with the adventurer-explorers while word of new markets and untapped resources inspired further exploration into the wilderness. In 1926, Thierry Mallet and his partner Del Simmons, working for the Revillon Frères Company, attempted to finish what Tyrrell started—descending the entire length of the Kazan River. They encountered the same Indigenous communities that Tyrrell had met twenty-eight years earlier. But their goal was to assess trading opportunities with the Inuit people. They didn't make it to the mouth of the Kazan River either but were forced to retrace their route seven hundred miles back to their origin due to the weather. Mallet's book, *Glimpses of the Barren Lands*, inspired me to learn more about the inland Inuit who lived along the banks of the Kazan River and instilled in me the idea that if North Country travelers ventured north into unknown country, they had to get back south against the current on their own power.

Meet the adventurer Prentice Downes. Adventurers are the travelers who push the limits of sport into newly discovered but seldom traveled country. These are the canoeists who read accounts of the explorers and saw opportunities to test themselves against those who came before them. In 1939, Downes launched where Tyrrell, Mallet, and Oberholtzer launched, but his goal was to re-explore the southern axis of the triangle between Brochet and Nueltin Lake. Unaware of Oberholtzer's trip, Downes traveled throughout the southern margins of the triangle when the people of the wilderness were leaving it. Indigenous people were moving to fixed communities, the fur trade was all but gone, and explorers had done their work. In his book, *Sleeping Island,* Downes mourned the passing of an era while trading posts that connected canoe routes were shutting down, and the keepers of tradition were vanishing. He viewed the past in 1939 like I viewed his trip in 1991 and how I view our own 1991 trip now. Downes infected me with melancholy and nostalgia for times past.

Meet us, wilderness tourists Jim and Laurie McNamara. Wilderness tourists are the travelers who follow the paths of the explorers and adventurers into wild places to appreciate the country for what it is and what it was. Motivations may be adventure, wilderness appreciation, nature, sport, or any number of personal reasons. I'm not sure where the boundary is between people like Downes and us, or even if there is one. I am sure many wilderness tourists traveled through the triangle in the decades between Downes and us, but I don't think anyone connected the route as we did. I like to think we were somewhere between adventurers and tourists. I didn't find any modern books about canoe travel based in the triangle, but I was inspired by contemporary accounts of long journeys into the Far North. In his book, *In the North of Our Lives,* Christopher Norment writes about a fourteen-month traverse of the Barren Lands north of our route, including an over-winter stay in a cabin on Thelon River, bookended by two summer-long canoe trips. Alan Kesselheim wrote about a similar journey in *Water and Sky*. Their stories motivated and reassured me, inspiring me to spend an entire paddling season as deep into the wilderness as possible.

The achievements of the previous characters were built on a foundation created by the First Nations people who preceded them. Two particular groups of the Dene and Inuit weave the people and the landscape together into a tapestry that defines my perception of the North Country. First are the Chipewyan group of the Dene Nation who occupy the northern boreal forest of Canada and historically range into the Barren Lands. The Chipewyan language, one of the Athabascan family of languages, is spoken over the largest area of any North American indigenous language. Recent studies suggest that the Dene may have been the first inhabitants of North America after migrating from Siberia about 15,000 years ago. From the first European explorer of the Barren Lands, Samuel Hearne in 1770, to Prentice Downes in 1939, and even to us in 1991, Chipewyan people guided, informed, hosted, and sometimes conflicted with seemingly every traveler who passed through that transitional country between the boreal forest and Arctic tundra.

Second, the Caribou Inuit, sometimes called Inland Inuit, "discovered" by Tyrrell in 1894 are part of the greater Inuit population that migrated from Siberia in another wave about 5,500 years ago. It's unclear when the Caribou Inuit separated and moved inland. But when Tyrrell met them, they had little contact with their coastal relatives. The Ahiarmiut, called Ihalmiut by Farley Mowat, are the subgroup of Caribou Inuit who resided in the Kazan River-Angikuni Lake region. Following a precipitous decline in their population during the nineteenth and early twentieth centuries, in 1959, the last band of Ahiarmiut were airlifted by the Canadian government from their home in the central Barren Lands and relocated to a community on the coast of Hudson Bay. No community has lived permanently in the Barren Lands since. Still, the historical presence of the Chipewyan and Ahiarmiut in their overlapping homelands create a platform for me to relate my own story to those of my heroes of the canoe.

The Dene and Inuit probably have their own heroes and legends. I only know of one, and he builds an arc through this whole story. Meet Casimir. An influential Chipewyan, Casimir's life spanned the decades from the first explorers to the early adventure tourists. He guided Tyrrell to the Kazan River, left evidence of his life for Oberholtzer to see, sketched a map for Mallet, and shared route knowledge with Downes on a chance encounter in his wilderness. His lasting influence was enough to immortalize him on our maps in Kasmere Lake (his name has many spelling variations). His actions, or those he represents, are directly or subtly pervasive throughout this story.

The vocabulary. Language in this story has evolved from the time of the early explorers to when we took our trip to when this book was completed. It is my intention to honor the Indigenous people with vocabulary that respects their identities as individuals, communities, and nations in this complex world. When quoting the writings of early explorers, I retain the vocabulary used at the time. The terms "Indian" and "Eskimo" appear regularly in these old documents, usually with the respect expected at the time. Even my own journals and writings from 1991 contain phrases that just don't feel right now. I have done my best to respect the people who saw this land first by using modern vocabulary that honors them.

The hope. In hindsight, ours was not such an epic adventure compared to the feats of today's adventurers. In fact, the thousand-plus miles we paddled are modest compared to others past and present. We paddled for an entire summer, while others paddled for years. There were no disasters, we ended with a surplus of food, and I weighed the same when I finished as when I began. But we set and achieved some big goals, saw some fantastic country, and collected a lifetime's worth of stories to tell. For sure, the trip remains one of the most significant events of my life, and I feel that this story can affect others. Just as the trip connected me to the web of northern travelers, it also connects me to those who feel as passionately about the northern wilderness as I do. I hope you come away feeling the same.

ACKNOWLEDGMENTS

It might not be customary for an author to thank the main character of a story, but I would be remiss if I did not thank Laurie McNamara, who not only paddled and portaged every mile with me, but endured thirty-three more years of chatter about publishing a book someday. Thank you, Laurie for all the miles we have traveled together.

On the shore of Wollaston Lake, David invited us into his home where he and Paula prepared our last home-cooked lunch. That meeting led to an introduction to John, which opened up the Chipewyan community of Wollaston Lake to us. Because of them, our trip transformed from a simple adventure into a purpose-driven quest. The many quotes in Chapter Two, and throughout the book come from transcripts of interviews conducted by the Office of the Prince Albert Tribal Council, bound in a manuscript entitled *Treaty Interpretation and Historical Investigations into the Rights and Interest of Chipewyan-Denesutine Bands (Saskatchewan Athabasca Region in the Northwest Territories*. Thank you David, Paula, and John.

The story would have likely faded away if it had not received a boost of energy when George Luste, a legend in Canadian canoe culture invited me to tell our story at the 2008 annual meeting of the Wilderness Canoe Association. Unfortunately, we lost George a few years later. Thank you for the inspiration,

George. I wish I had completed this in time for you to read.

Thank you, David Pelly, for sharing your vast knowledge of the north country and its people. Chapter Six shares a title with one of David's excellent books.

Three editors provided invaluable edits and insights to help me turn what was essentially a chronological trip journal of a twenty-six-year-old canoeist into a book. Thank you, Adria Perez, for the thorough developmental edit. Also, thank you to Richard Dionne for the thoughtful copy edits and your Canadian perspective, which saved me from more than one embarrassing mistake. Thank you, Tiffany Avery, for your attention to fine detail.

Thanks to CoverKitchen for your excellent work designing the book and for your patience through my many false starts.

Thank you, John Plum, for creating the beautiful maps illustrating our route and the routes of those before us.

CHAPTER ONE

SEEKING DEEP WILDERNESS BY CANOE

"There is no better way to recapture the spirit of an era than to follow old trails, gathering from the earth itself the feelings and challenges of those who trod them long ago. The landscape and the way of life may be changed, but the same winds blow on waterways, plains, and mountains. The rains, snows, and the sun beat down, the miles are just as long."

—Sigurd Olson

August 15, 1991: Laurie wandered toward the horizon where the tundra met the sky. She stooped to pick a cloudberry or examine a new flower and continued her trek, fading as the distance between us grew. She dropped over the edge of a distant hill and disappeared into the landscape, swallowed by the vastness of this barren land.

I sat in the center of an ancient circle of stones on a ridge overlooking a vast Arctic lake. The colors of water and land mixed into a blue and green scene, broken only by our flashing red canoe beached below. The treeless land rose to meet the sky in a distinct line, unbroken by modern structures. If I ran to the northern horizon and gazed toward the next, the view would have been the same—rolling tundra hills laced with interlocking waterways that enabled unlimited exploration by canoe. I would have to run to the Arctic Ocean before the scene would change. We were far beyond the boundary of the developed world in the land beyond the line.

The line slices across Canada from James Bay to Inuvik, marking the northern limit of the paved world and the beginning of the vast wilderness of the Far North. Northward, the forests yield to a treeless land stretching to the Arctic Ocean, so remotely desolate that it has the undeserved name of the Barren Lands.

I was alone in that circle of stones about as far away as a person can get from any road or coast, but I experienced a profound sense of connection to the people who extracted life from its vast expanse. We reached this Arctic lake six weeks into our trip by a six-hundred-mile circuitous canoe and portage route through the forest homelands of the Dene to the tundra homelands of the inland Inuit. That moment in the circle of stones, built by a traveler from another time, was the climax of a long physical journey and an even longer intellectual journey into the wilderness and history of the Far North.

A flash caught my eye as the sun's light glanced off the red canoe. Laurie was waiting, ready to go. I stood and breathed deeply. A herd of perhaps five hundred caribou caused a brown, shimmering wave on a distant hill to the north. More than anything, I wanted to keep paddling north. To let the current carry us downstream and the wind blow us across lakes until our paddles splashed up saltwater. But I turned my thoughts south and took my first steps toward the challenges of our return journey. We loaded the canoe, shoved off, and began the daunting five-hundred-mile upstream and overland route, southbound, back to the forests where we started.

Late July 1986: I sat on the stern of my beached canoe, feet soaking in the cold water of a lake in northern Maine. The Boy Scout troop I was guiding, lounging in their hammocks, seemed more mature than other groups. The typical camp games and moderate whitewater didn't inspire them. They came for five days of deep wilderness, and I brought them to Moosehead Lake. A wave from a motorboat towing a water skier rocked my canoe and the one next to me where the other adult in the crew sat. He was about ten years older than me—maybe thirty-one. He didn't say anything but sent a look over his shoulder that read, "You're kidding me?"

He did his best to conceal disappointment over the next two days as he talked about the true wilderness of times past. Being prone to nostalgia myself, I caught his bug. The wilderness of northern Maine inspired me, but if there was something deeper, even if it was in the unattainable past, I wanted it. I tried to express my feelings in a letter I wrote to my girlfriend, Laurie, who spent her college summers working on a strawberry farm with migrant workers in Michigan. I didn't have the words to express what I didn't really understand, and she didn't have the patience to read about how my vacation job could be better.

The idea of true wilderness took seed at that moment on Moosehead Lake and bore fruit in that circle of stones five years later. I spent the time in between, through graduate school and marriage to Laurie, crafting and pruning my own definition of wilderness, finding inspiration from the writings of those who thought deeply about it, fine-tuning it with my own trips.

I crave remoteness and the profound satisfaction when I find it. Maybe it's about a fascination with the natural processes governing this planet. Maybe it's about finding places with less of a buffer between humans and earth. Maybe it's just that I enjoy the effort it takes to stand in distant places. I felt all of that when I first worked as that canoe trip leader in Maine. The numerous lakes and rivers that crossed the land in a maze of unpopulated canoe trails provided an unlimited field of discovery for a kid who grew up where small towns and farms consumed the land. The camping, paddling, and trail companionship brought me back to that job for three seasons. I thought I had found the last remnant of pristine wilderness on Earth.

My expectations were already changing when that wise old man of thirty-one rattled on and on about what true wilderness could be. Dictionaries use words like "uncultivated" and "wasteland" to define wilderness. Cheers to the uncultivated; let's cherish this time when we still have land to waste! My definition includes size and accessibility. An uncultivated, wasting acre is not wilderness. I want large, roadless regions with no boundaries. Environmentalist David Brower called wilderness "country big enough to have a beyond and an inside to it." Parks and preserves are fine examples of nature but are small samples of what wilderness should be. I was now looking for a landscape wild by nature, not by law.

I found what I was looking for in an old, yellowed book by Sigurd Olson. It sat on a dusty shelf in what used to be a boarding house for loggers in the early 1900s and later served as the canoe base where I worked. I don't know whether a logger or canoeist left it there. Regardless, Olson's words expressed a fondness for canoe country that we all felt but lacked the depth to convey. He wrote about wanting something deeper, too. While guiding canoeists in the Quetico–Boundary Waters wilderness along the Minnesota–Ontario border, he listened to tales of those who had gone farther: "The more I heard about those places, the more powerful grew my longing, to see not only the rivers and lakes along the border, but the uncharted regions of the whole Hudson Bay watershed and Northwest Territories of Canada as far as the Arctic coast."

A fellow guide usually left Olson's book on the table in my tent when he was on the trail, with pages folded and inspiring passages highlighted. He also left an annotated book by Albert Camus, attempting to connect Olson's love of life with Camus's philosophy on life's absurdity. I responded with my own Olson passages but left Camus alone. That level of intellectual pondering was beyond me. Olson's words were simple, literal, and seemingly directed at me. For the first time, I saw in writing what I felt but didn't understand: wilderness exists and has value whether we go there or not. I was inspired to go.

Sigurd Olson led to Calvin Rutstrum and then into a tangled web of literature on the land, wildlife, and people who called the North their home. Stories of adventurers paddling into unmapped regions, encountering Indigenous cultures, excited my romantic desire to be part of the Old North, when a person had to understand the ways of the wilderness to see it. I wanted to live the lives of those early travelers who lived in times when self-propelled motion was the only way to explore new lands. But the prime of northern canoe travel was over. Even in the 1940s, Rutstrum lamented the loss of true wilderness, suggesting that "modern" canoeists can never know what he experienced. I suspect someone older than Rutstrum told him that, like that old guy in Maine who told me. But in a way, Rutstrum (or his elder) was right. After the World Wars, the Old North began to disappear. With it went a way of life. Indigenous people left the land and settled in communities. Outboard motors replaced paddles, bush planes reduced trips to distant places from weeks to hours, and the remote, working canoe routes were abandoned.

People pose a challenging conundrum in my personal definition of wilderness. On one hand, I cringe when I see people on a wilderness trip out doing the same thing I'm doing. I want the place to myself. On the other hand, I am enamored with human evidence from the past, as long as it's passed that undefined age when graffiti becomes historical art and trash becomes artifacts. Those signs instill visions of a wilderness society living by the paddle, traveling the old routes, creating the legends.

The Far North is thick with legend and tradition. In times past, a thriving community of wilderness travelers called that vast region surrounding the ring of stones home. Nomadic Dene inhabited the woodlands far to the south, Caribou Inuit populated the tundra, and a handful of adventurous explorers, traders, and trappers roamed the unbounded wilderness. Together, they developed an intricate maze of travel routes as they struggled to extract a living from the land. That was when wilderness travel was a necessary part of life, not an adventure vacation.

The canoe was a vehicle of transportation, not recreation, in a time and a place when a person's reputation was determined by the weight they could pack across a portage or by their knowledge of the vast canoe routes of the North. Stories detailing astounding feats grew into legends among a web of wilderness acquaintances. A fraternity of travelers rich with the traditions of the paddle spanned the North. That is the Old North, and the weavers of legends are gone.

That old man in Maine convinced me there was no true wilderness left, that it only exists in old books about older times. I believed that when I read Farley Mowat's *Tundra*, where he summarized several exploratory expeditions into the Barren Lands. He told stories about north-flowing rivers with headwaters far beyond the known world, Indigenous cultures living wilderness lives, and caribou herds roaming the Arctic plains. Then I studied the maps of those trips and discovered that the landscape still exists as it always had. Indeed, there is a line across the continent that no roads cross. It's a bit farther north than it used to be, but it is still there. The land beyond the line remains an uncultivated and uninhabited wasteland, wild by nature, where entire river basins lie beyond the extent of our road network. When the people of the wilderness left, no society replaced them. A few canoeists, hunters, and scientists still find their way into the region. But no towns aside from Baker Lake dot the vast expanse between the villages on Lake Athabasca straight north to the Arctic Ocean—a span of six hundred miles—or between Great Slave Lake east to Hudson Bay—a span of five hundred miles.

The Barren Lands and northern forests lie nearly as empty

of human life as when the great glacier first retreated and gave birth to that scarred and sculpted landscape seven thousand years ago. Caribou, the lifeblood of all who lived in the North, still flow in great herds across the land. Rivers that run hundreds of miles from headwaters to their mouths still flow freely over the glacier-scoured landscape. Each old track, campsite, and abandoned portage trail tells the fascinating story of this rugged land to anyone who will take the time to paddle and listen.

Angikuni Lake, the place far north of the line where Mowat visited the inland Inuit during their final years on the land, became a magnet for its remoteness, cultural history, and importance in the early exploration of the continent. Angikuni Lake is in the Kazan River system, approximately 350 air miles from the nearest road. The Kazan River traverses the Barren Lands from its remote headwaters near Kasba Lake, about 150 air miles beyond the line, northward to Baker Lake, a tributary of Chesterfield Inlet at the northwest end of Hudson Bay. Not a single road crosses the entire six-hundred-mile length.

When Samuel Hearne became the first European to see the Kazan River in 1770, its tundra banks harbored camps of the Dene Nation. A hundred years later, Joseph Tyrrell discovered a group of Inuit living along the Kazan who had no contact or traditions with the sea. Known as the Barren Lands Inuit, Caribou Inuit, Ihalmiut, or Ahiarmiut in various records, their existence was unknown to the Canadian government. I was stunned to learn about their fate.

The Ahiarmiut survived almost exclusively on caribou; they relied on the great herds for food, clothing, shelter, and even kayaks. They knew little, if anything, about any people south of their Dene neighbors in the forests when Tyrrell found them. Then, their population was around two thousand. In the following decades, the Ahiarmiut had increasing contact with outsiders from the south, primarily through the northward expansion of the fur trade. During this time, they experienced a series of tragedies that ultimately led to the collapse of their society. When Farley Mowat visited them in 1947, their numbers had dwindled to around forty people distributed among just a few families camped along the Kazan River. In 1956, the last band of Caribou Inuit were airlifted from the camps for permanent resettlement in a community on the shore of Hudson Bay. I was compelled to see their ancient homeland, paddle in the wake of their kayaks, and sleep in their abandoned campsites.

Angikuni Lake and the vast wilderness around it gave me a place to focus my wilderness fantasies where I immersed myself in a seemingly mythical landscape and absorbed the splendor of its wild, open spaces while I conducted my daily life. Gradually, the dream session became planning sessions and at some point in the winter of 1991, I acknowledged that I had to take my canoe to where the roads end. I had to cross the line.

***

There's something ritualistic about preparing for a trip. Obstacles are anticipated, joys are awaited, daydreams become visions, and visions become plans. My home office turned into a map room where I lost myself in the lore of the Canadian North. Topographic maps of the entire region covered all wall space. I plotted potential routes, computed mileages, calculated travel times, and determined river drops.

The general route evolved to encompass three anchor points with lots of uncertainty in between. Angikuni Lake was the first anchor. The canoe is no stranger to Angikuni's waters; in fact, a few Kazan River expeditions traverse the lake each year. The typical way to paddle the Kazan River is to charter a floatplane to fly to its headwaters at Kasba Lake or Snowbird Lake, paddle its six-hundred-mile length, and then fly home from Baker Lake. This flight-assisted method did not appeal to me. It would negate the whole concept of remoteness that I had longed to experience. In the past, just reaching the headwaters of remote rivers required weeks of rigorous overland travel from the nearest outposts of civilization. Few travelers ever made it beyond the limit of trees into the Barren Lands. Those who went carried the uneasy knowledge that they had to retreat south to the forest before freeze-up descended on them. There were no one-way downstream trips to awaiting floatplanes. When they returned, they had that gratifying feeling that only comes from closing the circle.

It is good that the hardships that the early travelers endured are eliminated when we fly out. We now do this for recreation, after all. But gone are the feelings of homecoming and accomplishment after a long upstream journey. Lost are the many skills of upstream travel when poling, paddling, and lining up rapids were once part of every paddler's repertoire.

I'm unsure if all this righteousness came from a place of honesty. Fact was, I just didn't have the money to fly. Regardless, the route would start and finish at the end of the road. Thus, the second anchor point became Wollaston Lake in northern Saskatchewan, the closest road to Angikuni Lake, three hundred air miles to the south.

Wollaston Lake uniquely drains toward two oceans, creating a hydro-continental divide. The Fond du Lac River flows northwest from Wollaston Lake into Lake Athabasca and then to the Arctic Ocean via the Mackenzie River system. The Cochrane River flows northeast from Wollaston Lake before turning south toward Reindeer Lake and into the Churchill River system to Hudson Bay and the Atlantic Ocean. Beyond this divide, all rivers flow generally northward and empty into the Arctic Ocean or one of its marginal seas such as Hudson Bay. Explorers returning from those north-flowing rivers faced weeks of upstream travel to headwater sources, then arduous portages over heights of land to the comfort of southward flowing rivers and the outposts of civilization that they harbored. Our route would do the same.

Wollaston Lake is home to a community of the Chipewyan band of the Dene Nation. In times past, the Chipewyan were semi-nomadic, traveling throughout the vast wilderness of the northern forest and up into the Barren Lands in search of caribou. Those times are over, but it seemed likely that there would be a canoe route north to the Kazan River for us to find. I studied maps and literature to plot the most efficient route. In doing so, I discovered what would become the third anchor point.

Nueltin Lake is approximately eighty air miles east of the Kazan River headwaters. It drains through the lower Thlewiaza River into Hudson Bay, about 250 miles south of Chesterfield Inlet, three hundred miles north of Churchill. Covering 880 square miles with a length of ninety miles, its importance in the exploration of the region, its geographic position straddling the forests in its southern reaches to the Barren Lands in the north, and the intersection of Indigenous and new world history made it an undeniable attraction.

The route connecting the three lakes creates what I called the "taiga-tundra triangle" covering approximately seven hundred air miles and connecting three roadless watersheds. The sinuous waterways and overland treks we would have to travel cover about a thousand miles. While considerable information was available in old reports about the lakes and the major rivers flowing through them, the country in between was mysterious. So we plotted our own routes using the coarse 1:250,000-scale (about one inch on paper equals four miles on the landscape) topographic maps from the Geological Survey of Canada. The triangle could be traveled in either direction. Either way would require a substantial upstream and overland return journey of about six weeks.

My pencil lines on the maps took various shapes over the months. I traced the streams we might be able to ascend and descend and connected small lakes and ponds by potential portage routes to cross watersheds. I plotted several auxiliary routes from the main loop in case we were traveling fast and wanted to see more land, and I identified all the turn-around points if we decided we could not make it back before freeze-up. I came to know the route in excruciating detail, but four particular problems consumed my attention.

First, the northwest–southwest limb of our triangle required crossing an eighty-mile forested gap between the Cochrane River and the headwaters of the Kazan River. Topographic maps show a mosaic of disconnected small ponds and streams in a thickly forested wilderness. A height of land must exist somewhere in the maze, but it was challenging to find with our rudimentary maps. How many miles could we travel each day through country dotted with lakes scarcely a mile or two long connected by portages equally as long? I could see an infinite number of potential routes through the forest, but was there an old route north established by the early travelers? If so, how could I find it? If not, could we carry our canoe through thick forests from lake to lake without trails?

Joseph Tyrrell reached the Kazan River from the south while exploring for the Geological Survey of Canada. He and his companions completed the most extraordinary exploratory canoe voyage in the history of the Canadian North, covering thousands of miles over two years. In his second summer, guided by a Chipewyan of note named Casimir, he reached Kasba Lake by first portaging from the Cochrane River northeast to the Thlewiaza River and then traveling upstream and portaging northeast to Kasba Lake. In his report, Tyrrell mentioned another "Indian canoe route" to the west through the forest over "a long chain of small lakes and portages." This was likely the route I was trying to map on my own.

The idea of reopening the "Indian canoe route" was exhilarating. It also seemed more direct than Tyrrell's route which went farther east than I intended to go. So we settled on what we would call the "pond-hopping route" through the forest gap—without opportunities like Tyrrell had to learn about the routes from the Indigenous people who developed them. Lacking that opportunity, we would instead figure it out when we got there.

Second, the northwest–east limb of our triangle required crossing a sixty-mile gap over the tundra between the Kazan River near Angikuni Lake and the north end of Nueltin Lake. Whereas the forest gap had a history of canoe travel, the tundra gap did not, as far as I could tell. I knew some explorers had been to both Nueltin Lake and the Kazan River, but I did not know if they visited them in the same season. There were some old trading posts on Nueltin Lake, and some of their trappers left records mentioning traveling in the Kazan region. Did they paddle or instead travel in winter by dog team? I could not find any hints of a paddle route between the two watersheds. Would the creeks and ponds be paddleable, or would we have to carry our gear across the glaciated rocky tundra for sixty miles? I mapped a theoretical route, but we would have to wait until we were there to know if it was possible.

The northern point of our triangle, Angikuni Lake, is near the spot on the continent that is farther than all other points from a road or coast. It is literally in the middle of nowhere. The Kazan River continues north from there. We would travel south into my third obstacle. Assuming we made it to Angikuni Lake, could we complete an upstream and overland return journey to Wollaston Lake in a reasonable time?

I had paddled upstream before, but only on afternoon jaunts for fun. Depending on the route, we would face an upstream battle of five to six hundred miles that would take us at least six weeks of ascending rivers and carrying over heights of land. We would have no firsthand knowledge about our route before attempting it. How many miles could we cover in a day? What if we didn't reach Angikuni Lake until fall? Could we get frozen in?

What if we got a few miles upstream and realized we couldn't do it? If we made it to Angikuni Lake our only bailout option would be to continue along the Kazan River another couple hundred miles to Baker Lake and hope there would be a plane to fly us south. We had no maps of the Kazan River beyond Angikuni Lake and no money to charter a plane. We would have to continue the upstream journey regardless of the difficulty.

Stories of tragic return journeys haunted my thoughts as I planned our own. In 1893, the summer before Joseph Tyrrell explored the Kazan River, he and his brother James and a small crew explored the Dubawnt River which flows into the Thelon River then into Baker Lake, west of where the Kazan River enters. They reached their northern goal but there was little time for celebration as it was already mid-September. They faced a 750-mile paddle south to Churchill on the treacherous waters of Hudson Bay. James Tyrrell chronicled the trip and had this to say about their arrival at the mouth:

> We passed out into the broad, shallow delta [of Baker Lake] and gazed over the deep blue, limitless waters beyond, the gratifying fact forced itself upon us that we had accomplished what we had started out to do— viz, to explore a route through the heart of the Barren Grounds where no other white man, if indeed Indian or Eskimo, had ever passed. We were still, of course, a long way from being out of the Barren Grounds country, but once on the waters of Baker Lake, the remainder of the road was to some extent known to us.

Still, they were 750 miles north of the nearest outpost

in mid-September with an ocean in between. That brutal trip pushed the Tyrrell party to the extreme limits of human endurance. Winter came early and trapped the explorers until they thought they would perish. Storm after wintery storm blasted the rugged shores of Hudson Bay, but they pushed on in the clearings with little food to fuel their weary bodies.

They ran out of food on September 21. They shot ducks but often could not retrieve them due to dangerous ice conditions. They tried to hunt caribou but could not reach them. They shot a polar bear, but it was starving, too. That was September 28 and they had nearly three hundred miles of ocean coastline to travel, in open canoes, in the winter freeze-up. Ice developed first in the bays then extended far out to sea, and the mist from the treacherous waves froze on their paddles. They were forced into a scramble for their lives when it became frightfully clear that they could not reach Churchill at their pace. They abandoned all non-essential items, including scientific collections, instrumentation, and most of their gear. Eight men boarded two canoes and paddled for their lives while the coast froze behind them. For ten days they struggled, living on ducks and ground squirrels.

On October 14, just a few days' travel from Churchill, Joseph was in "perishing condition" after spending a bitterly cold and wet night on the ice. They could go no further in canoes as the sea froze around them. Two brave men from the party went overland to reach Churchill while the others waited for a rescue party to arrive. A rescue party did come with dog teams and escorted the crew to the comfortable shelter of Fort Churchill where they arrived on October 19. But their return journey was still not complete.

After a short period of recuperation in the remote fort, the Tyrrell party began the final leg of their journey. In mid-November, the crew and some Indigenous guides began a winter trek of nine hundred miles by dog team and foot that brought them to Winnipeg on January 1, 1894. That seven-week journey alone would today be considered a great adventure. But its brief account in their reports indicates that these were men of uncommon will, conditioned to a life of hard adventure.

Leonidas Hubbard was not as fortunate. In 1903, he and a small crew attempted to traverse Labrador by canoe. They got off route and pushed forward too long before turning back on September 15. A month later, they still had not made it out. Like Tyrrell, exhausted, freezing, and starving, Hubbard's companions put him in a tent and raced out for help. But Hubbard's help came too late. His last journal entry was dated October 18, the same day his companions departed. In late-October, rescuers found his corpse in the tent buried under snow where it remained until his companions retrieved his body in May 1904.

Our return journey would not be as ambitious as Tyrrell's or Hubbard's. We would start earlier in the season and would be on inland waterways. Still, I didn't know anybody in recent times who had done anything similar—a simultaneously thrilling and terrifying concept.

I knew that in 1929 Thierry Mallet, a trader for the Revillon Frères company, completed the same return journey we would potentially attempt. He and his companion would have likely been the first to paddle the entire Kazan (Tyrrell didn't make it) if Yathkyed Lake, just two hundred miles short of their northern goal, was not frozen. They waited a few days for the ice to clear, but the thought of running out of food haunted them. In his report Mallet wrote, "Our caribou meat was gone. Our flour, tea, sugar, lard, and beans were very low. I tried to hunt, but there wasn't a deer in sight. I managed to kill a few partridges with a shotgun, but they were very scarce, and I had walked miles to find them. For some unknown reason, although we had a net down at all times, we couldn't get a fish, either in the river or in the pool of clear water in the lake. Finally, we had to give it up. Heekwa-Leekwa [Yathkyed Lake] had us licked. We decided to turn back."

I didn't have Mallet's report before our trip; I only knew from other sources that he returned from somewhere on the Kazan River approximately seven hundred miles back to his starting point. His report, written for *The Beaver* magazine twenty-one years after his trip, would have been of no help anyway since he lost his journal and wrote it from memory. Despite the lack of details, just knowing that someone else traveled up the Kazan River gave me confidence. What I didn't realize until after the trip, however, was that Mallet had a small outboard motor and a crew of Chipewyan guides to carry his load! We would have only our paddles, a rope, and our strength to work our way upstream.

Mallet's return journey was inspiring, but if we headed straight north to Angikuni Lake through the forest gap at the beginning of the trip, we would not return the same way. Instead, we would cross the tundra gap to Nueltin Lake and then return to Wollaston Lake along the east–southwest limb of the triangle. This limb was the most well-known section of our route. A thriving community of wilderness travelers came and went between when Tyrrell headed north in 1894 and when Farley Mowat visited Nueltin Lake in 1947. Traders, trappers, and Chipewyan families traveled the waterways from the distant camps and cabins to the trading post at Brochet. Mowat mentioned in one of his many influential books about the last days of the Indigenous cultures in the region when he and a companion traveled from a biology field station on Nueltin Lake upstream and overland to Brochet. This knowledge further inspired my confidence that we could complete a long upstream journey to Wollaston Lake if we decided to follow our route clockwise. I was certain that many other paddlers had traveled to Nueltin Lake in the forty-two years between Mowat's trip and ours, but they didn't write books or publish their stories as far as I knew. If they did, I was too disconnected to know about them. I found no new route descriptions but knowing that the old literature did have them gave me confidence that we could do it too.

The forest gap, the tundra gap, and the return journey combined for my fourth significant problem. Which way should we follow the loop? After about a week of paddling we would reach the point where the Cochrane River turns south. Near there, the old "Indian canoe route" through the forest gap heads straight north, putting us on a clockwise loop. The nearby portage route to the Thlewiaza River and on to Nueltin Lake heads northeast, putting us on a counterclockwise loop. Either way, we planned ten weeks to complete the loop and then a final week to repeat our route upstream to Wollaston Lake. Should we tackle the unknown forest gap first to ensure we could make it to Angikuni Lake quickly, but risk a longer return route across the tundra gap to Nueltin Lake and then up the entire Thlewiaza River? Or should we head northeast to Nueltin Lake first and risk getting stuck in the tundra gap?

I settled on the clockwise route in the final days before departure. I planned to leave the Cochrane River by the eighty-mile, pond-hopping route north to Kasba Lake. I knew the old canoe routes were long since abandoned, and any portage routes would be overgrown. Still, we preferred to tackle this stretch early in the season, despite the heavy load, rather than risk traveling unknown terrain while racing against freeze-up. We would paddle the length of Kasba Lake to the Kazan River and Ennadai Lake, our gateway to the Barren Lands. My interpretation of the maps showed that two rivers flowed north out of Ennadai Lake and rejoined at Angikuni Lake; they were the Kazan River and the Nowleye River. I decided to follow the little-known Nowleye River.

I hoped to reach Angikuni Lake by mid-August. We would start our return journey by ascending the Kazan River to a point upstream of Ennadai Lake where we would cross the tundra gap toward Nueltin Lake. We would then head south on Nueltin Lake to the mouth of the Windy River where we would leave the lake to avoid its notorious winds. We would ascend the Windy River to its source and then portage to the Thlewiaza River. We would then follow this river upstream, then portage to the Cochrane River to complete the loop.

Our mapped distance was slightly more than a thousand miles, a number not so impressive compared to the thousands of miles some expeditions complete in a season. But we were not following a single swift-moving river. The portaging from basin to basin and the lengthy upstream and overland return journey limited the miles we could cover. The daunting return journey, the forest gap, and the tundra gap weighed heavily on my mind while planning the trip. Given enough time, I was sure we could do each but I was very unsure about how long each would take. Each obstacle could add days or weeks to our trip and send us into early winter. We could complete the trip in ninety days, but I planned for a hundred.

***

Is it possible to carry a hundred days of food in one canoe? We usually survived on pretty meager meals on our short canoe trips, boiling some kind of noodle mixture, looking forward to the actual food we would eat when we got home. Hunger and cravings were part of the wilderness experience. However, we did not want to live like that for three months, so we devised a tasty and nutritious menu with a ten-day rotation of dinners with nice main courses, breads, and occasional desserts. We brought twenty freeze-dried dinners to cook on a stove for the month or so while on the tundra. We would cook over fires to save fuel while in the forests and use a stove while north of the tree line. Lunches would be quick snacks and peanut butter and jelly sandwiches with bread we would make the night before. Breakfasts would be cold granola cereal with powdered milk washed down with instant coffee. We would treat ourselves to a cooked breakfast of instant oatmeal, eggs, or pancakes once a week.

I planned a food budget of about two pounds per person

daily for a total target weight of four hundred pounds. I created a master list of ingredients, measured to the teaspoon and packed in bulk plastic bags and stuff sacks. Our homemade food dehydrator worked twenty-four hours a day in the weeks before our departure.

I read somewhere that small chunks of cheese can last for months if dipped in wax, so I brought home from a local deli a twenty-five-pound log of Colby cheese, maybe ten inches in diameter. Laurie boiled up a batch of hot paraffin and we spent an evening reducing the massive hunk into bite-size morsels that we would use on burritos, in soups, and as snacks.

We cut cheese rounds about an inch thick with a long blade, then sliced them into small cubes that we would hold in forceps, dip in the molten wax, and then air-dry before storing on wax paper. I watched Laurie grip the knife handle with her left hand then stand on her toes to put her weight into it as she used her right palm to force the blade into the cheese. I cringed but said nothing until her right hand slammed onto the counter after sliding off the blade and ripping across the knife's tip. She paused for a second, puzzled, staring at the fatty part of her palm just below her thumb where a cut should have been. Then it opened like parting lips; blood oozed like drool, then, well, like blood from a gaping wound.

I jumped into action, led her to the bathroom, and washed away the blood. I pinched the wound then guided her to take over while I searched for a butterfly bandage in a box of medical supplies my dad had sent. I finished the job with the calming presence of someone who rightfully earned a first-aid merit badge years ago. Confident, I then walked out of the bathroom.

The next thing I remember I found myself lying on the soft, carpeted floor with a cool, damp washcloth on my forehead. Laurie's concerned face filled my view as I gradually regained awareness.

"Are you OKAY? ... Jim?"

"Me? Are YOU OKAY? ...What?"

"You fell."

Confused, I stood with Laurie's assistance and returned to the bathroom. In the mirror I saw a bruisy cut, not quite a gash, running diagonally from my left forehead over my eye and nose, across my lips to my lower right chin. Laurie couldn't say what happened other than she heard a crack and then a jumbled thump. I had fainted, fell locked kneed into the corner of a wall, then crumpled to the ground. We soon reversed roles. Laurie became the nurse, and I became the patient.

We sat at the table, pondering what happened. I felt fine while tending to Laurie's wound. Baffled, I couldn't remember another time in my life when I reacted like that. But it happened. We laughed it off as a one-time thing. Then, while getting blood drawn for a routine health checkup, I watched the crimson fluid leave my forearm through a clear tube to a syringe, and it happened again. I fought it this time and didn't pass out, but my cool, clammy skin confirmed the humbling awareness that I had somehow become a fainter.

"You just rest here 'til you feel better, honey," the nurse said calmly as she went about her business with my precious blood.

Maybe I was always a fainter and never had the opportunity to show it. In retrospect, I couldn't remember a time when I had actually seen a nasty wound. I had never encountered the sucking chest wound that my Boy Scout merit badge trained me for or the bone poking from the skin that my fellow scouts and I knew we'd all someday face as our leaders prepared us for when we would be the first on the scene of a horrific accident.

Later, I sifted through the contents of the large box of medical supplies my dad had given us from the pharmacy he owned and operated. There were scalpels, sutures, a rib-spreader, prescription-level pain killers, gauze of varying widths, fake skin and cold compresses for burns, specialized bandages for lacerations, pokes, gashes, and the commonly cited but seldom-seen sucking chest wounds. There were splints, scissors, floss, pills, razor blades, and everything else an expert first responder could want in the wilderness. Laurie would have everything she would need to care for me if something tragic happened.

I laughed about it more than I should have over the following few weeks, trying to reassure myself that I would be fine in a crisis. Still, I knew my condition would be something to manage if I were called into action. Stay low and keep away from sharp corners.

***

Four large packs made of heavy-duty, water-resistant ballistic nylon held all our food. They were creatively named "dinner," "cheese," "lunch," and "surplus." The lightest was just twenty pounds lighter than Laurie at 110 pounds, and the heaviest equaled my weight at 135 pounds. We packed each ingredient in rubber-banded plastic bags and stored them with similar ingredients in a stuff sack, then placed them in the pack lined with a heavy-duty, six-millimeter plastic bag. The liner bag was goose-necked and sealed with a band cut from a bicycle inner tube for complete waterproofing. We were confident that our waterproofing system could handle any situation.

A fifth pack, a canvas Duluth pack lined with plastic, was supposed to hold all our clothing and gear. For clothing, I opted for a minimalist layer system from just shorts up to complete cold-weather protection. On the coldest days I would wear everything I brought except for one extra pair of wool socks and a pair of boots. Laurie opted for some extra clothing to change into at camp. I later envied her decision. For sleep and rest we brought thin foam pads rather than the more comfortable air mattresses that might pop. We also brought a three-person tent for the extra space and Thinsulate sleeping bags that could handle moisture.

We added a sixth backpack when we failed to squeeze everything in. A soup pot and a second small pot, a small Boy Scout mess kit to serve as a mini Dutch oven for baking bread, a mixing spoon, two bowls, two cups, a couple of utensils, and dishwashing supplies completed our cook kit. A tarp, a small grate for cooking over fires, a small stove and three quarts of fuel, a camp saw, rope, repair supplies, and a few odds and ends filled this pack. An ammo can held books, lighters, film, sunscreen, bug dope, snacks, and anything else we wanted to keep accessible and dry. A small dry bag filled with camera gear and more film, a shotgun for bear protection, three paddles, two life jackets, three compasses, and a map case rounded out the pile of food and gear we would shove into the canoe and carry across portages.

Portaging is a burden when accumulating miles is a goal. A

mile is a mile when you can portage in one trip. That, of course, would be impossible with our load. A mile is three miles with two trips, five miles with three trips, seven miles with four trips, and so on. Seven miles of walking for a mile of progress seemed dangerously long and threatened my meticulously planned route. Two loads, however, still seemed impossible. I reasoned we could get six packs, a canoe, and a pile of small items across a portage in three trips. Laurie would carry two food packs and the Duluth pack. I would carry the gear pack on top of the lightest food pack on my first trip (I'd seen pictures), the heaviest food pack on the second trip, and finally, the canoe solo on my third. We would strap paddles to the inside of the canoe, clip small dry bags to the large packs, and carry any excess items in our hands. We would grunt and sweat and curse our way across the trails while dreaming of the diminishing weight as we consumed the flour, lentils, beans, cheese, and peanut butter until we could condense to three trips, then two. This all seemed reasonable when I walked around with the heavy packs on my smooth, grassy front yard.

What kind of canoe can handle the lakes, rivers, and portages under the load of a three-month trip? My experiences had been with canoes provided by camps where I worked. If our trips focused on lakes, we used the aluminum Grumman canoes that were so pervasive across the North. We used ABS plastic Old Town Trippers when swift rivers exposed the canoes to rocks. The relatively new, lightweight Kevlar canoes provided a third option. While their thirty-five to forty-pound weights would be delightful on the portages, they were new on the scene so I questioned their durability. And they were expensive. I wanted something indestructible and affordable. Then Old Town offered me a cosmetically blemished Discovery 169 made of indestructible polyethylene—at wholesale cost. At just under seventeen feet, it could hold our gear, track well in flat water, and be maneuverable enough for whitewater. At ninety pounds, it would be a burden to portage. Having more strength and determination than money, we bought the Discovery.

Was it possible to complete the route within the short northern paddling season? Reports of ice cover on lakes into July in some years caused uncertainty, but a July 1 launch seemed safe. Reports of freeze-up dates varied from early to late October, meaning we would most likely be dealing with snowy weather on the way out. We would be safe if we moved fast. In late May, just a few weeks before departure, I contacted a lodge on Wollaston Lake to inquire about parking my vehicle for the season. I was startled to learn that freeze-up can happen in mid- to late-September. Without altering our route, that information haunted me throughout the trip and pressured us to travel hard.

What if things go wrong? We answered this question from friends and family by saying we wouldn't go alone. But none of our friends who were capable could commit to three months. In time, the decision made itself. We would go alone. We resolved the issue with much debate by bringing along an emergency locating transmitter (ELT). This small device simulates the distress signal of a downed aircraft when activated. I hesitated to bring it because it reinforced the idea that the modern world can find you wherever you go. With it, however, we would not be alone. Although it represented the modern world and the revolution to come, our responsibilities to each other and our families outweighed our prejudices.

John Hornby, a famed northern traveler of the early twentieth century, once said, "Northern travel is getting too easy. Soon only tourists will be traveling this land." Hornby and two companions later died of starvation after a poorly planned northern tour. Yes, northern travel is much easier than it used to be, and it is much safer. It is good that we can travel through the northern wilderness and not have to endure the hardships that the old timers faced, but something inside me longed for that time when the north was only for those who could endure. It would be foolish to deny such simple safety measures because of ego, so we brought the ELT and packed it away so I didn't have to look at it. Although this gave us some assurance, I didn't know if it would work so far out where air traffic was limited. It didn't help our case with our families when Laurie told her mother that if she didn't hear from us after four months, they shouldn't bother looking because our bones would likely be scattered under the Arctic sun (she said it more tactfully).

Should we bring a weapon? We debated about bringing a firearm to protect against the occasional grizzlies that roam the Barren Lands. There was a slim chance of needing it, but I heard enough pleas from friends and family that the whole idea was settled without question. We packed a 12-gauge shotgun which could provide protection and help secure a backup food source if need be.

***

Mid-June came fast. The trip that had been a dream was about to happen. We wrapped up our business in Syracuse, bought last-minute equipment, and fretted about the ordered equipment that had yet to come. An enormous pile of food and gear filled a corner of our living room, yet our packs had yet to arrive. Laurie was busy giving and grading finals, I was making final changes to my thesis, and we both worried about the implications of what we were about to do. Our apartment lease ended, and we would be gone too long to resume academic careers the following year. My efforts to line up work and housing upon our return failed. We left New York with nothing to return to, no home, no jobs, and little savings. All we knew was that we would live in our seventeen-foot canoe for the next three months.

Our stuff finally arrived. And the long-awaited day came when we loaded our vehicles and left New York.

We stopped in Michigan to visit family, store belongings, leave a car, and make final preparations. I spent a whole day reorganizing our gear, building "things to take" and "things to leave" piles. The things to take centered around a large tree and sprawled over most of the lawn in a pile that looked like it wouldn't fit in three canoes.

I watched Laurie attempt to move a 120-pound food pack to the take pile. She grabbed the shoulder straps, squatted, and thrust upward, intending to jerk the pack to her thigh. But her five-foot-two, 110-pound body could not generate enough force to get the pack off the ground—at all. I couldn't do much better. At five foot nine and 135 pounds, I wasn't a strong man. As a guide, however, I had developed strategies to get heavy loads on my back. We'd work on Laurie's strategy when the time came, I mused.

We experimented with different loading systems and finally, we squeezed the four food packs, two equipment packs, two small waterproof boxes, fishing gear, camera equipment, and shotgun into our small craft. It was a proud moment when I shoved the last item, our first-aid kit, underneath the stern seat. The crowning glory was my homemade, three-piece spray cover, complete with chest-high cockpits to seal out spray and waves in big water. I fastened down one side, stretched it over the immense load, and my heart sank when it stopped two inches from the gunwales on the other side. A few last-minute modifications with a sewing machine made it serviceable, but it was not pretty.

Finally, at 2 p.m., we backed the truck out of a driveway in Buchanan, Michigan, and began the 1,900-mile drive to Wollaston Lake, Saskatchewan. We dashed through the Midwest to the Canadian border, then straight north through the farmlands and prairies of Saskatchewan. Towns drifted by, each marked by the imposing tall grain elevators on the horizon. Far to the east at this same latitude, the land had already changed to the spruce and fir forests of the North. To the west, the geographical shifts from civilization to wilderness occur much farther north where the towns, the farms, the forests, and ultimately the northern limit of trees creep farther and farther north into Yukon and Alaska. Here in central Saskatchewan more to the south, the prairies gradually give way to the forests, the home of the Cree, and we soon entered canoe country.

The end of the pavement came after La Ronge, the last easily accessible community in Saskatchewan. Fifteen years earlier La Ronge was the end of the road, and the country to the north was accessible only by plane or snowmobile—canoe or dog team before that. Now, a three-hundred-mile dirt road slices through the heart of a fabulous mecca of wonderful canoe routes to Wollaston Lake. But those routes headed south while we drove north.

There were no instructions on what to do next when we reached the public campground at the end of the road on Wollaston Lake. No smiling greeters to welcome us to the North; no bulletin boards highlighting the attractions to see on our visit. We were at the line. Did the others there know they were at the edge of the largest natural wilderness area on the continent?

A sign at the check-in station asked canoeists to log their destination, route, and length of stay. The few entries per year mostly logged a few nights at various locations around the lake. Some longer trips to Fond du Lac caught my interest. However, I simply entered "the Barren Lands, two people, one canoe, returning in the fall."

A grocer in La Ronge warned that it would be difficult to find a vandalism-free place to leave our truck for three months. Several vehicles parked near a boat ramp had missing wheels and smashed windows, convincing me that the grocer was right. On the roadless side of the lake is a Chipewyan settlement. A barge travels the sixty-mile round trip daily to service the community. A barge worker suggested talking to his boss about freighting the truck to the village to leave it at the police station.

A rough dirt road ended in a gravel pit where I found a trailer that served as the summer home for the barge operator known to us as Skipper Jim.

"Come on in. Join me for some tea?" a voice asked from

inside the trailer.

Skipper Jim shared the same passion as I did for the history of the Far North. Our rambling discussion about historic travels, future trips, and life in the North led to an offer to store the truck at his place then ride the barge to the village where we would begin paddling. We gladly accepted and agreed to meet at the barge landing in two mornings.

We spent the next day repacking our supplies, adding additional food we purchased in La Ronge, and trying to put aside the nervous tension that mounted over our pending departure from civilization. It was almost a ceremonious event when I awoke and donned my wilderness garb. Here, the journey officially began as I put on my old orange-faded, wool-crusher hat that had been with me on every canoe trip I had ever taken. That second morning came quickly, and in a rush of activity we found ourselves aboard the barge with a fuel truck heading for the Chipewyan community of Wollaston Lake.

CHAPTER TWO

FROM PASSION TO PURPOSE
IN THE DENE NATION

MILE 0–25

"I once had a chance to meet with a Sayese elder. He told me in the old days things were tough, but we didn't think of it as such. The trips were long but many of us made it with just dog teams ... just like the ptarmigan they traveled all over. So if you put one of their feathers onto your dogs' harness, your dogs wouldn't mind traveling everywhere. Those are the stories I heard from my elders. So we traveled everywhere."

—Napoleon McKenzie, Dene, Black Lake Band,
May 1990

"Go home gringo!" a man about my age yelled as he rode past on an old Schwinn ten-speed.

"Excuse me?" I asked, a little shaken.

He then threw out some confusing, belligerent threats about the consequences of traveling on his land.

"Get out of here!"

"I'm leaving soon," I huffed, hoping to avoid further conflict.

"Go home now or you'll never leave!"

I wasn't going home, but I was definitely ready to leave. We would have started paddling immediately but needed to purchase a missing map from the Natural Resources office. We lingered and roamed the dusty streets of the village. Small shacks that housed the families of the Hatchet Lake Denesuline First Nation lined the way. Here, at the northern limit of our world, was a scene that resembled the back alleys (although unpaved) of most urban cities—graffiti, discarded soda cans and assorted other litter recklessly tossed about, mangy dogs sifting through garbage piles, youth roaming the dusty roads toting boom boxes. I walked past a few of the humble shelters and saw among the homes a quaint, white, ranch-style house with a plush green lawn. It was the only home in the area with a fenced-in yard, obtrusively setting it apart from its neighbors. A large satellite dish in the front yard looked conspicuously out of place next to the smoking teepees and outhouses in front of the other houses. It was the home of a police officer, a representative of the government sent to bring law and order. It stood out as an obvious symbol of the timeless conflict between old and new cultures in the north. I walked by the place trying to conceal my camera.

"We don't belong here, Laurie. We gotta get outta here!" I said.

"I don't feel comfortable here either. Can we leave now?"

"No, I didn't get the map yet. They won't be in for another hour."

Wollaston Lake is home to a group of Chipewyan, one of the five main groups of the Dene Nation. The traditional Dene territory stretched across the northern boreal forest from Hudson Bay to Alaska. The Chipewyan, also called Denesuline, occupy the eastern-most part of the territory, generally along the northern edge of the boreal forest, with Barren Lands Inuit to the north, other groups of Dene near Great Bear Lake and the Rocky Mountains to the west, and Cree in the forests to the south. The Chipewyan were traditionally nomadic until relatively recently, moving in small groups of extended families alternating between winter and summer camps. When the European fur trade came to the North, they organized into regions centered around trading posts. The group of Chipewyan living in Wollaston Lake and other nearby villages are known as the Edthen Eldeli, meaning "Caribou Eaters" in English. They speak a version of the Athabascan language, but the guy on the ten-speed spoke very clear English. I expected some curiosity, but I didn't expect hostility.

Perhaps others shared his resentment of outsiders in more subtle ways, but his outright anger and threats were not common, we were told. At that moment, however, blame for whatever conflicts existed between Indigenous people and outsiders seemed directed at me. Maybe we should have started paddling from the road.

I wanted to experience the ways of early travelers of the Old North who relied on encounters with Dene or Cree families for information about unmapped routes. It's probably insulting to the Dene for me to wish for those bygone times. The life they lived was not a wilderness vacation but a constant struggle for survival in a harsh environment. Perhaps that is why northern people sometimes seem unreceptive to transient visitors like me. Perhaps they are tired of being treated like museum pieces. Still, I could not help feeling a little disappointed when old Fords and Chevys motored by, kicking up suffocating dust storms in their wakes. Floatplanes and motorized boats lined the shores. I saw only one other canoe; a solo man paddled it in our direction.

The paddler was David, a missionary in town crossing the bay to check his mail.

"Looks like an expedition," he exclaimed, eying our huge pile of gear. "Where's the rest of your canoes?"

"There's just the one; the two of us are taking a trip north," I replied.

"That's all going in one canoe? Does it fit?"

"Well, I packed it the other day, and it all fit. I've actually never tried floating with it all, though." Saying that out loud sent an electrifying jolt through me. We were beginning a three-month canoe journey and I still had doubts about whether our canoe could handle the load.

Under scrutiny from everyone who walked past the landing, I scrambled to toss our massive pile of gear in the boat, intending to paddle off into a quiet cove where I could engineer the perfect load design. David interrogated us about our plan with hints of what I interpreted to be awe while I struggled to deadlift a pack up and over the gunwale. I grabbed the pack too high, misjudged the height, didn't have the arm strength to finish, and rolled it into the canoe with my body. I sent David an "I meant to do that" look. His nod told me his awe was actually suspicion.

"When you're ready, paddle over to that house for one last home-cooked meal," he insisted as he paddled away.

A couple of kids stood a few feet away and watched in

dispassionate silence while we piled the rest in. I settled our business with the map while Laurie found places for the things that didn't quite fit. A metal ammo can full of books was clipped to a pack strap, a bag of food that should have been in a pack was where Laurie's feet should have been. Still, we had to get off that landing.

Laurie waded to the bow and pulled while I pushed from the grounded stern. Lifting was pointless. Small curled bits of red plastic painted the gravel as we worked the boat into the water. It floated.

Old Town says the weight capacity of the Discovery 169 is 1,309 pounds. I did the math, figuring we were at about 850 pounds. No problem, this boat was designed to freight moose out of the Maine backcountry. But I wondered if I misread the specs as the boat rolled to the gunwales when I sat in the stern seat. Regardless, we were going. Like we'd done countless times before, Laurie looked back over her shoulder and asked, "Ready?"

"Let's go!"

The loaded canoe, seemingly reluctant to leave the comfort of its place, at first resisted our strokes as if still grounded. Slowly, inertia became momentum as the canoe came up to speed, maybe one mile per hour, and plowed through the water into the bay.

David's offer of one last home-cooked meal was not a draw as I was anxiously looking forward to getting this trip underway to our own fire-cooked meal. But I wouldn't pass on an opportunity to talk to a man who had an inside connection to the Chipewyan community, whose ancestors were a vital part of the story that brought us here. Another reason to meet David was, like the explorers, traders, trappers, and Indigenous people, missionaries were an integral component of the web that connected cultures through the canoe routes of Canada. And here was a missionary, working with the Indigenous people, paddling the only other canoe in sight.

***

Paula, David's wife, came to the door of their trailer. "We're so glad you came!" She beamed, opened the door, and welcomed us with an arm extended. Sandwich fixings were laid out on a table in their small kitchen.

David's awe-turned-suspicious look took on a tone of envy as we chatted about our trip. He knew the same stories that brought me north, studied maps of routes, and dreamed of days when his predecessors took long wilderness journeys to find the "unsaved" or to visit their parishioners. He may have even hinted that he wanted to come. When our vibrant conversation turned to the Chipewyan, David jumped to the phone and called his friend John, a Chipewyan from La Ronge, who was in town.

John's enthusiasm for our trip was inspiring. We chatted about the North Country, the history of the Dene people, and his own wilderness life with his family. He explained to us that we were about to travel through the heart of the historic existence of the Dene people, but a land under threat.

In times past, the nomadic Chipewyan followed the great caribou herds through forests and into the Barren Lands of the Northwest Territories. This was their homeland for as long as anyone could remember, and many families still hunted and trapped there. Theirs was a tough existence, a life of wilderness travel that depended on the whims of the caribou. In the early 1900s, changes began to take place for the Chipewyan people as contact with outsiders became more frequent. Treaties were signed and reserves were established. The Chipewyan adapted in their own way to the new world and began to settle in the newly established communities centered around trading posts. Some families maintained their wilderness lifestyle to an extent, but by the 1950s, they were no longer nomadic and had permanent homes in the villages. But the southern Barren Lands remain their ancestral home.

A group of inland Inuit known as the Caribou Inuit, now living in coastal communities, also have memories of their own history on the Barren Lands. They, too, are a people of the caribou. And they, too, extracted life from the great herds that migrated past their camps. The Caribou Inuit lived primarily on the barrens. As a result of their remoteness, contact with outsiders came late, and they lived in their traditional ways well into the 1920s. Soon, they too were enticed into abandoning their old ways and came to depend upon trade. Although the existence of the Caribou Inuit was well known to the northern traders, they remained a mystery to the government. When the fur trade collapsed, the Caribou Inuit fell on hard times. Starvation and disease spread through their camps and their population dwindled. No treaties were offered to them; by the time they were recognized as a people, they were nearly extinct. By the 1950s, the last of the survivors were relocated to villages on the shores of Hudson Bay. The Barren Lands, their home, became a land of ghosts.

When we visited Wollaston Lake, the Dene Nation was in negotiations with the Canadian government over a massive land claim by the Inuit to establish administrative control over their ancestral homeland. The Nunavut Land Claims Agreement began in 1976 when the Tunngavik Federation of Nunavut filed the largest Aboriginal land claim in Canadian history. The Inuit claimed approximately over half of the Northwest Territories, which at the time reached from Hudson Bay to the Yukon, north into the Arctic islands, and south to the 60th parallel, which far overlaps traditional Dene territory.

While Wollaston Lake is south of this border at 58.2 degrees latitude, the Chipewyan and other Dene nomads once roamed far north as part of their ancestral patterns following the caribou herds. The land north of 60 is now seldom visited but remains a vital part of the Dene identity.

The deal was essentially done when we visited Wollaston Lake in 1991, but was not signed until 1993. In those years, the Dene were implementing a major effort to document their use of the land north of the border to be part of the land act. Scores of elders who still remembered the old ways were interviewed by a consulting company working to assist the Dene. They compiled maps to show where the Chipewyan had lived, died, camped, hunted, and trapped in earlier days.

John gave us the interview transcripts and maps and asked us to help them by photographing any evidence we saw of Dene land use in the North. We were honored to accept the commission.

***

The transcripts[1] were more than just printed words. They were an open invitation into the past and present lives of the Dene people, commentaries from their point of view on the land, and their struggles to extract a living from it. I didn't get a chance to fully read the interviews until after we returned from the North, but just paging through them quickly on that day sent my imagination to places and times I had only read about earlier. Even the places of birth given at the top of each transcript were intriguing: Kegelton Lake, Sahaye Lake, many listed as unknown, a few in some of the established communities, but most on some remote wilderness lakeshore in a tent far away from the nearest outpost of civilization:

Babies were born away from the main camp. Spruce boughs were put on the ground. Once a baby was born, the mother would bring it back to the main camp. That's how most of us were born. Not like the white man.

My dreams of finding a connection to the past were being fulfilled. Many of the people interviewed were old enough to have lived and traveled in the times I had read so much about. Their words provided valuable insight into the days that held my fascination:

1Quotations in the remainder of this chapter come from transcripts of interviews conducted by the Indian Governments of Saskatchewan, Office of the Prince Albert Tribal Council, bound in a manuscript entitled *Treaty Interpretation and Historical Investigations into the Rights and Interest of Chipewyan-Denesutine Bands (Saskatchewan Athabasca Region in the Northwest Territories.* Names are excluded to protect privacy.

Wherever people heard there were caribou, that's where we lived, no matter where. If there were caribou out on the Barren Lands, no matter what the weather conditions ... we always lived like that, just like the animals we hunted. There were no boundaries in the old days.

Food, shelter, clothing, and everything they needed for survival in their wilderness world came from the animal that they recognized as their source of life. Their devotion to the land was, and is still, profound:

We treat this land in a sacred manner because it is sacred. It gives us food, water, and shelter. It gives us life. If you destroy the land you destroy the people. We want to continue living in harmony with the land and all things on it ...

When the first foreign explorers ventured into the Far North in the early 1700s, the Dene Nation covered the northern forests from Hudson Bay to Great Bear Lake and extended far north of the tree line onto the Arctic tundra, land we now think of as Inuit territory:

The first time the white people came into this country was in Fort Churchill. That's where the first trading post was. That was the time of Thainaltther, a Slavey woman [Slavey is another branch of the Dene Nation living to the west of the Chipewyan]. That must have been about two hundred years ago now. Thainaltther was captured by the Cree, she was almost killed with a spear but got away. From there she made her way to Fort Churchill. There, she was taken into the Fort. She was asked what kind of person she was. Her reply was, "I'm Dene ..." Thainaltther was asked to locate where the rest of the Chipewyan people were ... Since that time, Dene have come from all over to trade at Fort Churchill. Chipewyan from Kazan Lake to the North, the southern bands, and the western bands also made their way to do their trading.

That contact at Fort Churchill came as an outflow of the fur trade that connected Canada and its Indigenous cultures to the world. The Hudson's Bay Company (HBC) was central to those connections in the Far North. Established in 1670, England granted a corporate monopoly to the HBC to operate the fur trade in all rivers draining to Hudson Bay, an area known as Rupert's Land. That monopoly lasted two hundred years until England sold Rupert's Land to Canada, after which trading posts proliferated throughout the region, pushing deeper into unexplored country as competing companies sought to intercept Indigenous trappers closer to their homelands. Traders established canoe routes from their sources to their posts and from their posts to their trade partners. Then came the missionaries following the trade routes to lost souls, then the government seeking to formalize boundaries and agreements that had evolved through mutual use of the land.

I was oblivious to the greater sociopolitical implications of those interactions when I first envisioned a trip north. As a young American, I had never even heard of Rupert's Land. I didn't care about trapping and trading, I just saw the culture of wilderness canoeing that developed around it, the legacy of routes, and the wild lands that they led to. The interactions with Indigenous cultures was a romantic addition to the mystique of the North Country and an example of my conflicted view of people in the wilderness. A deeper awareness of the implications of those interactions came later, and was made personal by these interviews of people living when we arrived there.

At the time of first contact, the Dene Nation was strong and vast, sprawled across the Far North in several different bands. They were people of common blood but traveled the land as individual families or camps with little official tribal organization. They traveled by dog team in winter and primarily by foot in summer. They built small canoes to ford rivers or hunt caribou at the crossings, but they didn't use boats as a primary source of transportation like their neighbors, the Cree. The Dene did not live in large, semi-permanent camps like the Inuit but were constantly on the move following the migratory caribou herds. As contact increased, they became trappers for the fur companies, guides for the explorers, and middlemen between the traders to the south and the remote populations of Inuit to the north.

In 1782, a smallpox epidemic brought from the south swept through the Dene Nation and devastated their population. Small bands formed and maintained little contact with each other. The strong middlemen that the traders had relied on were no longer, and contact between the southern newcomers and northern people was lost. Many Dene moved south into Cree territory around the newly established trading posts on Lake

Athabasca in the final decades of the eighteenth century while another group clustered around Fort Churchill. These groups continued in close association with the changing world to the south. But another group of Dene remained in their homeland and continued in their ancestral ways. These are the people that came to be known as the Edthen Eldeli, the ancestors of the people we met at Wollaston Lake.

The Dene people never fully recovered from that tragic year of 1782, but for over a century to follow, the Edthen Eldeli lived their lives with little or no interference from the new world to the south. They continued to travel north of the tree line, but the far reaches of the central Barren Lands would never again be known as the land of the Dene. One band of the Edthen Eldeli who continued to live their lives north of the tree line came to be known as the Barren Lands band. Another band centered their activities around Hatchet Lake, a small lake just north of Wollaston Lake on the Fond du Lac River. By 1856, both bands were thought to "belong" to the newly built post located on Lake Brochet, about eighty air miles directly east of Wollaston Lake.

The Brochet post was built by the HBC to serve primarily as a meat supply for the voyageur brigades of the fur trade farther south. The fur trade had not yet reached the Far North, but it was not long in coming once the Brochet post was established. The Edthen Eldeli were persuaded to trade their caribou meat for goods from the south including new clothing, new foods, and new weapons. A flour and sugar diet replaced a mostly-meat diet, and the rifle took the place of the spear. In time, the fur industry realized they had a new potential force of cheap labor. They persuaded the Edthen Eldeli to hunt for fur instead of meat. This new method of survival had to be learned by the people because in times past, they did not need to trap small game. The spear provided them with caribou, and occasionally a bow and arrow provided ptarmigan or rabbit. The traders taught them to trap and bring the cured pelts to the posts. This began a new era of relations that would never end, although the Edthen Eldeli still had little actual contact with outsiders other than the few trading post managers. Many elders interviewed in the transcripts spoke of the rare occasions they saw outsiders in their youth:

> In the old days we never had too much contact with people from the outside world ... Once in a while one would come by boat ... we were amazed at their fair skin ... they set traps all over the place on our land ... we didn't know what they had come for.

But their style of living had begun to change as they became more accustomed to the peculiar habits of the newcomers:

> There were no white men when I was young. Then they came here to trap. They passed through here to travel up to the barrens. They came here only to trap. Soon, they were everywhere. Not too long after, they came to fish. After that, it was harder for us. Too many people fishing. They brought their bad habits, too. There was lots of booze. They used to use 45-gallon drums to make their brew. Since then, Dene began to pick up on their habits.

Around the turn of the twentieth century, the South began

to see the North as an untapped resource. Soon men came into the camps of the Edthen Eldeli carrying papers with promises. Another interview included:

My grandfather used to say, the white people will come from the south like a big flock of geese. Once they arrive, things will change forever.

Treaties were explained through the interpretations of a priest from Brochet. He told them that the government wanted to ensure the rights of the Dene "as long as the sun shines, and the rivers flow, and that big rock exists across the lake [Lake Athabasca]." They would be allowed to hunt and fish and live exactly as they had always done. Once a year, they could come to the post to receive the treaty obligations of supplies and money. Why wouldn't they be allowed to live on their land as they had always done? The concept of boundaries and ownership of land was strange and unsettling, but to the newcomers, unclaimed land was equally unsettling. The Dene, new to the concept of signing papers, debated for days and discussed the implications of what they were getting into. Many of the elders warned of the consequences that might arise in future. Nevertheless, they were soon persuaded:

The elders spoke highly against taking the treaty. Then, one of the party members asked an old woman if she wanted five dollars. She was told that the money could buy anything that she wanted from the store [trading post]. Old people did not get any kind of help in those days, so she took the money and that's why the rest of the people went along with it. I don't know what might have happened if she didn't take the money.

The government needed a chief to represent the people and disperse the treaty funds. The people elected Casimir, the man who guided Joseph Tyrrell northward to the Barren Lands. The Chipewyan didn't really have chiefs before the treaty. They existed in relatively autonomous family units that came together when needed to share resources. The Canadian government, however, needed centralized leaders to accept and disperse treaty obligations to the groups.

Boundaries were drawn on paper maps defining and restricting the land that they were allowed to use. The Dene now officially held land in the eyes of the government, the implications of which would not surface until much later as the land outside the treaty boundaries was unclaimed territory:

> The [C]rown said treaties should be negotiated with
> the Chipewyan for the land. Let them live on it, but
> the [C]rown will be in charge of it. So for five dollars
> a year, the [C]rown is in charge of our land.

Many of the old people remembered the days when the first outsiders came by boat with their promises, and certainly anybody of respectable age heard from their parents or grandparents of the events of those days. Nearly all elders interviewed claimed that there were never any discussions about treaty boundaries. They were simply told that the annual five dollars and supplies were given as a gesture of peace. The Dene were to continue living as they always had:

We were not asked for anything in return. The treaty commission just told Dene to ask for anything if they ever needed it, like gunpowder and basic supplies. I don't know if it was fully understood what the Dene had to give up in return. If they wanted land, probably that is what it was. But there was no mention of any transfer of lands between the whites and Chipewyan.

As word spread about the treaties, the annual trek to receive their benefits became as regular a part of their lives as their treks north to follow the caribou. Families still lived independent, subsistence-style wilderness lives but began to travel more frequently to their traplines instead of to the caribou-crossing places. People began to build cabins in the wilderness to use as base camps, especially for their traplines. Once a year, they headed to Brochet to receive their treaty money, but that was all they saw of the village:

Ever since I can recall, each summer people traveled to Brochet for the treaty. After that, they headed back north into the Barren Lands. We stayed 'til Christmas when a small party would travel back for supplies.

They still lived their rugged wilderness lives, but their independence and self-sufficiency began to diminish:

Those supplies were given as welfare .... My father told me go get a packsack to put these things in, like flour, tea, sugar, those things were given out once a year. Bacon and nets, twine and bullets, now we have welfare checks once a month. Then it was different,

my mother used to make a net with the fish net twine
... they knew how to do those things ...

The Edthen Eldeli no longer relied entirely upon their own resources, but many families lived a unique and impressive blend of lifestyles, taking full advantage of the benefits of both worlds:

> We didn't use bullets in the old days. After we left here [treaty collection] by boat up to the barrens, we hunted caribou at the crossings. Here people made dry meat, collected hides for blankets and tents. If some of the men got a few furs they came back [to trade] for supplies.

This wilderness life of partial dependence upon trade goods continued well into the 1950s. The new boom in the fur business in the 1920s brought increased contact as several new posts were established throughout the North. The Dene worked alongside the new trappers and made their living hunting fur-bearing animals or freighting supplies by canoe to the outposts (the Edthen Eldeli had adapted to the ways of the canoe, perhaps from the influence of the Cree).

The fluctuating popularity of furs in the cities had devastating effects on the people who had become hunters of fur. In the 1930s, nearly all the fur posts had collapsed and those who had become dependent on trade goods began to starve. More sickness and disease spread through the famished camps and the Dene population was once again greatly reduced:

We had two big sicknesses which killed off a lot of people. The last time, seventy elders died together, so a lot of knowledge died with them.

The government saw the hardships that the Dene were facing and established reserves. They argued that if they could get the Dene to live in one place, they would be able to assist them more easily. But some did not see it that way:

> My father told me, if you give the government what they want, they're going to keep you on a piece of land. Just like sitting in this cup. Don't give them the chance, he said. Now all our land is given away. He said someday everything will have a price. People scoffed at him. Now look.

By the 1940s, the Dene began to establish permanent camps around Brochet and other settlements such as Wollaston Lake. Over the next few decades, they abandoned their migratory ways:

> I remember it. It was only recently after we settled here in Wollaston Lake that things began to change. Houses were built, so we couldn't travel like the old days. That's why the Inuit don't see us up around Kazan Lake anymore.

Today, the Edthen Eldeli consist of five bands living in communities in northern Saskatchewan and Manitoba. The transcripts suggest both good and bad have come from the radical changes those elders experienced, but nearly all of those elders interviewed spoke of the days of their youth with fondness:

In the old days we fended for ourselves. Now, when I look back at it, I'm living in two worlds. The land is still the same, but the way it's being done is different. We never saw money in the old days ... up north .... In the old days people lived on the land off the land .... Now young people don't even think of those things ... my canoe just sits in my yard. I've asked that a new canvas be put on it, but it just sits there. It's just going to rot away ... I'm living in two worlds ... the old way and the new way ... It's hard for me to live like that ... That's why elders from today choose the food of the old ways to what they can get at the store. That's the way I am ... I'm content with just a bit of caribou ...

The "old days" that they spoke of are the days of the Old North that captured my imagination. Today, there is very little of the old wilderness life left in the Dene communities. Who wouldn't turn down life-changing conveniences? We certainly can't expect Indigenous people to continue living in the old ways when a new and safer world is right next door. Progress and development have a way of traveling on their own. Certainly, the young people who were raised in the communities have no desire to return to the old ways, just as I don't want to give up the lifestyle that has evolved with my own society. As a transient southern tourist, I'm in no position to form any sociological theories concerning the state of the Dene, but the words of the elders speak of the problems that have developed with slow assimilation to the new world. Many of the elders still held to the survivalist, subsistence-living attitude that was vital to living in the wilderness, but this attitude creates problems in community living:

We Dene were always like we are today; we survived from day to day. If you look around, that's pretty well the same as those days.

Meeting daily needs used to be a full-time act of survival. Now, the Dene have the luxury of time. This young generation is the first of the Dene that has had to think about anything other than daily survival. Even the elders realized that their daily life was easier:

People get lots of benefits today. We get help for housing, medical assistance. In the old days, there was nothing. We were poor. Some women died due to pregnancy complications. Now we get help for everything. Sure, it benefits us.

Many expressed the sentiment that with the change in lifestyle, they lost their identity. Their views of themselves changed when measured against the new wealth—money:

We didn't know we were poor. We were put on this earth to live and love this land. That's how we lived, and the people knew no other life. We didn't crave for anything. We were happy living out on the land.

The generation gap and disappointment of the elders that is typical of all societies that experience change were certainly present in the Dene community. Many elders felt that the youth abandoned their ways, while the youth thought the elders were stuck in a forgotten world:

We're still trying to live the old ways, especially us elders. I think it's been harder for us because we just live here in one place and on welfare. That's another headache for us. Those things just keep us here. The young people don't even want to hunt anymore; it's too easy for them. I only want to live back in the north. There I can do whatever I want. That's where I was raised. I don't like living here in the community.

The subsistence lifestyle of the earlier times, however, was hard. Periodic starvations, deaths from the elements, and daily struggles for survival were common:

In my younger days, when I still lived at Ennadai, I traveled everywhere in this country. After I came back [from a long journey] I found that one of my children had frozen to death. I remember I had a couple of chocolate bars for my children in my pocket. Once I had come home, I found out that the news was grim and true ... that was the time I lost two boys. One froze and the other died just as I had come home. That's what I can tell you about the old days.

There was a tone of resentment in many of the interviews. Despite the acknowledged advantages of their new life, many blamed the new world for their cultural destruction:

Right now there's mines all over the place, tourists lodges on most of the big lakes. Who's paying for the use of our land? Everything is being destroyed from us. All this started to happen once the white trappers arrived here. They started to poison the wolves, kill off the foxes ...

When we showed up in 1991, the land that these elders recalled so richly as part of their youth was being taken away. The treaty being arranged for the Inuit, who also, but not exclusively, used the land in the Far North, would strip away any rights to the land north of the 60th parallel, the southern boundary of the Northwest Territories. The Dene were being told that they legally surrendered their rights to non-treaty land despite the clear documentation of historic and recent Dene use in the North.

Political boundaries didn't exist before outsiders came north. Homelands overlapped as people followed wildlife. People lived their lives with a knowledge of where they were from and respected everyone's rights to the land. Now, territorial claims and artificial boundaries resulted in widespread anger and confusion among elders:

In the old days, we all shared the land; nobody bothered each other. The Inuit, the Whites, Dene all shared the land. We were all happy. Dene and Cree alike. Nobody talked about the land. Now everyone seems to be at each other's throats. Look in the south; there's no land for anyone anymore. Now, it seems everyone wants all the land for themselves. Because of that, even the Dene and Inuit are at each other now. If it was like the old days, we wouldn't be doing all this today.

***

John spoke quickly and intensely, standing as he explained the problem that the Dene were facing. My eyes widened, and I had to force myself to refrain from interrupting with a thousand questions. I listened, grinned at times and teared at others, until our conversation broke when he was called to other commitments.

Later in the afternoon, John brought us to the office of Chief Joe, a young man in his mid-thirties wearing the typical attire of younger people up here: blue jeans, sneakers, a nylon jacket, and a baseball cap sporting the emblem of a mining company. After the initial introductions, there was silence until the chief declared, "I hear you are taking a trip."

"Yes, we are."

Silence. More silence. Joe nodded and stared at something up in the corner of the room. I looked, then broke the silence and talked about some route problems that we had not resolved. Joe had no knowledge of the land in question but thought some of the elders might be familiar with it.

The room quickly filled with old men and we spread our maps out on a large conference table. John translated our questions to these elders who spoke no English. Soon they were lost in their own conversations about the land. Some of these men were old enough to have experienced Dene life before communities were established. They traveled the wilderness with their families and had memories that transcended the current problems of their people. Their comments reflect those in the transcripts:

I used to travel with my grandfather. One day he told me, "We've traveled a long ways and I've shown you the land. One day you're going to be a man and you're going to have to do this on your own."

Joyful expressions of reminiscence crossed their faces as their old, weathered fingers traced routes on our map with familiarity as though they had just been there this morning. Occasionally, one would burst into laughter. Perhaps they were recalling a humorous incident on the trail. This was an exciting moment as it resembled many stories of early travelers depending on the knowledge of locals to secure route information. Although this meeting was in a small office and not on the shoreline of some remote lake, the spirit of the meeting felt the same.

One old man caught my attention. Age is difficult to judge among these older people; their outdoor life weathered their faces in ways that mask their true age. He appeared to be about eighty. He could have been one of the Chipewyan who helped Prentice Downes reach Nueltin Lake in 1939, an occasion recorded in the book *Sleeping Island*. He wore thin wool trousers held up by suspenders over a dark green shirt of the same material, very similar to the clothing I wore except for the polypropylene underwear that covered my skin. His footwear told me that he was indeed a part of the Old North. He wore moosehide moccasins that extended about six inches above his ankle. These were covered to the ankle with rubbers, a specially designed overshoe to fit a moccasined foot. I wore the typical footwear seen on warm-weather canoe trips in the south: wool socks and canvas sneakers (I had calf-high boots for cold water). This old man stood silently as the other men seemed to be arguing about one particular route.

I asked John to query the men on whether anyone knew the route through the forest gap. Was the old "Indian canoe route" mentioned by Tyrrell in the memory of the men here? John said nobody goes there anymore, but the old man with the moccasins took the pencil and sketched a line through the ponds and streams from the Cochrane River to Kasba Lake along a path I would not have chosen. Learning the ancient route from the people who developed it gave me a strong connection to the place and times I thought had been lost.

We spent a couple more hours visiting with our new friends. Physically and spiritually, these people were living on the edge of two worlds. To the south was the vast new world, the modern society, a civilization to which they had full access. Medical care, education, popular music, videos, they could get it all and have adjusted their lives to accommodate the changes that have taken place in recent years. To the north stretches their vast wilderness homeland, unchanged from when they roamed its expanse. Speckled throughout the northern forests and Barren Lands are their graves, campsites, cabins, and travel routes that they knew for centuries but now lay abandoned. And in their daily lives are traces of their connection to that past. Caribou still stir their instincts for the hunt, and they still depend on that creature for survival, not for clothing or shelter, but for food in the face of extremely high grocery prices at the local store. Most cabins have teepees set up in the back for smoking their wild meat, and many families still travel north to operate traplines during winter.

The men then dispersed and we practically skipped back to David's trailer. We would have accepted his invitation to stay the night, but our meetings with John, Chief Joe, and the elders amplified our enthusiasm to get on the water. We fussed with gear, tied things down, made foot room, pointed our bow north, and at 4:30 p.m. on July 2, 1991, paddled out of town with the vigor of the first day of an expedition. Still energized by our time with the Chipewyan elders and exhilarated by our expectations for the coming months, we paddled through the afternoon and into the evening across the perfectly calm lake as the sun hung high in the northern summer sky.

***

Sometime that evening I took the first of perhaps a hundred similar pictures of the view I would have for the next few months in that canoe: ten feet of red packs stretching to Laurie's back, her arms flexing a paddle, and her long red hair tumbling out from her green felt crusher hat over her blue, army-navy surplus wool shirt. Sometimes I'd see the profile of her face as she gazed at the view or wanted to make sure I heard her words, but usually I'd hear just murmurs as she looked forward, talking into the wind, while we traveled toward the next distant point.

That evening was punctuated by long periods of silent appreciation and gratitude for where we were, and giddy chat about the scenery, the boat, and our plans to come. At around 9:30 p.m., we floated in a quiet bay, scanning a topographic map, deciding if we should find a place to camp or push past one more point. Just a few miles from town, the silence of the North Country was heavy until the distant sound of a motor grew louder. A boat entered our bay. Its engine shut down and it floated alongside us.

John and David were ending their evening fish and tracked us down on their way back to town.

"Hello!" announced John. "How's the paddling?"

"Beautiful! The calm water is nice ... gives a chance to get used to the boat."

"Well, the word is out that you've started north."

"To who?"

"The town. Everybody is excited for you. A lot of people come through here and just get off the barge, take some pictures, then leave. The elders were happy that you asked for their help and got them involved in your trip."

He couldn't know how gratifying it was to hear that, particularly after our first encounter at the barge landing. We chatted a bit more about the weather and such things important to lake travel, then David expressed some concern about our direction of travel.

"The river is that way, you know," he said, pointing in a direction off our course.

"Yup, we're a little hesitant about paddling in open water so we're sticking very close to shore until we get comfortable with this barge."

"Good idea," David said, but his slow nod expressed doubt about our navigating abilities.

Before they motored off, John, who had revealed himself to be a great-grandson of Chief Casimir earlier in the day, tossed a gallon-size ziplock bag onto our packs. I slapped it down before it skittered off and smelled what it was. The bag was full of smoked caribou meat, a bid of goodwill and a nod of approval from the Edthen Eldeli, the Caribou Eaters.

CHAPTER THREE

THROUGH THE FORESTS
OF THE FAR NORTH

MILE 25-45

"The movement of a canoe is like a reed in the wind. Silence is part of it, and the sounds of lapping water, bird songs, and wind in the trees. It is part of the medium through which it floats: the sky, the water, the shores."

—Sigurd Olson

The first strokes into canoe country always feel familiar, even if I'm launching into waters I've never seen. When I grasp my paddle, I become part of the tradition that surrounds it. It brings me all it has seen, the long rapids, the windy lakes, and the silent, magical places where its splash is the only sound. I know it's not as mystical as that. It's just that when I hold my paddle it mingles my experiences with the legends of the North Country and takes me to distant, wild places. Bill Mason called it the "path of the paddle," and Sigurd Olson called it the "song of the north." Whatever it is, it teases me when I'm away and guides me when I'm there. I wasn't consciously thinking of all those things on that evening we first paddled north, but the spirit of it all manifested in my wide-open smile. That's the way it always is at a trip's genesis.

If not for dusk, we could have paddled north into our new life for hours. As the sun hung low, we directed the enthusiasm of our first day on the water to the puzzle of finding our first night's camp. There were no established sites with picnic tables and fire rings; we could camp wherever we could find room to pitch a tent. We rejected a few sites, searching for that idyllic scene to celebrate. Our standards dropped, however, as we competed with darkness and tried to nose our bow into the thick shrubs that guarded the shoreline.

With its six hundred pounds of gear, the boat ground into the submerged rocks and sand inconveniently far from shore. We tied to a branch, found a clearing within a spruce stand about thirty yards inland, and received our first dose of the reality that we signed up for. Calf-deep in the cold lake, I struggled to extract the packs from their snug positions. We twisted, pried, and cursed the packs out of the boat for twenty minutes until we dropped them in the bushes, exhausted. On land I grabbed the straps of a food pack, slid it up my shin, and rested it on a bent knee. With an upward heave, I slipped my right shoulder through a strap and staggered under the downward force of the 115-pound load. I stumbled for stable ground as I took a few bracing steps, then teetered like a newborn calf as I searched for balance in my awkward, hunched stance. I hoisted this same pack with pride back in Michigan and strutted around the yard like a peacock. Here, the shrubs grabbed my ankles and the moss sapped my energy. I dropped the first pack without regard for its contents and returned for the next.

We collapsed with the packs a little closer to the camp site each time and left them where they dropped. Humbled, we sat in the shrubs, leaned against the packs, and giggled as darkness enveloped us.

"We might need to rethink our portage strategy," I chuckled.

"Do we have a lot?"

I studied Laurie's expression for a second, deciphering whether her question was sincere.

"Some. Not for about a week though."

I stood to get back to work, thinking we needed to have a serious discussion about our route. Laurie had been consumed with her job as a schoolteacher during the planning months. She knew how long we would be out and jumped all in on prepping food and gear. I wondered, however, if I wasn't as open about the magnitude of the trip as I should have been. She liked the two or three multi-day canoe trips she had been on, mostly for the wildlife and scenery.

She'll be fine, I thought to myself.

Laurie set up the tent while I returned for "the beast," our heaviest pack. I tried propping it upright, stooping to place my arms through the straps while still on the ground, then doing a leg press with the pack on my back. Instead of standing, I rolled over and wound up face down with the pack's total weight pressing my chest into the ground. At that moment, I discovered the tenacity and fierceness of the North Country mosquito.

The notorious bugs didn't bother us on the water. As I lay in the moss, helpless under the crushing weight of the pack, they made their domineering presence known. They swarmed and pinged off my face with ferocious intensity. I rolled the pack off my back and jumped to my feet, desperately trying to escape. A brief second of relief, then the cloud of mosquitoes followed and the night air filled with the blurred movements of a legion of bugs. The forest resounded with a deep, guttural, constant drone, the busy sounds of a billion tiny wings. If I could have separated the noise from its source, it might have served as a nice tool for meditation. A bug lodged in my ear, the forest exploded in chaos, and I lost my composure in a fit of flailing arms.

The small fire that I lit only kept the bugs away if we risked burning our faces. Hurriedly, we erected the tent and slipped inside, unzipping just enough to squeeze through for fear of welcoming the swarm in. Peering out through the mesh netting, it bothered me to see our haphazard camp. *We'll work on that*, I thought.

Mosquitoes mounted a night-long attack that mimicked the sound of driving rain on the tent. I busied myself with killing the several dozen bugs that entered the tent while Laurie tried herding them to the door to release them into the night. Our efforts, although inspired by a common goal, canceled each other out. We settled into our bags, adjusted to the wavering noise of the swarm, and took a break from the hectic events of the evening.

***

Night one. Thrilled to be on our way, we lay in the tent ecstatic over the events of the past couple of days. We told each other stories about what had just happened until we quietly drifted into our own spaces. I nibbled on some caribou jerky while Laurie wrote in her journal.

It wasn't just the excitement that kept me awake. Instead, the tightening chest and churning stomach that kept me staring at the tent ceiling late into the northern night were telltale signs of anxiety. I would come to know its many forms over the next twelve weeks, but that night it was new and puzzling. I couldn't pinpoint a specific cause; the list of potentials was too long. So I treated the symptoms and listened to the fabric of the tent respond to the breeze, pictured the tops of the pine and spruce moving together, and hoped for a loon call that never came until the sounds of the night turned to the sounds of morning.

Day two. Laurie already had the food packs opened, their contents spread across the shrubs, when I roused at 5 a.m., donned my head net, and left the tent.

"Good morning!" Laurie greeted me with excitement.

She pointed to a bowl of granola and powdered milk on top of a red pack. I added water, stirred, and enjoyed my first breakfast next to Laurie at the boat.

"Thanks. Why is everything spread out?"

"I couldn't find the dried fruit. It takes so long to sort through the packs."

Our food system needed refining, but that would wait until we were at a better site.

The lake was perfectly calm. Somewhere to the north was the entrance to the Cochrane River. In between here and there was about twenty-five miles of lake with islands, bays, and open water that enticed us to get moving.

Despite the simple camp, it was an hour before we had the

boat packed and ready to paddle. Simultaneously frustrated and amazed at the immense load, I laughed and moaned until we finished stuffing packs into their places. Laurie took her place in the bow while I pushed and dragged the canoe over rocks until it floated free. I overtopped my boot and felt the water soak my sock as I shoved off and settled into the stern. We were floating, and soon we were paddling north.

We paddled a conservative route along the eastern shore of Wollaston Lake for two days, reviving the skills that had diminished over the winter. Familiar actions and modified techniques surfaced as we strove for efficiency. But nothing was familiar about how our canoe handled the heavy load. Fortunately, the lake greeted us each morning with a glassy sheet of water that stretched northward to the horizon and gave us a chance to learn the subtleties of the balance of our craft. The gentlest waves started a slow, heavy roll to one side and then the next that lasted long after the wave passed. The slightest lean brought the top-heavy boat to its gunwales which were just a few inches out of the water when the boat was flat. We experimented with the limits of stability and gradually grew accustomed to the gentle undulating motion as we plowed through the smooth water.

We crossed larger bays and connected islands as we became more comfortable with the boat. The north end of Wollaston Lake is speckled with numerous small islands that provided the secure feeling of being close to shore even though we ventured several miles out. We repeated the same safety discussion each time we encountered a large crossing.

"Do you think it's okay to cross, or should we hug the shore?"

"I think it looks pretty good. If the wind picks up, we'll head toward that other island."

"Okay, but let's travel hard so we don't get stuck in anything nasty."

And with renewed energy, we pushed hard toward the island or across the bay until we were safe from any wind dangers. If the slightest breeze blew, I would regret embarking on "such a foolish crossing."

The wind picked up from the south around 3 p.m. on our first full day of paddling while we were in the middle of a four-mile crossing to an island. I took a few hard strokes to build momentum until we reached a smooth glide; the canoe surged forward with each stroke. I watched Laurie, as I had done many times before, dip her paddle in the water, forty-five degrees off vertical, pulling it through the water in a long, slow, arching stroke.

"Can I give you a tip?" I asked as cheerfully as I could.

"Okaaaay ... is something wrong with my paddling?"

"I'm not really feeling much back here."

"Sorry, I'm not that strong!"

"Neither am I, but there are things you can do to get more power out of your effort."

My blade caught the surface on the return stroke and sent a dose of cold water to her back. She stiffened and shrieked.

"Really?!"

"Sorry! Didn't mean that."

I dug in a couple hard strokes to feel the boat move; she kept her own style while we moved through the open water for a few more minutes until I broke the silence.

"It's just that if you held your paddle more vertical, you'd get more power," I said. "And take short pops instead of long drifts. Paddle with your gut."

"I've always paddled like this!"

"I know."

We pushed toward a small island to beat a threatening storm. Laurie quietly swallowed her pride and experimented with technique. Soon she was delivering crisp, smooth, powerful strokes. I matched her cadence until we glided into a cove on the lee side of the island.

Soon, the lake that had been so calm throughout the day whipped into a violent tossing of white as a thunderstorm moved across the water. We planned to eat dinner while waiting for the storm to pass and then travel into the evening so as not to fall behind on day one. We paced with paddles in hand along the granite shore, the wind howled as the hours passed, and darkness settled on the small island where we eventually resigned to spend the night.

The small island that held us captive rose from the lake about two miles from shore as a manifestation of the Precambrian Shield, a geologic term for the formation of igneous rocks that underlie much of the northern continent. "Precambrian" refers to the period of history before around 541 million years ago when earth experienced an explosion of animal diversity. So significant was the Cambrian Explosion that everything prior, approximately 80 percent of earth's history, is lumped into the name Precambrian. The rocks on this island are among the oldest in the world.

"Shield" implies that the region is tectonically stable,

although it wasn't always so. Eons of tectonism and volcanism produced mountains taller than the Himalayas are today. Mountain building ceased around a billion years ago before climate took over the role of landscape architect. Wind and rain eroded the landscape over time, gradually moving material from mountain tops to valley bottoms. Glacial cycles accelerated erosion until around eight thousand to nine thousand years ago, scouring and scraping rock during glacial advances, dropping sediment and sculpting canyons from meltwater floods during glacial retreat, leaving a landscape riddled with U-shaped valleys, eskers, moraines, erratics, kettles, and jumbled piles of glacial material strewn over a smooth igneous core, creating the immense system of streams, ponds, lakes, and rivers we now know as canoe country.

Inland from our granite beach, a circle of pine and spruce trees ringed the island and enclosed a small bog. Although scenic, the island offered little space for camping. We set up our tarp in the brush between some trees at the edge of the solid rock beach and spent the evening cooking over a small fire, watching the storm roll through. Periodic rain episodes hammered the tarp. Lightning flashed in the distance. We tracked the storm's movement across the vast expanse of the lake. Dark, ominous storm clouds built up in the southern sky. Long, gray steaks of rain arched to some point beyond the far shoreline.

With no room for a tent, we strung our large army-surplus mosquito netting under the tarp and nestled among the shrubs. Mosquitoes again rose from the boggy ground and overwhelmed our campsite as the evening progressed. We both spent most of the night in a fitful sleep, killing the occasional mosquitoes that crept under the netting. Without the nylon sound barrier, each hint of our activity triggered a crescendo and decrescendo of the maddening swarm. Thousands of insects searched for passage through the netting that hung just inches from my face. They grouped in masses so dense that they partially blocked the light from the bright moon.

Sometime in the night I succumbed to the temptation to smack the netting. The sky filled with the chaotic swarm while dozens slipped in. Rather than fight them, we just pulled the tandem sleeping bag tight around our faces and rolled around searching for our own defensive positions to withstand the siege, which put us nose-to-nose.

"Why didn't you show me how to paddle right before?" Laurie asked.

"Didn't really matter before."

A lingering storm thwarted our plans for a 4 a.m. departure. It had been light out for an hour already, prompting us to get moving. I had to remind myself that just because daylight was longer than at home, that didn't mean we had to paddle farther. The waves that told us to wait seemed to come from a storm that passed during the night. By 8 a.m., the lake had returned to the calm water we had known the day before. A breathless day enabled us, even at our slow and tentative paddling pace, to reach the end of Wollaston Lake and enter the Cochrane River.

***

The Cochrane River flows north from Wollaston Lake for about twenty-five miles before it meanders northeast, then turns south and flows into the Churchill River. The first thirty-five miles are more like a series of long lakes connected by short, narrow waterways. Sometime in the middle of the afternoon, we sensed a slight temperature drop, a subtle change in wind direction, and a touch of humidity heralding the approach of more storms. With these signs, we would drift, almost unintentionally, toward the shore, seeking a comfortable shelter.

The sandy beach we chose for camp was a striking contrast to the solid granite shoreline we paced along the night before. This sand was part of an esker, a ubiquitous landform in the Far North. These long, sinuous ridges of sand and gravel cross the land in patterns embracing the drainage paths of ancient sub-glacial meltwater streams. Scoured rock debris were transported in these "rivers" until the channels plugged with sediment. The results when the glacier finally melted were symmetrical, steeply sloped ridges resembling inverted river channels snaking across the terrain for miles; sometimes they reach heights two hundred feet above the surrounding land.

Neither gravelly eskers nor granite uplifts provide enough soil to support thick stands of vegetation, so the forest in the North is generally open with little underbrush to discourage off-trail wandering. The ground cover is usually a variety of mosses that are comfortable to walk on. But scattered through the open forests are moist, boggy patches that sport dense stands of trees and shrubs with a ground cover of thick, spongy sphagnum moss that sucks the energy from anyone trying to hike through it. Shorelines are often lined with these boggy areas guarding the solid ground several yards inland. On this night on the esker, however, we had immediate access to a fine campsite. With easy unloading and no slippery boulders, we sought esker campsites whenever we could.

These early camps on the first few days gave us time to experiment with methods and refine routines that would provide daily structure to our wilderness lives. I had camped a lot as a kid in Boy Scouts in the farm country of southern Michigan. We drove to nearby wooded lots and set up weekend encampments. The adults kept a fire burning all weekend, drinking coffee all morning, other drinks all afternoon and evening. We didn't hike, we just ran around in the woods, chopping down trees and burning things. We lashed poles together into tripods to hang cookpots over huge fires. We built lifeguard towers, toilet stools, tables, and anything else that might make our maximum-impact camping more comfortable. We pushed over dead trees, uprooted boulders, and rolled them into ravines. Once we found an old car abandoned in a gulch. Unsure how it got there, knowing it would never get out, we spent an afternoon smashing its windows, breaking off mirrors and doors, and beating everything dentable with clubs fashioned from the forest.

Backpacking was an exotic concept that may have been mountaineering as far as I knew back then. My first attempt at other travel-based camping away from vehicles was in a canoe-camping class in college. As the big weekend approached, the instructor didn't like the weather forecast and changed the plans. Like we did in Boy Scouts, we instead drove into the woods where we set up a base camp. Fifteen of us loaded into five canoes and paddled down a stream for a few miles until a boat tipped over. Four people in blue jeans swam to shore while the contents of their aluminum canoe floated away. They sat in the mud trying to warm up while a cold sleet fell. The instructor ran back to camp and returned with the van to pick us up. Later, around the drying fire, the instructor told stories about his time out west, hiking through the mountains for days at a time, carrying what he needed on his back. It was spellbinding. How could there be so much land to hike through that would require carrying your gear? As evening approached, the instructor asked if we wanted to get out of the rain and go into town. Why not?

He took us to a presentation by someone from my home-town (Lansing, Michigan) named Verlen Kruger who had just completed a three-and-a-half-year, twenty-eight thousand-mile canoe trip connecting almost every major river in the country. How was this possible? Kruger and his partner Steve Landick started in the headwaters of the Missouri River and then followed it until they worked their way into and across the Great Lakes. They followed the St. Lawrence Seaway to the Atlantic Ocean, and then paddled the entire east coast around the tip of Florida and along the Gulf of Mexico to the mouth of the Mississippi River, which they then paddled *up*. They worked their way through Canada to the Arctic Ocean, and then down the entire Pacific coast and around Mexico's Baja Peninsula into the Gulf of California to the mouth of the Colorado River, which they also paddled *up*. They eddy-hopped upstream through the Grand Canyon, then across the Midwest to Lake Michigan and the mouth of the Grand River, which they followed *up* to Lansing where they ended their trip.

I was transfixed, but Kruger's trip was so massive that it didn't occur to me that anything remotely similar was possible, or even desirable. We drove back to the woods to sleep in our soaked tents and complete the trip for our one college credit.

The instructor's stories were also intriguing. Are there really places where a person can just wander off and camp anywhere? How does someone even know where to go? Even if I knew where to go, there was no way I could pay for such an extravagant trip. I asked the instructor if it was possible to work in the wilderness; he suggested applying to be a guide for a Boy Scout High Adventure base. I learned what I could through the mail, and I applied to the little-known Maine High Adventure Base where I thought I would guide hiking trips in the Appalachian Mountains of northern Maine. It wasn't until our guide-training trip that I learned I would be a canoe-camping guide, which put me on a path that eventually led to Laurie and me sitting by this fire in a sandy esker campsite en route to the most remote region on the continent.

My camping techniques had evolved considerably since those early days. Still, the prospect of living in the wilderness for up to one hundred days with whatever we stuffed into our canoe was simultaneously exhilarating and intimidating during those first days and nights as we honed our routines.

We tried to rise early in the morning, which would have been tough to decipher without a watch. The sky in the hours between sunset and sunrise turned to a dusky gray that seemed always ready for the new sun. The first one out of the tent, usually Laurie, would prepare breakfast, which was often a light meal of granola or oatmeal, a hot drink from the boiled water that we stored in the thermos overnight, and a few handfuls of dried fruit. On rare days, when we didn't feel pressured by time, we had powdered scrambled eggs heavily spiked with Tabasco and powdered potatoes.

The second person up packed the tent's contents and emerged to a prepared breakfast. We milled about, moving slowly to escape the mosquitoes while lifting head nets to swallow our food and discuss our goals for the day. We tore down camp after breakfast, filled the packs, and loaded the boat. Laurie took her usual seat in the bow, I in the stern, and we paddled off into whatever plans we had for the day.

This morning's routine took about an hour to an hour and a half. If the weather was threatening, we might move faster or wait to see if it would calm. We aimed to get on the water around 7 a.m. so we could get as many miles in as the midmorning winds picked up. Sometimes we packed and paddled before breakfast to get on the water earlier. We could usually remove head nets after about fifteen minutes on the water when our personal clouds of insects dissipated.

The day's events varied according to the travel conditions. We typically stopped a few hours into the day to eat breakfast bars that Laurie had thoughtfully stashed. By midafternoon, we were ready for another stop. Lunch usually consisted of bread cooked the night before with peanut butter and jelly and a handful of "good old raisins and peanuts," or gorp. Our mixture contained a healthy proportion of M&M's, so we dubbed it "mm-gorp," and it became somewhat of an addiction for me as it was the only treat to satisfy my sweet tooth. Laurie filled a rigid plastic container with a week's supply of mm-gorp and regulated my doses. Later in the afternoon, we'd have another snack break with a bar of some kind. I nibbled throughout the day on the dried caribou, which lasted the entire trip.

Each day brought challenging navigation problems as we

learned the limitations of 1:250,000-scale maps. Large islands provided positive location points, but our maps blurred many minor features. Sometimes small islands would be shown as one large island, and other times islands weren't recorded at all. I kept the map and compass strapped with shock cord to the thwart before me and kept a constant eye on our position. We would fix our position on the map, plot a line from where we were to where we wanted to go, measure the bearing, adjust for magnetic declination, then let the compass point to our intended destination. Islands and bays blended into one hazy horizon from a distance so the views looked nothing like the picture on the map. But as we followed the course toward our goal, ignoring the small islands that did not appear on the map, the scene would gradually unfold, and we could identify our desired point by shape.

Our ideal time to camp was around 5 p.m., but we rarely stopped that early. Pressure to travel just a bit farther around the next bend kept us moving. Early in the trip, when the traveling was particularly difficult, we often traveled until 8 p.m. Then we would fall into a tough cycle of traveling late, sleeping in, then traveling late again to make up for the late morning. This style of travel left little time in the evenings for relaxation.

Selecting a campsite depended more on access than anything else. Flat tent sites and good views took second priority to the need for a safe place to unload the boat. We would paddle up to a potential spot on the shore, and one of us would get out to scout the location. If it was favorable, we began unloading immediately. We tossed the loose items ashore, and then I would usually pry the first pack free and load it on Laurie's back. We hauled the rest of the packs, dragged the boat to shore, flipped it over, and tied it down. We dropped the food packs where the kitchen would be and the Duluth at the chosen tent location. One person became the tent-and-wood person; the other was the cook. I set up the tarp if the weather looked threatening.

It seems a simple thing, setting up a tarp, but I've always regarded it as an engineering challenge, a skill that every North Country paddler must master. A quick, serviceable job can be done by haphazardly stringing it up between some trees. But a solid, weatherproof shelter crafted to shed wind and rain is a pleasing symbol of old-style campcraft like in the old books that filled a shelf at home. I like the skill and tradition of doing it right.

A tarp is just a square piece of material with some tie loops and grommets. Still, you need rope; and you need to know how to tie a good knot. I run a long rope along the centerline of the tarp, tied through the edge grommets with a half hitch. This centerline rope will take the stress of tension instead of the tarp so that the tarp will not get stretched out of shape. The ends of the rope are then tied to trees. On one tree, I use a clove hitch, a bowline, or some other secure, non-adjustable knot that I feel like tying. To the other tree, I tie an adjustable knot. A taut-line hitch will work, but I prefer a trucker's hitch that can be tightened down and will not loosen over time. The trucker's hitch should be finished with a slippery half hitch so it can be untied with a simple yank. If there are no convenient trees to serve as anchors, poles or paddles can be used by tying a clove hitch to the pole immediately next to the tarp so there is no slack. I use taut lines or figure eights to secure the ropes to the stakes. The tarp can take a typical A-frame style or canopy-type structure from this position. The A-frame is fine if the centerline is high and the weather is not too stormy. But I usually prefer a canopy so I can build a small fire at the tarp's edge. Maybe I spend too much time worrying about proper heat retention from the fire, calculating drainage points, and constructing the most efficient geometry. But the finished tarp is something to admire for its function and style. During storms, I sit in front of my fire under the tarp's protective shelter, listen to the patter of the harmless rain, and watch the run-off fall away from my gear. If my tarp fails, I can still hear the rain inside our new, wind-proof, free-standing, semi-domed tent.

While one person arranged dinner, the other collected wood before setting up the tent and arranging the bags and pads. When Laurie was on dinner duty, I admit I often took a bit too long to test which end of the tent our heads should lie.

"Jim, what are you doing?"

"Oh, uh, I'm almost done. The zippers on the sleeping bags are stuck."

We laid the foam pads on the tent floor and zipped our two sleeping bags together. We placed the Duluth pack, now containing only our clothes, in the vestibule, and arranged our rain gear on top for easy access in the morning. Journals placed near our heads, a candle lantern hanging from the ceiling, assorted loose items in their familiar places, and home was ready for the evening.

After building a fire, the cook boiled water to fill the thermos for morning and to cook the evening meal, which consisted of a main course and some bread. Main courses were built of a primary grain (rice, lentils, couscous, barley), bean (powdered refried, powdered black, dried pinto), and cheese. Together with a collection of spices, dried vegetables, and sweets, we had a menu of ten different dinners and four soups to build from ingredients packed in bulk. This method saved space and pre-trip preparation over individually packed meals, but shopping for ingredients from the packs added time at the end of our long days. Still, this routine allowed for creativity with our meals.

Our typical bread was the traditional bannock occasionally spiked with nuts, garlic powder, or any berries we could find. Sometimes we splurged and made banana bread with home-dried bananas, cornbread, cinnamon rolls, or whatever we could invent. We usually made an extra loaf of bannock for lunch. If the main course was some kind of soup, we would plop the dough mixture into the soup to make dumplings instead of bannock. On those nights we made chapattis (fried cornmeal and flour patties), or tortillas for the next day's lunch.

Bannock is just a big, pan-fried biscuit, but it's as much a part of the North Country environment as the spruce that burns to bake it or the mosquitoes that inevitably end up in the mixture. With the availability of better-quality quick meals, bannock has fallen into the class of ancient relics, like the tumpline for carrying loads without shoulder straps, and the pole for traveling upstream. But it remains a mainstay in the paddling diet for those who still wear wool, use a pole, and sometimes even tump loads.

We tested most traditional methods described in the old books before we settled on our techniques. An old Boy Scout mess kit that I bought when I was ten worked wonderfully as a mini, 8-inch-diameter Dutch oven. We spread a thin dough mixture in the greased bowl and covered it tightly with the frying pan. Sometimes we'd bury the kit in coals to cook slowly. Usually we needed it faster. Laurie kept the pan on the grate over a low flame or far to the side of a moderate flame. She rotated the pan every few minutes to ensure even heating, occasionally checking it by poking a twig into the center until the twig came out dry. She consistently produced smooth, lovely, golden-brown loaves. The flavor was enhanced by the simmering anticipation as she cooked it to perfection. This took too long for my liking. I placed the pan on the grate directly over the hottest part of the flame and shuffled it around like popcorn until just before I thought the bottom would burn. Then I took it off the heat, removed the lid, and used a rock or log to lean it toward the flame to brown the top. My bannock wasn't as aesthetically pleasing as Laurie's; it was usually lumpy and partly burned on the bottom. But I had hot, edible bread within seven to ten minutes of mixing the dough. It was always done in the middle— and with enough squeeze-bottle margarine, we couldn't taste the burned parts.

When the food was prepared, we would find comfortable spots on the ground under the tarp, maybe lean back against a pack, and enjoy a relaxing hot meal. The smoke that gathered under the tarp usually kept the bugs away enough to eat without our head nets on. We began evening chores immediately after eating. Dishes had to be washed and food packs packed to ensure a quick morning. I storm-proofed the tarp, Laurie arranged the packs in a neat cluster, and we inspected camp for stray items.

We didn't hang our food in "bear bags" like we typically did on our week-long trips in the south. Even if the scraggly trees in this region offered limbs to suspend them, the spindly append-ages couldn't support the hundred-pound packs high enough.

Despite being useless for supporting food packs, these sparse, sometimes sickly-looking trees are as characteristic a signature of the northern forests as sand dunes are in the desert or wheat fields in the prairies. Wherever I am, my thoughts drift northward when I see their image. I envision the distinct silhouette of a tall jack pine leaning over a sloping peninsula of granite that extends into a small lake; a canoe beached on the smooth, weathered shore; up the slope, the granite yields to the spruce and pine forests; its floor is carpeted with moss, and the smoke of a woodsman's campfire hangs low in a clearing. The trees provide shelter from the wind, fuel for the fire, and back-rests for the weary traveler. Alone, a jack pine appears homely and unappealing, but a forest full creates a comforting shelter from the open waters. From a campsite, the dispersed straight trunks of trees lead the eye into the hidden recesses of the forest. As the sun dips low, long shadows merge into darkness, and the forest at the edge of your clearing becomes a mysterious place. The dark shapes of the trees against the starry sky mark the boundary of your home for the night.

Instead of hanging, we packed our food in a way that we thought would not attract bears, then set the packs on the ground at a safe distance within earshot of the tent. We sealed everything in plastic bags, tried to keep an immaculate campsite, and counted on the supposed scent-proof packing and a bear's natural fear of humans to keep our food safe. Some people who use our same method recommend dispersing the packs far from the site. We chose to keep them all together, mainly because we didn't feel like moving them again by the time the boat was unloaded and the packs set down. Plus, if we could hear any intruders, we might be able to frighten them away.

We camped near some fishermen on our third night while still on Wollaston Lake. They told us that every night for a week black bear invaders rummaged through their gear searching for fish scraps and even broke the canopy on their boat. That night, we did what many old timers recommended and strung our cooking pots between the packs to make noise if they were disturbed. We went to sleep knowing that we would either wake up confident in our system or fretting about requiring a new one. All night, each harmless noise of the forest had us ripping open the tent door, ready to catch the intruders in their vandalous act. But each time, our flashlights shone on the silent and undisturbed packs. That night, as all others on the trip, passed without a problem. The neighbors' camp, however, was ransacked again. We later abandoned the extra hassle of stringing the pots as we gained confidence in our method.

I'd walk to the water's edge most nights, before slipping into the tent, to determine the wind direction (the only meteorological observations I could make), and craft a statement like, "Hmmm. Winds are picking up a bit from the northeast; looks like we might get some rain by midafternoon." Each correct prediction was a testament to my expertise, and each failure resulted from being "new to the region." In the Far North in early summer, the wind typically comes from the southwest. As the season progresses, it shifts around from the north. This little bit of valuable information helped us plan our days, but my predictions weren't really as useful as I would have liked. We would use them to decide what side of a lake to be on, but generally, we proceeded as usual until the event, predicted or not, actually happened. I think my attention to the weather was really just an acknowledgment of our dependence on its whims.

Inside the tent, we hung all of the damp clothes in the mesh gear loft, arranged our clothes for the morning, then settled in for our journal time. Before we slept, we reviewed the previous day and discussed our goals for the next. We rarely read our entries to each other except for factual updates. Laurie would give her count of how many eagles or loons she saw until those sighting became too commonplace. I studied the maps, calculated our daily mileage, and computed how far we had to go the next day to keep on track. My last thoughts each night were usually about upcoming route decisions.

***

It seemed as though an entire season had passed during that night at our first esker camp. A cold, sleety rain fell, and the wind blew straight off some still-frozen lake to the north. I regretfully didn't bring a thermometer, but it's easy to identify freezing when the falling rain carries an occasional snowflake. We lingered in camp until midmorning, encased in rain gear, knit hats, and gloves, waiting for conditions to change while the skies grew darker and the wind blew stronger. Neither of us could tolerate losing a day so early in the trip since we expected even harsher conditions later. The mile width of the river was not enough to build threatening waves, so we loaded the boat and paddled straight into the screaming wind and icy rain.

Rain beaded and drained beautifully off our Gore-Tex rain jackets, but I wished we hadn't bought the cheapest ones we could find from a mail-order catalog. The extra cost for sleeves that cinched tightly around the wrists would have been welcome. When paddling, the raised grip hand exposed a funnel that caught just a few drips with each stroke. After the first water molecule finds exposed fabric, its companions follow. The wicking nature of polypropylene, sold as a benefit to draw sweat away from the body, pulls the relentless drips from the wrist to the elbow, then to the shoulders and chest and back. The damp base layer under an otherwise dry fleece extracts heat from the body, which slows down to conserve energy then shivers to warm up. Paddling technique suffers when keeping the grip hand low, and by keeping the head bowed to the wind to avoid a similar invasion at the neck. We float, battered by the elements, approaching listlessness, until we heed Sigurd Olson's advice to "remember, no matter how cold and wet you are, you're always warm and dry."

Attitude goes a long way toward overcoming adversity, but so does good gear. My homemade spray cover for the canoe was invaluable. I designed it to keep out waves so we could paddle in big water. The more important benefit that emerged, however, was the warmth it retained for our lower bodies and feet. With the spray cover tunnels cinched around our waists, our Gore-Tex jackets properly adorned, and our comfort levels adjusted, we were a solid, buoyant unit, confident in the most challenging conditions. We paddled hard in the wind and rain, generating warmth which in itself inspired more motion. In time, we learned to greet all conditions with a joy that comes from embracing the environment around us so that only unsafe, not uncomfortable, conditions slowed us down. Still, when one of us would slip and complain about the conditions, the other would throw out the line about adjusting comfort levels. The conversation would usually degrade from there. Sometimes it's fun to wallow in perceived misery.

"Suck it up! Cal Rutstrum would have been fine in his wool shirt and waxed cotton jacket."

"Cal Rutstrum can ..."

"Hey now, be careful who you curse!"

Maybe Rutstrum and those travelers sat out in this weather. After all, they did not have the gear that we have today. In fact, he wrote about traveling for months with only his camp kit, a rifle, some fishing line, bannock mix, and a bag of sugar!

The North Country has seen changes, but some things have remained as steadfast as the granite of the Precambrian Shield. Wind. On this fourth day of our journey, the sleety rain fell nearly horizontal, directly into our faces. We took the small waves head on as we inched forward. Landmarks on shore lingered next to the canoe indefinitely. One particularly twisted and gnarled birch tree off our bow caught my attention just before I lost myself in a bizarre daydream about the fifteen years of my future life until a strong Arctic blast sent some sleet down my collar. I snapped out of it and noticed the same birch tree I saw a lifetime ago. Each stroke took full exertion as the canoe nudged over the next wave, then a quick paddle recovery before we blew backward.

We traveled the shoreline and set goals of distant points

to seek shelter from the wind. By 3:30 p.m., we had progressed a meager four miles and rested in a small cove at a narrows before a large lake. After a short break, we paddled into the open water where there were much larger waves coming from a more threatening angle. Progress did not seem worth the effort so we decided to stop and try again later that evening or early next morning. The most promising campsite, and the safest location to reach, was at our last rest site a hundred yards back.

We held our position in the rolling waves, waiting for the right moment to pivot the boat. A large crest threw Laurie's bow high; then I followed as she plunged into the trough. Water poured over the gunwale and collected on the spray cover in Laurie's lap. A few more waves rolled through while we learned their frequency. Each wave was as good as any other to make our turn, so we readied ourselves. We rose on the face of the chosen wave and then executed the maneuver.

"Okay, sweep!" I yelled to Laurie as I performed a strong reverse sweep.

We spun on the wave crest, then plunged into the trough sideways. The next wave hurled us skyward, then a rapid series of whitecaps came out of frequency and our maneuver was cut short. The wind hurled us toward the boulder-choked shoreline at an alarming rate. Large waves sloshed under the spray cover and water began to fill the boat. Before we could pivot entirely, we crashed into the boulders hidden by the waves about thirty feet from shore. The boat broached on a large rock. Powerful waves complicated our effort to paddle away and repeatedly lifted us up and dropped us down onto the rock. We both leaped into the water to push free. Sharp boulders came to the surface, but the depth of the frigid water between the rocks was to my waist. The shoreline was unapproachable through the rocks and our attempt to push away resulted in more water crashing into the boat. Explosions of white drenched us as we aligned the boat into the waves, jumped in, and paddled hard away from shore. The water sloshing up to our calves magnified the boat's instability. Now in deeper water, we dared not turn again. We ferried away from shore and let the wind blow us backward while leaning heavily to avoid capsizing. After the wind blew us past our desired landing point, we paddled hard forward until we reached the quiet shelter of the cove.

An hour passed under a tree, then another under a hastily pitched tarp, then another next to a fire, until we abandoned thoughts of paddling further. With smoke and warmth collecting under the tarp, Laurie fanned the flames, stood, and with a joyful cheer said, "Happy birthday!" before walking into the rain.

***

Laurie shopped for ingredients from the food packs while I rendered dry wood from the soaked forest to keep the reluctant fire burning.

"Okay, get out!" she commanded from under the tarp so she could prepare a birthday meal.

I was twenty-six and a few days into the only plan I had for my future. It was early enough in the trip that I would still think about things other than our daily goals. I took the maps to the tent to study routes but lost myself in various versions of my future, pondering my fate.

Maybe I would return to graduate school to complete a

PhD. I was a decent undergraduate student but not particularly talented. I started college as a pulp and paper engineering major thinking I would spend my days walking around in the trees assessing their potential to be turned into paper. I accepted an internship in the North Maine Woods of as an environmental engineer, but eventually figured out that working as an environmental engineer for a paper company dealt more with effluent from the mills than trees in the forest. I went to Maine that summer but took that job as a canoe trip leader instead. I changed my major to geology, intending to go to graduate school to study hydrology, then work as an environmental consultant, whatever that meant. But I needed a 3.0 GPA. Somehow I finished a math minor without ever really understanding what calculus was. Those classes did irrevocable damage to my GPA. Then I aced the geology major in three loaded semesters and eked out a final GPA of 2.997. Close, by my standards, but not by those of many graduate schools. Fortunately, one professor who felt that my talents were not reflected in my early grades called a colleague and wrote a glowing letter of recommendation and I moved to Syracuse, New York. There I discovered that research can be a career. I dug deep into my thesis topic, inspired by the integration of geology, biology, and ecology that studying water in the environment requires. I finished my degree in two and a half years, then spent a final semester converting my thesis to a scientific publication. I was hooked. I wanted to be a research scientist. I left Syracuse knowing I would return to graduate school but not knowing where or when. I'd figure that out later. Tonight, however, I enjoyed the uncertainty and the fantasies about what career I might have until I heard:

"Ding ding ding ding ding … That's a dinner bell in case you can't tell!"

Back under the tarp, Laurie produced a steaming stack of hand-made tortillas, refried beans, and a creative salsa made from dried veggies, reconstituted tomato leather, and spices.

Laurie doesn't suffer from uncertainty. She took a French class as a freshman in high school. She loved the teacher, loved the topic, loved kids, and never once questioned her desire to be a French teacher. Sometime during college she'd added a Spanish major and an English certification. At twenty-six, she had already acquired and quit two jobs for me; once to leave her beloved northern Michigan to come to Syracuse, then another to paddle a red canoe to the most remote region on the continent. She would join me again wherever I ended up, of that I was certain.

Wax that I peeled off a few chunks of beautifully preserved cheese sizzled in the fire. Something baking filled the tarp with a delicious aroma while we ate our backcountry burritos and chatted about the day, the weather, and our plans.

In a few days, we would need to make a decision that we had already made and remade—clockwise or counterclockwise around the loop? Our plan was to go counterclockwise, northeast to Nueltin Lake then northwest to the Kazan River and Angikuni Lake, then make a straight south return journey. But we started to acknowledge that we might not have time.

"If you had to choose … would you go to Angikuni Lake or Nueltin Lake?" Laurie asked.

"Why?" I knew what she meant but asked anyway.

"I think … if we keep this pace, we might not have enough

time to do the loop." Hesitantly, she continued. "If we picked one, we could go for it, but just turn around if we're going too slow."

I came to the same awareness but didn't acknowledge that it was decision time. I didn't answer. It felt like I was making a preemptive decision to give up on the full loop on just day five. I made another burrito and poked at the fire while Laurie carried the hot baking pan balanced on two sticks to the other side of the packs. She returned a couple of minutes later with a beautiful chocolate pudding cake made from melted M&M's, adorned with a few burning candles, and delivered with a light-hearted poem that perfectly captured our ambitions, the evening, and our melancholy mood before it vanished into the past, as oral traditions do.

"Angikuni. Let's take the pond-hopping route north after the Bigstone portage," I said. "It might be a hard week."

CHAPTER FOUR

CANOES ARE FOR PORTAGING

MILE 45–125

"Almost imperceptibly the trail led down the ridge, and it was then I caught the first sight of blue, just a glimmer through the trees but enough to take away the weariness and fill me with the same old joy I had known thousands of times in the past, an elation that never grows old and never will as long as men carry canoes and packs along the waterways. In spite of the labor, it is this that makes portaging worthwhile. There is no substitute. If someone transports your outfit for you, it is lost."—Sigurd Olson

"Anyone who says they like portaging is either a liar or crazy."

—Bill Mason

In 1936, Sigurd Olson published an article in the *Minnesota Conservationist* called, "The Romance of Portages." In it, he lamented the "artificialization" of his beloved canoe country in northern Minnesota as the Civilian Conservation Corps set about straightening, smoothing, and otherwise improving the portage trails connecting backcountry lakes to make them more accessible. Olson viewed portage trails as evidence of humanity's deep association with wilderness as they provided connections to the travelers from times past. He cautioned that altering these monuments from the days of the past disturb values that can never be replaced.

I believe him. A worn, but rough trail that hints at times past is far more intriguing than a trail newly graded and graveled. However, the difficulties we had simply unloading the boat and carrying packs to camp every night tested my faith. On the night of July 7 there was some excitement, but no romance, in our conversation about the upcoming portage around Bigstone Rapids, a two-mile stretch of whitewater.

We spent that evening camped on a small island about eight miles before Bigstone Rapids, sorting gear, devising the most efficient way to pack for the portage. The load felt immense. Then it occurred to me that we would face Bigstone a second time on our return journey in the fall. It made sense to lighten the load and leave a cache.

I liked that word *cache*. It shows up in old stories and explorers' journals documenting long wilderness journeys. Caches left by travelers or their acquaintances sometimes months or years earlier served as beacons of hope as the weary traveler struggled to escape the wilderness.

Theirry Mallet strove for his own cache on his retreat from the Kazan River in 1927. With rapidly diminishing food supplies, his report stated that the "last four days were grim." Fortunately, they found a cache that Mallet had placed by dog team the winter before. They feasted for a day then continued their upstream journey refreshed and rejuvenated. Maybe we'd need a similar gift to ourselves in our final week to get back to Wollaston Lake.

A quarter mile from shore, the small island would be a great bear-proof place to cache a week of food. We sorted through our supplies for two hours, thinned out the excess, and eliminated about thirty pounds of food, the useless bug net, some other non-essentials, and a Bundt-cake pan that a how-to book said would be useful for baking bread. We left the non-food items loose on the ground and suspended an army-surplus waterproof bag of food between two trees. Satisfied with its height, we repacked the supplies and loaded the boat. A few pounds off a hundred-pound pack doesn't make much difference. They all felt the same. Still, knowing the packs were lighter made the prospect of the upcoming portage easier to take.

The time we spent building the cache robbed us of a brief stretch in the morning when the wind wasn't howling. Its direction was consistent, but ours wasn't as we followed the bends of the wide Cochrane River. The wind came from our sides, bow, and stern, forcing us to adjust our strategy, trading lee or windward shores to minimize exposure to open water. When the waves came from the side, we followed a zigzag to keep our bow or stern at forty-five degrees to them. We paddled out into the rolling waves until we were uncomfortably far from shore, then we would pivot on a crest and surf back toward shore, adding miles and time but keeping dry, except for the incessant drizzle of the day-long storm.

The uneven load of our boat compounded the difficulties of paddling in the wind. Our bow-heavy load, forced by space restrictions, acted like a wind vane. This was wonderful when the wind came head on but so frustrating when the wind came from anywhere else. Steering was more keeping a line in the moment rather than reaching our goal. We battled and cursed the wind, continually changing our technique to rest weary parts of our bodies until the river bottle-necked and the entire volume of water poured through a narrow channel where we stopped. This was the beginning of Bigstone Rapids.

Laurie spotted a cut log jammed upright in some boulders in a small bay on river left. It was midafternoon, a couple hours later than I had hoped. The windy paddle sapped our strength. Still, I trotted down an overgrown path scouting the way. Glimpses of the river confirmed that assessing the rapids would be a waste of time. There might have been paddleable stretches between bigger rapids, but this path was here for a reason. I sat for a moment on a damp, moss-covered rock listening to the wind and the rapids, enjoying the opportunity to take a break in solitude. I knew Laurie was probably huddled in a wind-break doing the same. Revived and inspired by this next phase, I strolled back to the boat where Laurie had a bannock peanut butter and jelly sandwich for me. We could have camped if there was a pleasing option, but it was too early in the trip to relax for more than those brief moments. It was 4:30 p.m. At just under two miles per one-way trip, we could complete the ten miles by nightfall if all went according to plan.

I helped Laurie load her pack and gave her two paddles to lean against. Her back was parallel to the ground while she waited, her head between her hands gripping each paddle. I hoisted the Duluth to my back, balanced the supply pack on top, and grabbed my camera bag in one hand, keeping the other free to balance the two-pack load. We wandered over the spongy moss until we located the trail, then I darted away. Within minutes, the boggy, wet trail sapped all energy from my legs, and the leather pack straps of the Duluth dug deeply into my shoulders. I used the tumpline to relieve some pressure, but the pain did not dissipate. *That's okay*, I thought; the pain of the portage is nothing new. It's a part of wilderness canoe tripping, and that's what we came to do. That attitude disappeared down the path and with a desperate lunge, I had to free myself from the burden and rest. Laurie was nowhere in sight. I sat silently, envisioned the remaining load, and got my first inclinations that we might not finish this portage. Concerned, I walked back and found Laurie about fifty yards from the beginning of the trail, hunched over, clutching her chest with tears in her eyes.

"Jim, my chest hurts. This is too heavy!" She was struggling to speak.

She carried one of the heaviest food packs, probably 110 pounds. With an ammo can full of books in one hand and a dry bag in the other, she had no way to adjust the immense load.

"Are you having a heart attack?" It was all I could think to say. She was panting hard, had turned pale, and could barely speak. "Let's get that off you!" Her pack was heavier than mine, too heavy to set down gently. A shoulder strap dragged her to the ground when I dropped it. She breathed deep, composed herself, and asked, "How far up did you drop your pack?"

"Not far. Maybe I can carry all the packs and you just get all the hand items."

"No, that would be dumb. I'm going to finish this, but I

need my hands free."

I helped her load her pack on her back again. She hitched it up and tightened the waist belt. The pack, a few pounds heavier than herself, rested on her lower back and slid to her butt; the shoulder straps kept the pack from falling backward. Focused, she leaned over, arms dangling low, upper body nearly parallel with the ground, and waddled away. I walked back to the boat to get the beast. We didn't cache much from this pack; it still probably weighed around 130 pounds. I surprised myself by hoisting it alone, buckling the waist belt, grabbing two spare paddles, and stumbled along.

The shoulder pain was intense, but I hardly noticed it over the pressure on my hips that felt like they would pop out of joint at each step. After ten paces, I had to stop and convince myself that this load was not unbearable. Laurie's slow, steadfast pace was impressive compared to my sporadic thrashings. I leaned forward, took off at a brisk pace until the pressure and pain built to a maximum, then stopped, bent entirely over to rest, and burst forward again. I dared not set the pack down for fear I could not shoulder it again. Once, I bent forward too far and let the momentum of the top half of my body carry farther than the lower half until the mass drove my knee to the mud, then my chest to the gravel. My extended arms did nothing to slow the fall. The pack pinned me like a mean uncle who takes a game too far. In time, I reached Laurie resting where I dropped my first load. Two more shuttles each got the whole load together, except for the various hand items that had been discarded along the way. Laurie returned to retrieve those while I went ahead with the next phase.

A long, brutal haul brought us to a calm bay about halfway

through the portage where I dropped my pack. I turned back and found Laurie about three-quarters the way down the path, sitting with that same exasperated "heart attack" look.

"Just leave it there; let's go back and get another load and I'll get this one later," I said.

By 8:30 p.m., we had everything except the canoe at the halfway point. I was too exhausted to return for it. Unfortunately, I had left my nice, hand-crafted, comfortably padded shoulder blocks at my birthday campsite a few nights earlier. Consequently, I had to carry the boat with just the bare wood of the center thwart on the back of my neck. I wore my lifejacket for padding, but the ninety-pound boat dug into the top of my spine. I couldn't do it again that evening, so it spent the night where I dropped it.

We camped in a boggy clearing with the tarp pitched over the entrance of the tent to shelter a small fire from the drizzly rain. We made a quick mushroom soup dinner and enjoyed the bug-free atmosphere in the smoke that collected under the tarp. The background rumble of the rapids seemed a sharp contradiction to the calm, misty bay we could see. Two loons floated into view. My awareness heightened, anticipating their eerie, satisfying call. It never came. They went about their business while we went about ours. Despite the long day and late hour, we stayed up late chatting and planning, alternately reliving the joy and pain of accomplishment and hard work.

I wrote in my journal that night:

It's funny how at the end of the day when the pack and paddle are laid to rest, and a snug camp is built, the pains

of the day are instantly gone. The quiet of the forest over-
whelms me and I feel renewed as if I never needed to stop.
Every evening is thoroughly enjoyable, despite the weather
or conditions of the day .... I've looked over what I've
written, and it seems I've only recorded the hardships. We
are having a grand time. The wilderness provides freedom.
We have food and time. We can do whatever we want.

We wanted to make progress. So we decided to leave another cache to eliminate as much weight as possible. We would sort that out in the morning. We had other things to talk about.

"We need to do four trips," I said, breaking a long silence as Laurie stirred the coals.

"Or five!"

"Yeah. That would add too much time. This is the longest portage we'll have for a while. And the packs will get lighter."

"It's just so crushing," Laurie bluntly stated. "I mean ... I can do it. I'll do it. But I think I'd go faster with lighter loads on more trips."

A fourth trip would add 40 percent more distance; a one-mile portage increases from five to seven miles. But the quicker pace, and more importantly, the improved attitudes, would make the portages tolerable.

More importantly, the eighty-mile pond-hopping route to Kasba Lake, with at least thirty portages, began the end of the Bigstone portage. Even with four trips, that many portages seemed insurmountable with our full load. We changed our plan once again.

Rather than tackle the forest gap now, we would portage into the Thlewiaza River system toward Nueltin Lake. If need be, we could abandon the primary goal of reaching Angikuni Lake and turn around at Nueltin Lake. This would still be an epic trip retracing the route of the traders, trappers, explorers, and Indigenous people who forged these routes north. We would have stories to tell. I justified this to Laurie, but I knew that if we reached Nueltin under challenging conditions, worn out, and ready to be done, I would push it to Angikuni anyway as summer turned to fall. Laurie knew it, too.

A warm, sunny sky greeted us in the morning, adding to the feeling of a new beginning, although we had half of the Bigstone portage to complete and our canoe was still stashed along the trail. We relaxed over our first hot breakfast: powdered eggs, a side of instant oatmeal, and instant coffee.

Refreshed and enthused, we split tasks and got to work. I retrieved the canoe while Laurie redistributed food, intending to eliminate thirty more pounds. When I returned, I saw squeeze bottles of margarine, hunks of cheese, a few cups of every type of grain we carried, and a larger-than-necessary bag of mm-gorp set aside from the pile.

"It's not much, but I just don't think we can afford to leave more," she mused.

"We'll be in big trouble if our survival depends on that little amount of food."

I looked forward to shedding every possible pound, so I packed the discarded food in a bag and slung it hastily from one of the few amenable trees. I considered suspending the bag between two trees because there were no branches long enough to place the bag far from the trunk, but didn't want to leave that much chord behind. The bag, and the mm-gorp it held, dangled out of reach from only the shortest bear as we prepared for the second half of the Bigstone portage.

We worked through the portage in two stages, four trips in each. On the first trip, we each took one of the light(ish) equipment packs with assorted hand items. On the next two trips, we each took a food pack with perhaps a paddle, and then we tandem-carried the canoe on the final trip.

The loaded carries were long, but the return trips often seemed longer, perhaps because when carrying a pack, it took all our mental energy to convince our bodies to keep going. Hunched over, I strained to raise my head high enough to get a long forward view. The springy pace of the first few minutes faded each time as the expected pains found their way to their proper places. It helped to readjust the load from my shoulders, hips, and back, but I eventually searched in vain for a non-tender spot. The crushing weight of the pack passed right through my back, translated through the femur, right to the knees that jarred with each lumbering step.

With seven trips across a trail, familiar landmarks emerged to mark progress. A pile of bear scat marked the first quarter, a downed tree across the trail was about halfway, a deep, mucky section that gripped our ankles was about three-quarters, and a funny-looking white blob of some kind of fungus meant only two hundred yards to go. It helps to grunt at every other step, establishing a rhythm. A glimpse of the water through the trees temporarily motivates, then the pack gets heavier at that damn fungus as the finish takes longer than it should. Restless impatience turns to anger at those landmarks, my rhythmic pace collapses, and I shuffle bent-kneed until my body fails coincidentally and luckily at the end of the trail.

Liberated from the weight, my back straightens, shoulders expand, and I breathe deep. The sweat chills my relaxing body as I sit on the pack, a prized trophy of my accomplishment. It doesn't feel right to rest while Laurie is still working, so I trot back where I find her taking a standing break in the muck.

"You're done already?" she asked.

"Yup, it's not far," I crowed. "Lookin' good!"

There might have been a tear in her eye, but she smiled, propping up her body with two paddles, knees locked under a pack heavier than herself.

"How far to the mushroom?"

"Minutes! You got it!"

I grinned, watching her painfully but cheerfully shuffle away. *She'll be fine*, I thought. We got this.

I suppose Sig was right, there's something romantic about walking these old paths. On the lakes and rivers I can *sense* a connection to those early travelers. On the portages I can *see* it. My footprints build on previous footprints maintaining the worn path built by the Chipewyan, explorers, voyageurs, adventurers, and us. We carried mostly food. Others could have carried anything imaginable. On the working freight-canoe teams employed by the trading companies, men were explicitly employed as packers. The tool of the trade was the tumpline, two eight-foot straps of leather connected with a canvas headband. The straps bound their loads, which could have been crates of ammunition, sacks of flour, a wood stove, bales of fur, or anything to support life and trade in canoe country.

The standard load for the voyageurs employed by the trading companies was two ninety-pound bales of pelts. The load rested on their backs, supported by the canvas headband. In one story, a trader working a remote post four hundred miles west of Hudson Bay, ordered some fine china to make the cabin nicer for his family. When a few plates arrived broken after being transported for an entire season across the lakes, rivers, and portage trails, he complained to the HBC that the portage men of the day weren't like they used to be.

I felt like a packer when I carried our Duluth, a canvas duffel bag contoured to stand upright in the canoe. It had leather shoulder straps and a tumpline attached to the upper corners. The Duluth pack was a signature piece of gear for those who knew the ways of the North. There's hardly a more pleasing image of the North Country than an old canoe beached on a granite shore with a faded Duluth crumpled next to its bow. When I put it on my back, adjusted the headband to take the load off my shoulders, and strode down the trail, I felt a bit of that romantic connection to those packers. But within minutes, I wondered why it took so long for the world to invent hip belts. Give me a couple of bales of fur and I'll stuff them in my modern Grade IV portage pack with a hip belt, padded shoulder pads, and adjustable suspension system and trot on down the trail. Well, give me one bale and I'll get it there with less complaint than if I used a tumpline.

Regardless of those old stories, I was proud of our work on the Bigstone portage. We finished it at 5:30 p.m., one mile of forward progress, and camped where we dropped our load.

Lentil chili, bannock, and tea by the fire.

My journal entry that night records a modified version of a familiar refrain:

It's funny how when you lay your pack and paddle to rest, the hardships of the day disappear, and we settle into the splendor of the North Country.

***

July 10: Twenty-one miles! Marvelous day. Hard work followed by a wonderful dinner at an excellent campsite ....

July 11: Fantastic North Country day! Seventeen miles, two portages, ran three rapids ....

Our skills and confidence coalesced after Bigstone in ways that let us experience the grandeur of the wilderness as we worked down the Cochrane River, which had narrowed to a width that actually deserved the label "river." The weight of our gear challenged our whitewater paddling technique. Still, we ran several minor rapids, portaging when we had to. Once or twice we portaged only our gear and then paddled the empty canoe through fun, technical, but manageable rapids. Exhilarated, the warm, sunny weather inspired us to spend long, hard days on the water, knowing that the northern sun would still be high late into the golden evening. Laurie eventually stopped recording the number of bald eagles she saw as they seemed to appear around every bend.

On July 12, we aimed to make it to the north bend of the Cochrane where we would begin the portage route to the Thlewiaza River. During the afternoon, the morning's clear skies clouded over, the wind died, and the water became perfectly calm. The pastel blues and grays reflected on the water from the overcast sky were disturbed only by the parting wake of our boat as we silently glided along. After seventeen miles, we pulled up to a beautiful sandy beach to camp. It was 4:30 p.m., our earliest time yet. We considered pushing on but faced a long portage in just a few miles, so we opted to enjoy the evening.

Two loons floated together in the calm water as we went about our camp business. Although we had seen loons daily, we had yet to hear their eerie call. Maybe they were different up here from those icons farther south whose call is as emblematic of canoe country as the canoe itself. When Laurie heard a loon for the first time on her first canoe trip, the bird instantly became a part of her identity. But the loons here seemed silent. Still, we watched them float together, diving and resurfacing under the northern sky. Then one surfaced without the other. After a moment, a haunting wail seemed to originate from the depths of the loon's soul. Then a series of yodel-like notes rose and fell in a rhythm that rippled across the calm lake. I grinned silently while Laurie held her hands to her mouth and whispered, "Ooohhh!" Another distant loon's call blended with the echoes of the first. It seemed too far away to be the partner we saw; then a third loon, probably the partner, joined in the chorus. The sounds bounced across the lake, through the trees, and around our camp for several minutes until echoes faded into the evening.

Laurie walked to camp to cook dinner after a few minutes of contemplative silence. I felt compelled to float on the water, so I pulled out my fishing rod for the first time and launched the boat. I wasn't too interested in the fishing but that pristine surface beckoned me to glide across its expanse, paddling slowly toward the loons until they dove and popped up elsewhere. Distant storm clouds and their reflections compelled me to paddle aimlessly, tracking different illusions as they traveled across the water. I wrote in my journal that night:

This scene would be stunning if not for the constant buzzing of the horse flies that shatter the silence ...

It was true; the horseflies, also known as bulldogs, were with us constantly during this hot weather. We could leave the mosquitoes behind once on the water, but one or two horse-flies—all it takes to ruin the silence—kept up with us wherever we went. They're about the size of a large thumbnail and buzz like an electric razor. They constantly circled around our heads, much too fast to swat in the air. They rarely landed, but the bite was painful and bloody when they did. It was a proud moment when I had my first bulldog kill. It happened a couple weeks into the trip. One landed on my thigh, and with practiced, lightning-fast reactions, I gave him a smack. It fell off my leg and drowned in the water in the bottom of the boat. I stood up, rejoiced, performed a victory dance, and shouted to all horse flies within earshot, "I dare you! I dare you to come at me again! You see what your pal got?" I think the blood that pumped through my veins soon attracted every horsefly in the region.

I lasted about an hour in my attempt to fish until the annoyance of the flies overcame the beauty of the scene and I took refuge in the smoke of Laurie's fire. She had anticipated my lack of success and had already prepared a tasty cream of vegetable soup with white sauce. Anticipating our trek to the Thlewiaza River, we nodded off and slept long and hard that night, satisfied to have completed the first phase of our trip.

**

We portaged north where the Cochrane River turned south. Here, we stepped off the hydro-continental divide that separates the road-accessible watersheds from the vast network of roadless rivers of the Far North. This southwest-east limb of the taiga-tundra triangle was once a nexus of intersecting canoe routes and cultures rich with the traditions of the paddle. Explorers, traders, trappers, Chipewyan, Cree, and Inuit traveled the network of routes as they worked by canoe. Indigenous nomads set the routes in pursuit of caribou and fish; explorers used them as pathways to new lands; traders and trappers expanded them as commerce drove the fur trade north. The records they left connect early explorers to present-day recreational canoeists through common names and acquaintances that span decades. Together, the people, the trails, the waterways, and the canoe created the interconnected web of paddling history we came to experience.

Our path to the Thlewiaza River followed a large esker-moraine complex through a tributary series of ponds and streams until the water became too shallow to float on. We plotted a route that seemed like the most likely path that Joseph Tyrrell would have followed with his Chipewyan guides, but signs of the passage were faint at best. The shore of the small pond seemed too thick with shrubs to harbor a portage trail. A gray weathered axe blaze on a rotting tree stump protruding from the brush caught my eye. A faint depression in the moss led through a thicket to a steep sand embankment. This was the first portage on the route to Fort Hall Lake.

The trail, worn through the moss to the gravelly substrate of the esker, cut through the open forest for about a mile before it dropped steeply down the other side to Smith House Lake. We traversed the lake, then followed a second portage over a steep esker to an excellent camp. We set up here at 7 p.m. We had been traveling twelve difficult hours.

Eskers, such as this peninsula, laced the region, providing prime portaging conditions. Trails typically began and ended with steep climbs to ridgetops through open forests. High hills ornately landscaped by patchworks of sand, moss, and trees surrounded the small lakes between portages. We hoped to complete the third portage of this series and make it to Fort Hall Lake on the Thlewiaza River the next day. We slept late thinking it would be easy. The morning's events changed our minds.

We were supposed to pass through a few narrows to some ponds. Our 1:250,000-scale maps looked sufficiently detailed, but the complex matrix of small lakes, streams, and ponds does not translate well to maps of this scale. Shorelines were roughly sketched, numerous small ponds were not shown, and the lake's shape only vaguely corresponded to reality. We searched for the small bay to follow out of the lake but only found several false bays leading to uncharted ponds. I climbed a small hill to get a view and saw a remarkable network of waterways that seemingly led nowhere in all directions.

We dragged the canoe from pond to pond for three hours

searching for a route through the maze. Perhaps we had portaged into the wrong lake? We considered going back but made another attempt to force our way north. We went to a point that I was reasonably confident I could locate on the map, took a compass straight to where the portage trail was supposed to be, and traveled in that direction, traversing whatever was in our path—land, streams, ponds, or swamps. Occasionally, the shape of the land resembled what was on the map, but then we would be paddling where land should have been. Winding streams took us through thick stands of trees in directions that did not seem natural. Then I saw what could have been the largest beaver lodge on the planet. The crafty engineers had created their own flow system.

We continued northeast, holding our compass bearing over water and land until one of the many dead ends sported a small, cut sapling. The remains of an old campsite, some weathered caribou bones, and a fire ring lay on the other side of some thick shrubs. A mark on John's map confirmed that we were on a historical Chipewyan route north.

This brief episode reinforced the respect I had for travelers before us who willingly experienced map-less wandering before satellite-based mapping created modern topographic maps. A Chipewyan man in his thirties I met after our trip told me he and his family traveled through this same region by canoe in the summer and dogsled in the winter with only the maps imprinted on their memories. He said, "We just always knew where to go." Another older man said, "We didn't have maps in those days ... but it was our land, and we knew it well."

Early outsiders coming into the region lacked that historical knowledge as well as the modern knowledge recorded on maps. They brought confidence in their abilities and hope in their chances of encountering Indigenous people from whom they could extract information. Prentice Downes brought such confidence and hope along this same route from the Cochrane River to the Thlewiaza River and Nueltin Lake. He traveled for several days in this style, always heading northeast, exploring every bay for an outlet, walking inland, searching for signs of ancient trails. Well-worn caribou trails confounded efforts to find human paths.

Downes wrote in 1939 that "any divergence [from the correct path] could lead us into a complexity of near inter-locking bays and lakes that would prove fatal." Although inac-curate due to the flood, our maps gave us the insurance that he lacked. "Lakes, lakes, lakes innumerable. Some seem inter-locking; some do not. This is all a crazy jigsaw puzzle of sand and water, dry potholes, coulees, and kettle holes. God help the man who gets off route in this country! Nothing to go by, just up and down, around sand hills and dry washes, and thousands and thousands of caribou trails."

Downes and his crew followed signs left by ancient trav-elers—a piece of peeled birchbark to mark a trail, a keel print in the sand to mark a very recent passage. They encountered Chipewyan families and exchanged information in mixed Chipewyan and English, sharing tobacco and meat.

Downes described this "Land of Little Lakes" as an "extraordinarily forbidding and sterile country." I saw instead a rich, beautiful taiga forest. The trail began in the dense lowland forest of the lakeshore and climbed over a sand ridge that gave way to a sparsely forested hilltop covered with boulders. The surrounding moraines (hills created from glacial ice that had pushed debris into piles) offered little soil to support any rooted vegetation, and they stood rugged and stark against the forest backdrop. Moss-covered boulders lined the path but created no difficulty for walking.

The third portage trail remained flat for a while, cutting across a maze of boulder fields interspersed with thick stands of pine and spruce. It descended along an increasingly forested slope until it dropped into a small, gorge-like lake called Blue Lake, a former important fishing locale for the Chipewyan. Tyrrell called Blue Lake a "beautiful narrow land of quiet water a mile and a half long, the eastern side of which is low, with a high ridge of boulders in the background, while on its western side is an even sandy esker thirty feet high, the face of which is wooded with white and black spruce, birch, alder, willow, and straight aspens ...." Thirty-five years later, Downes remarked that the forest had burned some time ago, and the trees had not yet grown back. "It was all very grim. The rolling, gray waves of rock, the fire-blackened, dead spikes of spruce, the gleaming white ghosts of birch all backed by a lowering dull sky streaked with rifts of lighter gray added a Goyaesque touch to the scene of abandonment and desolation." We experienced the weather of Downes but the beautiful surroundings of Tyrrell. A fine mist created a luscious appeal that softened the mosses and added vibrant life to the forest.

Soon after we reached Blue Lake, the clouds released a shower that kept us under the shelter of the trees. Our packs provided protection from the rain while we hunched under their bulk. The warmth of the day kept us comfortable despite the soggy conditions. The shallow shore extended into Blue Lake for about thirty yards before it dropped off sharply into a deep, rounded pool. Just as sharply, the lake became shallow again before it continued through the mile-long, river-like channel to its end. (I've seen a similar lake reportedly formed by a great, ancient waterfall that tumbled off large ice blocks and developed a deep plunge pool at its base.) The glacial features of the banks here create a canyon-like atmosphere. Tyrrell and Downes both noted this region's unique diversity. The rich turquoise color of the water, even in sections just a few feet deep, is an anomaly in this region of clear lakes.

A cool, misty wind blew as we paddled slowly toward the end of Blue Lake, enjoying the striking scenery while another thunderstorm approached from the south. We took shelter on shore under a hastily erected tarp to wait out a dramatic downpour, complete with explosions of thunder and lightning. Calm returned around 4:30 p.m. We packed and pushed on to make up for our morning wanderings. A narrow stream, marked as a single blue line on the map, drains Blue Lake toward Fort Hall Lake, or so I thought.

A wide, swampy area separated the lake from the stream. We weaved along a meandering route, sweeping around fallen trees, dragging over logs, and pulling over the shallow gravel bottom in search of passable routes. The stream narrowed to little more than the canoe's width. The vegetation grew thicker, but the current carried us along nicely. I stood and guided the bow with an outstretched paddle while Laurie pushed from the stern because that channel was too narrow for standard steering.

A large rock in the middle of the stream blocked passage with just a few inches of water on either side. In hindsight, this should have clued us into the fact that we were not on a canoe route. It took several more obstacles before we came to that realization. I cleared logs with my axe and kept going. We pulled on the branches through shrub thickets until the stream disappeared into a flooded shrub garden. We saw no evidence of previous travelers.

I climbed a high hill to survey our situation and saw that we were still farther from Fort Hall Lake than Blue Lake. Thunder, lightning, and heavy rains returned; we were stuck in a boggy stream with the evening approaching swiftly. That steep hill I had climbed was on one side of the stream; a wet, thickly forested bog with barely enough room to walk was on the other. Camping was out of the question. From the hill, I could see our canoe wedged tightly between some boulders with no passable route ahead and not much better behind. We could continue dragging along, portage through the bog to the lake, or turn back over all those obstacles back to Blue Lake. What lay ahead couldn't be any worse than what we had passed over, so we pushed on, dragging along the shrubs, pulling with ropes to round the turns, and scraping between boulders. At each obstacle, frustration and fear of getting caught in this mess at dark caused us to second-guess each decision. As night and cold approached, we dragged the boat over rocks and through channel-wide bushes without regard for its plastic bottom until a large boulder blocking the entire stream stopped us. A hard rain dripped off my felt hat and down the collar of my soaked shirt as we sat, contemplating our choices. Laurie's face barely hid her frustration at my determination to keep going forward. We retreated. We couldn't turn the boat around, so we paddled it backward. I straddled the packs in the stern and we clawed upstream until we reached Blue Lake, wet and defeated, just as darkness was falling. Just fifty yards down the shore from our stream we found the fourth portage, a well-worn path up the embankment that we should have followed. That portage would have to wait until morning. A quick meal of ramen noodles took the edge off our appetite before we fell asleep. We gained five miles in fourteen hours of physically demanding traveling.

This sobering lesson had profound implications for our upcoming routes. The squiggly blue lines, streams too narrow to have an actual width on our coarse topographic maps, were as likely impassible as they were ten feet wide. These "one-liners," as we called them, gave us grave concern. In just a few days we would face a fifty-mile stretch of one-liners interspersed with small ponds before Nueltin Lake. In two weeks, we would face the tundra gap with sixty miles of one-liners. In a month, we would confront the forest gap with a hundred miles of one-liners.

The mathematics of our one-liner routes consumed my subconscious. Every joyous moment watching a sunset or cooking bannock over a fire was tempered with how that time would impact our progress. In quiet times, paddling across a peaceful lake, the subconscious would surface with random statements about mileage rates: "Eight miles today drops our average to eleven, which puts us back to Wollaston on the third of October." Or, "If we do five miles a day through the one-liner stretch, we need three twenty-mile days to get back to twelve." These comments would catch Laurie by surprise as if she missed part of a conversation. She learned to treat these like the chatter of ravens in the forest, just part of the sounds of canoe country. I learned to let the tension simmer in the background of my mind ... most of the time.

CHAPTER FIVE

THE WEB OF THE FAR NORTH

MILE 125–184

"A good woodsman has patience. He realizes he can't change nature nor hurry her. He doesn't fret because a river runs the wrong way for his journey, doesn't cuss over being windbound for a day on an island in a big lake. He knows he can't lower the hills to make a portage easier, and in the winter he won't try to fight a blizzard. He learns only that rushing does not often get you where you are going any faster than taking it quietly. Wise in the way of the woods, he realizes that often, the longest way is the *shortest* ... Just watch a good woodsman pick up a canoe and walk away with it and you'll know what I'm driving at."

—John Rowland

We approached Fort Hall Lake through a small, weedy tributary in the lingering cold and wind from an overnight storm. Known to the Chipewyan as Thanaitua, or "Sand Ridges Around the Shore" Lake, it's a long, narrow sheet of slack water that occupies a flooded section of an old river. Its shores come within thirty yards of each other at a point where the old river cuts through an esker, then again a few miles later in a long transition to Thanout Lake, where the old Fort Hall actually is, or was.

Drifting slowly along the shore, I spotted a dilapidated footbridge across an inlet stream. The man-made structure seemed foreign after so many days, but it excited my nostalgia for any emblem of the Old North. I stepped into the water and scrambled up the bank as the canoe glided into the bushes under Laurie's guidance. Tufts of caribou hair and clumps of fishing line decorated the shore. The location didn't seem right, nor did it seem fort-like.

"This might not be the fort," I said more to myself than to Laurie.

She brought the map case with her and put it down on the damp moss, sat on a rock and opened the bag of gorp. John's map indicated that this was a Chipewyan campsite.

I followed a trail lined with stumps of felled trees to a small cabin built from logs, mud, and gravel. The single room housed a bunk bed, a barrel stove, and not much else. A large crosscut saw and several caribou racks hung on an outside wall. Snowmobile parts, discarded clothing, and other litter cluttered the hilltop. This was the winter trapping cabin of a man named Peter from Wollaston Lake. Each winter, he and his family traveled here to work their traplines. He ran a small fishing operation on the lake during the summer, and each fall, he procured enough caribou meat to last through the winter.

There was no cabin when Downes found this same site in 1939. Chipewyan in this region were just beginning the transition to permanent houses. Downes found an old spear used for killing caribou where I found spent shotgun shells and a broken belt from a Ski-Doo. One elder described his early life this way: "At the end of each day, we chopped twenty poles for the tent. Once that was done, the tent was set up. The men would arrive back from the day's hunt. The next day, the men went ahead to break trail. The women followed after breaking camp. We walked 'til lunch. The men left for the hunt, and we set up camp again at an appropriate sight. That's how we lived ... snowshoes in the winter, birchbark canoes, and dogs with packs in the summer."

Lifestyle changes began for the Chipewyan when they started trapping for the fur industry. One elder said, "Wherever we were when the lakes froze, we built small cabins and lived most of the winter there. For windows, we used caribou hides ..." Trappers typically traveled by canoe to their trapping grounds, hauling a whole winter's supply with their sled dogs running along the shore. They spent little time in their winter cabins since they usually traveled by dog team along their trapline, camping where they stopped. They returned to their cabins every few weeks for rest and to freight their harvest. They left the bush in spring to sell their goods. Summer was the time to repair equipment, visit friends, and prepare to repeat the cycle.

Permanent communities gradually developed around the more prominent trading posts. Still, most families maintained trapping cabins at various places in the North. Each fall would be a great send-off as the hunters and trappers departed by dog team to the bush, not to return until Christmas or even Easter. Soon snowmobiles replaced dog teams, and fewer families traveled north. Peter's family was among the last to continue extracting a living from their wilderness cabin.

It was too cold to stand around for long. We pushed on into the wind that had grown to a gale. Icy rain pelted our faces and dripped down our sleeves as we worked toward the esker narrows a few miles away where we could rest. The shelter of the trees on a beautiful sandy beach created a quiet, calm bay that contrasted sharply with the violent, noisy rage on the main lake. Our progress wasn't worth the effort. We rested under our tarp by a warm fire for the afternoon. The wind calmed after dinner; we packed and paddled to Thanout Lake at 9:30 p.m.

The cold, gray morning tempted us to build a fire and linger over a hot breakfast. Instead, we ate granola with powdered milk, broke camp before the threatening rain fell, and cruised along the shore of Thanout Lake. Distant trees emerged from the mist; a small unnatural shape interrupted the forested profile of a sandy ridge on the western shore near the end of the lake. These were the remains of Fort Hall. The structure was nothing more than the sagging remnants of a small cabin with some outbuildings. A traveler passing by would hardly take note if its history didn't inspire them. We pulled ashore.

It was a simple place with a few log structures that only a handful of people ever saw. Hidden in its rotting structure were the ghosts of a fleeting bit of history that had a resounding impact on the Canadian North. These forts and the trails that led to them were places where people of different worlds and times intersected. Old ones surviving in a changing wilderness and new ones extracting fortunes from the land shared a commonality strong enough to build a transient wilderness community with its own customs and traditions.

Fort Hall was supposed to be built on Putahow Lake, about forty-five miles northeast in Nueltin Lake country. Around 1907, the HBC commissioned Herbert Hall to build a post as a resupply point for traders and trappers working the country along the forest–tundra transition. I don't know what happened, but Hall built the post on Thanout Lake in a cabin Tyrrell noted as the winter home of Red Head, the chief of a local band of Chipewyan. Some Cree with Hall found humor in the situation and called his intended destination "Putahow," which means "the place he missed."

Fort Hall had been abandoned for a few years when Downes passed through in 1939. Even then Downes saw the weather-beaten fort as a symbol of times past. The short life of Fort Hall and others like it scattered throughout the North testify to the fleeting nature of that enthralling wilderness culture that Downes tried to find. He was close enough in time to feel the fresh loss. Fifty-two years later, enough time had passed so that the old fort created the joy of discovery for us. It was a manifestation of the old tales of the wilderness. Still, I commiserated with Downes. Only the weathered, gray walls of one small building stood, empty and abandoned, with gaping, cold spaces where moss chinking had once filled between the logs. A broken door and a vacant window revealed the guts of the shack to be overgrown with weeds. Gusting wind battered the fort, and a melodic, whistling tune rose out of the abandonment that seemed to revive the memories trapped in the rotting structure. Where our canoe was beached on the shore below should have rested a dozen boats; a young trapper in the storehouse should have been gathering supplies from an old trader to see him through the next leg of his journey. Today, there was just us and the wind, no stew boiling on the stove to give us a break from our trail meals. We pushed on, a little disappointed, as if we expected some welcome or acknowledgment that we had reached the fort. Soon, the fort was out of sight and later out of mind.

***

The Thlewiaza River turns sharply west after Fort Hall Lake, then east, and pours through the dramatic gorge of Kasmere Falls. Distant sounds warned of a powerful rapid long before we reached it. It's a fun game, though, figuring out what the sounds will reveal. The barely detectable hiss sometimes announces just a small riffle that passes quickly. Other times, the hiss grows to a rumble, then thunder that warns of something bigger. Every time the sound demands attention. This time, there was no mistaking the power of Kasmere Falls. The violent crescendo had us searching for a place to scout and likely portage before we saw any whitewater.

A nearly indiscernible path across a quiet backwater on a prominent granite beach led nowhere. I was sure that a portage route must have existed; this was a well-traveled route at one time. We combed the woods for three hours searching for a manageable route, but we only followed random animal paths into dense thickets and boulder piles. We paddled along the shore and discovered an opening in the shrubs in a small bay. A slight, uncharted stream worked its way over some rocks and emptied into a large pond half a mile from the river. On its shore we found a small clearing with a few rock fire rings in its center. A trail that had eroded to the gravel from historic use led away from the clearing over the crest of a hill.

We began the work at 4 p.m. The initial climb up the well-worn sandy trail brought us to the top of an open hilltop and continued for a mile and a half over rolling terrain, through woods, rocks, and bogs before its steep descent to a weed bed at the end of the rapid. Despite the excellent trail conditions, the sweltering late afternoon heat, thick mosquitoes, and heavy packs made for a difficult time.

Since losing my portage yoke, we had not yet devised a comfortable way to carry the canoe. The center point of the contoured plastic seats dug into the tops of our spines as the canoe bounced with our stride. Although the weight is shared on a two-person carry, balancing the boat's load in a way that satisfies both is usually impossible. The weight seems to grow heavy on one side as you march along. Frustration builds until you tongue-lash your partner for improper carrying, who, of course, is experiencing the same difficulties and blaming you all the while. We completed each trip with the packs without resting. But we tossed the canoe aside twice to massage our necks. After far too long, we passed the giant mushroom, our marker of just one hundred yards to go, crested the final ridge, and dropped down in the cool grass at the river's edge.

The evening wore on as we trudged back and forth across the path. Three miles, six miles, nine miles, and then the final, painful one-and-a-half-mile trip with the canoe, collapsing at the end of the trail at 8:30 p.m. The mosquitoes that forced us to sweat in our head nets cut our needed rest short. Exhausted and frustrated by our late evening, we paddled just a hundred yards before unloading the boat we had just loaded. We then camped at the base of an esker.

I wanted to collapse in the moss, but rest waits until the work is done when there are only two people. I made a tasty pizza with our bannock mix, tomato powder, and dried vegetables; soon, the difficulties of the trail were behind us. The bugs dissipated with the smoke of our fire, and the calm evening brought peace.

The temperature dropped through the evening, and morning came with welcome warmth. This was the first morning that didn't have us hopping around to circulate heat. Surprisingly, the bugs that had been so fierce the day before did not bother us. We packed up and paddled just a few hundred yards before hearing another distant rumble of a rapid. The current quickened; we saw the dancing of waves cresting over a drop in the river, and we pulled ashore to scout.

We went through the usual questions about scouting a rapid. How's the approach? What route do we follow? How's the washout in case of a mishap? This rapid was just a dancing wave train requiring little technical maneuvering. When alone and everything you need to survive is in your boat, you stop at the slightest hint of danger. We were confident in our skills but wary of potential outcomes. This time, confidence prevailed, and we paddled the rapid. A few back-paddles at each wave to keep water from coming over the gunnels, an occasional low brace, and some hurried draws and pries to keep us straight got us through without difficulties.

Downes described this section of the river as "a wicked looking, confused stretch of boiling, mad water that shot down a narrow channel and then foamed up into a curling, white wave parted by several glistening black boulders." Perhaps the water levels differed, but in my journal description of our day, I recorded, "We ran a minor rapid." The river gradually widened below the rapid until it emptied into the southwest arm of Kasmere Lake.

***

I can't distinguish what I knew when we paddled across the lake from what I learned from books and journals later. Still, Kasmere Lake, with its beautiful setting, rich canoe history, and namesake, Chief Casimir,[2] inspires my imagination to conjure stories about life by the paddle. Shaped like a distorted letter X, Kasmere Lake is a nexus of several old routes to the Far North. Called Theitaga Lake by Tyrrell and Thynara-tueh by the Dene, the intersection of exploration, adventure, Indigenous history, deep wilderness, and the canoe elevate Kasmere Lake to iconic status in my library of special places.

Casimir was the Chipewyan elected as first formal Chief of the Edthen Eldeli in 1907 when the Canadian government needed a treaty representative. Soon after that first treaty, Casimir argued with the commissioner claiming he was entitled to a new canoe. When the commissioner granted his request, Casimir took his followers to live in the Thynara-tueh region and shunned the census and treaty money for several years. They clung to the traditional ways of Chipewyan life much longer than those who had continued to rely on the treaty. Casimir's

---

2 Names frequently have different spellings in old accounts. Here I use Casimir to distinguish the person from the place Kasmere Lake. Casimir and Kasmere are used interchangeably in many sources.

resistance was an ongoing source of frustration for government workers attempting to distribute treaty funds to everyone on their list and balance their books.

If Casimir lived to be eighty, he would have been born around the time when the HBC built Fort du Brochet in 1859 on Reindeer Lake, a center of Chipewyan life. The company needed a new meat supply to make pemmican for their voyageurs after buffalo became scarce. They saw an untapped meat resource in the large caribou herds of the north, a workforce of hunters in the Chipewyan, and a communication pathway through the missionaries. With this new base, the unknown Far North came within reach of the new world. The route between Brochet and Kasmere Lake formed the neck of an hourglass where travelers from the vast canoe routes in the south passed through, exploring and seeking commerce and adventure in the new world of the Far North. Casimir seems to have had a hand in much of that action. He was respected enough that Joseph Tyrrell hired him and another Chipewyan named Thebayazie to guide his small crew from Brochet through the forest gap to the Kazan River. While Tyrrell's records name his guides as Xavierseese and Thebayazie, other sources have equated Xavierseese and Casimir.

In 1894, just a few months after his near-tragic Dubawnt River expedition, Tyrrell, his companions, and the two guides paddled out of Brochet in three canoes seeking to reach the Kazan River and then follow it to wherever it led. They reached Kasmere Lake along the same route through the Blue Lake system Laurie and I followed. They turned into the northwest lobe and ascended the Thebayazie River, now called Little

Partridge River, to its source, then portaged west to Kasba Lake and the headwaters of the Kazan River. Casimir had a relative take his place somewhere along the way. Both Chipewyan left the group at Kasba Lake, leaving Tyrrell and his men without guides to find their own way down the uncharted Kazan River. Each paddle stroke brought them farther north than any explorer had ever been, armed with only a hint of knowledge about where it would take them.

Sixteen years later, the twenty-six-year-old Ernest Oberholtzer also paddled across the waters of Kasmere Lake where he faced an agonizing decision. Should he continue down Tyrrell's path, unguided, to become the first known person to reach Baker Lake via the Kazan River, or should he heed the advice of the old-timers he met in Brochet and head east down the Thlewiaza River to Nueltin Lake and Hudson Bay? Laurie and I faced this same decision, with much different consequences. We at least knew where the rivers went!

Of all the characters who ended up in books about this country, I identify most with Ernest Oberholtzer. We were the same age, both introduced to wilderness canoe tripping by working as camp guides, shared a passion for deep wilderness, and were inspired by Tyrrell's writings. We both loaded up one canoe with one partner and enough provisions to last long enough to get as far as we could go and back.

We probably shared similar day-to-day experiences, but the seventy years between our trips encompassed perhaps the most condensed technological changes in human history so that Ernest Oberholtzer's accomplishment can never be repeated. We traveled a little over a thousand miles in three months; he went two thousand miles in five months. We had maps; Ernest had chance encounters with Indigenous people. We knew where the rivers went; Ernest paddled away from Brochet not knowing how he would get back home. But in those seventy years, the wilderness community between Brochet and Kasmere Lake came and went; the country was likely emptier for us than it was for Oberholtzer.

Ernest Oberholtzer intended to finish what Tyrrell started and become the first known explorer to reach Baker Lake along an inland route. He was not sponsored by a government or company; he was just a twenty-six-year-old from Minnesota seeking adventure in a wild place. It might be difficult for many now to appreciate the magnitude of Oberholtzer's desires. Then, the unmapped land of the Far North rested out of reach of even the most ambitious, hardened travelers. The HBC had recently established a post at Baker Lake where the Kazan River was suspected to flow, but it was accessed by sea from Hudson Bay through Chesterfield Inlet. The five hundred linear miles between the forests surrounding Reindeer Lake and the tundra surrounding Baker Lake remained mysterious.

Oberholtzer recruited Billy Magee, a Cree canoeman and friend, to join him. The two set out from Cumberland House in one eighteen-foot wood-and-canvas Chestnut canoe. As an avid conservationist, Oberholtzer carried all his food with him. This style of travel was foreign in his day when living off the land was the rule of wilderness travel. The struggles of those early portages without the convenience of modern packs—tumplines tugging at their foreheads with crushing loads—must have been heartbreaking. They needed five trips to transport their supplies

across portages. En route to Brochet, they had the grand experience of seeing the North in the prime of its canoeing tradition. They traveled with a Revillon Frères freighting company,
stopped at HBC posts to resupply, and reached Brochet in late
July after nearly five hundred miles of paddling.

Somewhere south of Brochet, Oberholtzer and Magee
encountered a party of canoes heading south. It was led by
Herbert Hall returning from a four-year stay at the post he built
on Ennadai Lake after he built the misplaced post on Thanout
Lake. They advised Oberholtzer to turn around; the wild country
was too much for a newcomer to handle without a guide. Regardless, Ernest and Billy pushed on.

In Brochet, Oberholtzer found his way into the tangled web
of northern canoe culture. A man whose brother had been with
Tyrrell inspired him while others warned him of the dangers.
Father Egenolf, renowned for his epic months-long travels by
dog team visiting his Chipewyan parishioners, encouraged him
to find Chipewyan guides or change his route.

Oberholtzer and Magee left Brochet, guideless, paddling
up the Cochrane River toward the same point of departure that
Laurie and I sought from Wollaston Lake, still uncertain of their
ultimate route. His anxiety must have been heavy, heading north
into unknown terrain with so much uncertainty. Perhaps he
pondered the same dilemma about the forest gap I did eighty
years later. On Thanout Lake near Fort Hall, Oberholtzer
observed a hill where "at the top-most point, some Indian has
built a new conical lookout of spruce trees, from which he can
see the surrounding country for miles." This, of course, was
Chief Casimir. Inuit from the north used to pass through the

Kasmere Lake region to trade at Brochet. Casimir, from his lookout, would keep track of all who traveled through his land and demand a toll for passage. Maybe this gave Oberholtzer some assurance people would be nearby if his route choice went wrong.

Somewhere in the Kasmere Lake region, a Chipewyan in a birchbark canoe paddled to their camp to trade and share their fire. He must have finally convinced Oberholtzer to abandon his plan to find and descend the Kazan River. Following that encounter, Oberholtzer and Magee headed east down the Thlewiaza River toward Hudson Bay. Their trip was nothing less than astounding. With no knowledge of the land, the two men found their way along the Thlewiaza, crossing its many small lakes, each time scanning the far shore for the river until they arrived at the immense Nueltin Lake.

Laurie and I made this same decision, unaware of Ernest's and Billy's dilemma. We also considered heading north along Tyrrell's route as we paddled across the bay where Little Partridge River enters Kasmere Lake, but we stuck to our modified plan and headed east toward the Thlewiaza River in the faded wake of Ernest Oberholtzer.

We found minor signs that marked the passage of the old ones throughout the Kasmere–Nueltin region. Old campsites gave hints to techniques no longer used. A fire ring with a stick thrust diagonally into the ground, extending over the fire to hang a tea pail, showed how they cooked. Several old bough beds worn into the moss showed how they slept. These discoveries injected little bits of joy into my days. I imagined that our life by the paddle somehow bought admission to that club and that maybe I could share a fire with a trader as he traveled the routes between the expanding network of trading posts.

Maybe I could have talked to Thierry Mallet about his return journey that had been heavy on my mind. Maybe I could have met Del Simmons, who, as an independent trader, established a few trading posts on the tributary waters and Nueltin Lake. He could have told me who was managing the posts and outlined the portage routes to get there. I could have clarified some of the curious but somewhat troubling gossip about Cecil "Husky" Harris, George Yandle, and Alfred Peterson.

Harris had built the HBC post at the site that Hall missed on Putahow Lake. He supposedly spent fifteen years in the bush without getting to the outside. On one of his trips, he brought his three Inuit wives to Winnipeg. It's a rough statement about how Indigenous women were treated then, but in Winnipeg, Alfred Peterson purchased one of Harris's wives, and George Yandle bought another. Stories like this inject some harsh reality into my romanticized version of frontier life and its impacts on Indigenous culture.

***

Wilderness as a healer is a common theme for couples who write books about their trips. I don't know if we healed anything; our marriage was too new for us to recognize any lingering troubles. We weren't driven to seek solutions to any internal conflicts. The long days toiling under our packs and moving with our paddles subdued any conflicts that might have been. After three weeks of shared solitude and the foresight of nine more, our lives became wholly consumed by where we were.

The shared hardships and joys that Laurie and I experienced together, and the impacts that every one of our actions had on the other, strengthened a bond that we didn't know was weak. Of course, our experiences as wilderness travelers in 1991 differed significantly from the couples and families who lived and worked together in the wilderness in the 1920s. I imagine, however, that their experiences were even more bonding.

Sydney Keighley brought his family and nineteen-day-old son with him when he departed Brochet by canoe in the fall of 1927. He was bound for Putahow Lake to trap for the winter. Keighley was somewhat of a nomadic post manager for the HBC, accepting short-term assignments throughout the vast country west of Hudson Bay and traveling between posts by canoe and dog team, crisscrossing the southern margins of our triangle route. His routine trips, and those of others at the time, make today's expeditions seem trivial.

On one trip, Keighley met Charlie Planinshek, an immigrant from Yugoslavia, at his small wilderness homestead somewhere south of Brochet. Charlie and his family were legends for a remarkable canoe trip they had completed years earlier. They traveled from Reindeer Lake through the forests and waterways of southern Canada to Minnesota and the headwaters of the Mississippi River. They continued down to the Gulf of Mexico, around Florida, up the Atlantic coast to New York, then to Montreal in just over three years. Along the way, the children performed a dance routine for pay. Proceeds went to their education.

Charlie had built his little cabin to begin a recluse life after his wife died and he died alone there sometime in 1943 or 1944.

Marcel Chappuis, a constable for the Royal Canadian Mounted Police, discovered Charlie's bones on one of his legendary patrols of the North approximately eighteen months after Charlie's death. Chappuis buried Charlie Planinshek in front of the cabin and placed some of Charlie's own flowers on the grave.

Keighley's next assignment was at Poor Fish Lake where, just a few years earlier, a previous trader dismantled and moved the whole building to escape the grizzly scene of a tragedy. Upon returning from a routine freighting trip to Brochet, the trader discovered the corpses of several Inuit dispersed around the post. They had traveled to the post to find relief from a winter of starvation in a year when the caribou failed to appear. Without meat for the long Arctic winter, the Inuit used their last resources to reach the post, only to find it empty. Depleted of resources and out of strength, they succumbed one by one, waiting for the trader to return.

Sadly, grim events like this were not uncommon in what has been called "the land of feast and famine." Mallet sledded north one January to convince an Inuit trapper to trade at his post. He traveled for twenty days by dog team until he found an encampment of igloos on an inland lake where a few Inuit families, seventeen people total, were fishing through the ice.

Inuit fished in winter only when the fall caribou hunt failed. They were starving. Mallet and his small team left what food they could spare. Six months later, he traveled by canoe to the same lake to rendezvous with one of his employees. The encampment was gone. Mallet waited a week before his employee arrived. The man's expression told Mallet the conclusion of the tragic story he was about to hear.

Sometime in the spring, the man visited the camp but found only a trail in the snow heading south. Discarded items littered the trail—traps, a telescope, bundles of fur—then he found the first grave. He followed the trail for seven days, finding more graves, then just bodies in the snow, until he found the seventeenth. The farthest along the trail, the last to succumb, was a twelve-year-old girl lying beside a rifle.

Stories like this erode my nostalgia for times past. We paddled through this same region where Inuit left their corpses along trails, and Chipewyan buried their own who perished from smallpox, famine, or any number of hardships, all while taking delight in signs of the past. That the Keighley family thrived that winter while in other years Inuit families perished, illustrates the harsh, fickle nature of the northern wilderness we traveled through.

***

I took a year to plan this trip, obsessing over maps, measuring a hundred days of food to the teaspoon, and studying mail-order catalogs for gear. Prentice Downes showed up in Brochet with scant provisions, no canoe, and no partner. He wasn't going as far as us, but his goal of Nueltin Lake was still somewhat mysterious.

Downes wasn't part of that old network, although he was well known in the small outpost of Brochet as a hard North Country traveler. He was there at the tail end of the working North and on the leading edge of wilderness tourism. Like Tyrrell, Mallet, and Oberholtzer, Downes spent a nostalgic evening at the HBC post exchanging stories about the Old

North with traders, trappers, and other sorts of people traveling through. I imagine Downes might have approached the conversation from an outsider's perspective relative to the men who lived and worked there. The canoe routes that Downes undertook as lifetime adventures may have been routine for Sydney Keighley or men like him who might have been at that table.

Father Egenolf was still in town and gave Downes a rough map of the Nueltin Lake region that Sydney Keighley sketched a few years earlier. Downes borrowed an HBC canoe and convinced a trapper from Wollaston Lake, John Albrecht, to join him. The two men launched one canoe and paddled up the Cochrane River, headed for the portage across the Land of Little Lakes.

They encountered a group of the Barren Lands band of Chipewyan camped on the shores of Misty Lake. One Chipewyan in the crowd was significantly older than the others. He wore a flour sack as a head cover, with the corner of the sack pointing upward, giving him a gnomish look. The old man, Chief Casimir, appeared strong and in charge. Downes traded tobacco for information from Casimir and left the camp with a little more insight than Keighley's rough map provided.

Chief Casimir died just a few months after Downes met him. His body was buried vertically on a hill on the eastern shore of Thanout Lake at the esker narrows where Laurie and I had spent a windbound afternoon. A few versions of his dying wish appear in different accounts, but the gist runs something like, "When I die, bury me standing up. Bury me on the high hill at the narrows. For there, I shall stand and watch you, my people, as you go north to hunt the deer. I will see you all as you pass, and

I will wish you luck in the killing of the deer." A small wooden cross marked his grave where John's map indicated it should be.

When Laurie and I paddled across Kasmere Lake deciding whether to head to the Kazan or the Thlewiaza, we had topographic maps, whereas those men had the knowledge of Casimir and the information of the web; they had fresh connections to the people who lived their lives by canoe in the wilderness. Maybe that's what motivated me to invite Farley Mowat to join us on the trip. I was delighted when he responded and disappointed when he turned us down, stating he was devoting his last breaths to completing his autobiography. Mowat introduced me to the Far North through his books about the plight of the inland Inuit. In hindsight, I'm happy that Laurie and I were alone, building that bond, living our wilderness life by the paddle that may have approximated in a small way what those who came before us lived.

We found just a few overgrown signs that anybody had traveled through the Kasmere Lake region in recent years. The Chipewyan moved to communities, the traders and trappers pursued newer, more lucrative opportunities, and the few hardy recreational paddlers who made it here left few traces of their passing. There were no Chipewyan families to talk to about routes, but John's maps, his direct lineage to Chief Casimir, and our interactions with the Chipewyan at Wollaston Lake gave me a hint of pride that maybe I had built another strand in the web.

Likely, John had never met his grandfather since Casimir died in 1940. So instead, I'll build my strand in the web to that quiet old man in that office meeting who sketched the route through the forest gap. He could have known Casimir sixty years ago, possibly in the camps that aided Downes. Maybe his family traded with Keighley or listened to the sermons of Father Egenolf. They were all gone, but the deep, compelling wilderness I longed for remained as wild as ever.

CHAPTER SIX

THE OLD WAY NORTH

MILE 184–251

"But the old-time canoemen are very few today. They are not needed anymore, and the War got a lot of them. Some have just disappeared. And the happy, careless voyageurs, gay caballeros of the White Water who whooped and laughed and shouted their way down or up unmapped rivers, and thought their day would last forever, have gone, vanished like the snows of last year, their long-dead fires all overgrown."

—Grey Owl (Archibald Delaney)

A glassy sheet of water stretched before us, a warm sun soothed our backs, and the bugs seemed occupied with other things. Sixteen days of hard traveling took a mental toll. Still, this spectacular North Country day inspired commitment and bathed us in the glory of deep wilderness. I stood shirtless on a small rock island where the Thlewiaza River enters Kasmere Lake, plotting a compass bearing toward our goal. To the northwest stretched the bay Joseph Tyrrell followed to find the Little Partridge River en route to Kasba Lake and the Kazan River.

We then headed east toward where the Thlewiaza River continued its tumbling path to Nueltin Lake. We skimmed across the lake with little worries and re-entered the river. The swift current carried us through a shallow rock-garden rapid, then a few more miles until the river cut through an esker and turned sharply to the south. There, we faced a tough route decision.

Nueltin Lake, about forty-five miles downriver, would be our gateway to the Barren Lands. It's an intimidating piece of water approximately eighty miles long and fifteen to thirty-five miles wide. When the wind gathers in the barren northern reaches of the lake, its relentless intensity produces a water surface that rivals a stormy sea. It can hold canoes captive for days.

Fearing wind would stifle our pace, we planned to bypass the southern part of Nueltin Lake by leaving the Thlewiaza River via a portage route through the Putahow Lake and Windy River systems to Nueltin Lake's northern end. "Planned," however, is a generous word.

I vaguely knew from Downes's book that traders and trappers used a route somewhere west of Nueltin Lake, but details were lost when they left the country five or six decades ago. I didn't know that Keighley brought his family there, or that Planinshek spent his last years there. If I did, I might have been more persistent in finding their route. Instead, I sought the route that I charted in the comfort of my map room at home; a fifty-mile stretch from this esker northward, riddled with one-liners.

I recorded in my journal:

We are camped at the northern point of the Thlewiaza, just before where I was planning on portaging, and I haven't found any evidence of human passing. There are no old campsites, no axe blazes, or no old stove parts. I'm a bit worried.

Sleep was evasive that night. I lay on my thin foam pad, pulling my bag around my head to keep out the cold and the sounds of Laurie's deep, restful breathing. She either wasn't worried about tomorrow or was too exhausted to let her thoughts hold back sleep. I counted mosquitoes on the white tent ceiling until my back hurt, then settled into my more natural sleeping position on my side until my sleep envy turned to annoyance. I was thinking we might stumble around between here and Nueltin for weeks without ever finding the old path; or maybe we could stay on the Thlewiaza River to Nueltin Lake. I had not considered that possibility; I knew little about the river other than Downes's description as wicked and nasty. The map indicated at least fifteen rapids; many more could exist at each narrows. Plus, we lacked maps for the southern portion of Nueltin Lake. Both possibilities were equally daunting. I would wait until morning to dump some of my anxiety off on Laurie.

On July 17 we woke to cold, gray skies after a chilly, winter-like night. The tension of indecision gnawed at my mind as we ate our granola breakfast, loaded the canoe, and paddled into the bay. We let the wind make the decision and drifted toward the small stream at the end of the bay. On the map, it looked like we could ascend this stream a few miles to a small lake where we would find a short portage into the Putahow system. We scraped up the creek for about thirty yards until it abruptly ended. Nothing continued, not even a muddy stream. The one-liner on the map did not exist.

We found hints of an old trail and set out to explore. The barely perceptible path led to a large, burned area that obscured any evidence of travel. Still, we found our way to the small lake where bits of rope, caribou bones, and other signs indicated human passage. This could be an old portage or a winter trapping trail. It could lead anywhere.

After an hour, we returned to the boat with the heavy awareness that we would likely have to portage at least six of the ten miles to the Putahow watershed on abandoned trails through thick, burned forest. Beyond Putahow, the route to Windy Lake was even more obscure on our coarse topographic maps. Somewhere in that blue maze of streams and ponds on the map was an old route. The persistent pressure to travel fast, however, forced me to consider our other possibility.

Was it really that important to find Windy Lake or to avoid the wind on Nueltin Lake? Windy Lake attracted me for more reasons than route efficiency. Its shores harbored Windy Post, the trading post that was last active in the region; its last occupants played a vital role in assisting the inland Inuit during their final days on the land. Its history was my first introduction to the Barren Lands through the writings of Farley Mowat. I wanted to find the post and connect to Mowat's words that first inspired our journey north. Prentice Downes reached Windy Post by paddling up the Windy River from Nueltin Lake. *Maybe we'll do that*, I thought, as I ruminated on the options.

Laurie snuggled into the shrubs, letting the sun warm her

skin, while I stared at our canoe grounded midstream on a rock, defeated by my nagging inability to make a damn decision. Was this a time to follow through on a decision or be flexible to change? Laurie later recorded in her journal:

I'm seeing personality traits in Jim that I've never seen before. He's usually so calm and confident. Maybe because he's always been the leader, guiding youth groups in Maine and with me on earlier trips. Now that I can participate, he can let the pressure show. I feel bad for his frustration, I felt good about my participation today. This was the first decision that I feel I actually contributed an idea and input. It was a good feeling.

"This is silly," I finally said. "This is not that big of a deal." But in my mind, I couldn't reduce the problem to the scale that it was.

"Well, let's look at the maps again, make a new decision, and just do it," Laurie flatly stated.

"Okay. There are a lot of rapids on the Thlewiaza, but some of them could be paddleable. On the other hand, we might be portaging most of the forty-five miles. Nueltin shouldn't be that bad; we've had wind problems before."

"Yeah, and I don't really want to wander around looking for some old path that might not even exist."

The appeal of traveling downstream won the debate in my head. The burden of decision lifted, and a surge of confidence energized my strokes as we retraced our route through an icy mist to the river. Windy Lake lingered in my mind.

***

The first of many rapids came quickly. It began simply enough with a series of small cascades emptying into a large pool, then into a narrow chute where water rushed over large boulders with thunderous intensity. Waves far too powerful for a loaded wilderness canoe told us to find another way.

No portage path was evident on either shore, but the lower rapid was clearly unrunnable. Uncertainty returned. I knew that Oberholtzer went this way seventy years ago, but I didn't know that in the early 1900s this route to Nueltin Lake was regularly traveled by those traders and trappers from Brochet. Some went through the Putahow portage, and some descended the Thlewiaza, but neither route showed signs of recent use.

We sat in the soft moss between some still-fruitless cranberry bushes, ate our bannock, and debated whether to portage through the untracked woods or take our chances on the river. I ate a handful of gorp, stood up, then walked to the canoe and sat in the seat, ready to paddle. Laurie nodded and followed.

We cautiously paddled the first section of the rapid to scout our options, knowing but not acknowledging that we couldn't turn back. We rushed over the cascades and approached the main rapid at an alarming rate. The eddies along the banks were jammed with hidden boulders that threatened to snag and wrap our loaded boat. Still, we had to stop before the main drop. We clawed into an eddy onto the rocks. The rapid loomed just below our safe spot; the left bank was unreachable. A difficult ferry above the drop would get us to the seemingly friendlier right bank. We rehearsed our strokes, pointed the bow upstream, angled into the current, and paddled forward with the most powerful strokes we could muster. The current grabbed our bow, but we kept the angle and successfully ferried across.

The right bank was much worse. A jumbled pile of boulders covered by a few inches of water kept us twenty yards from the bank. We inched our way downstream, thinking we saw a safe channel but floated closer to the drop without getting to safer waters. With the wisdom of hindsight, we scolded ourselves for even attempting this rapid. Accepting the work of a difficult portage would have been far better and quicker.

"I thought this would be quicker," I said. "I guess I was just trying to avoid a portage. That's what got us on this river in the first place, trying to avoid portages."

"Is that why we're not going to Putahow?" Laurie asked. "I thought it was because the route was too uncertain. It's because of laziness? Man, this is pathetic!"

She was right. I sighed, slumped a bit, and took some deep breaths while standing in knee-deep water above a dangerous rapid with a loaded canoe. Our only safe option was to portage along the rocks, in and out of the water to the end of the long rapid. Laurie held the boat while I unloaded two packs.

"I don't know if I want to carry those packs over the slippery rocks," Laurie said with apprehension. She had taken a few falls earlier and was never confident with her footing.

"Well, I'll carry all the packs. You just bring the smaller stuff."

Light rain made the rocks slippery and the depths between the boulders loomed as potential ankle-breaking traps. After just one load I agreed with Laurie that the rocks were probably more dangerous than the rapid. We sat on the gunwales, literally stuck on rocks with a very hard rapid just downstream. We each took a rope toward shore, pulled until the boat broke free, then lined through the drop that was too scary to paddle. With skill that surprised me, we pulled the boat into a surging eddy, hopped in, and paddled the lower rapid successfully. The whole event took us about two hours.

An even more powerful rapid confronted us within minutes. True to our resolve, we immediately began the work of portaging. Again, no portage trail was evident.

It wasn't just this portage that caused me to spiral. Our slow pace, route indecision, safety, responsibility, fear, the upcoming map-less route, and maybe even the early morning with yet another instant peaches-and-cream oatmeal break-fast—it all left a gnawing tension in my stomach. I sat in the damp moss, head in hands, elbows on knees, and let out quick shallow breathes to control my body.

My previously rare but increasingly present breakdowns manifested in anger and self-loathing rather than tears. Typical, I suppose. I got mad at the portage trail for not being there, furious at the packs for being heavy, angry with Laurie for not being mad, and enraged at myself for being enraged. Anger evolved to self-pity, and I sat, gripped in indecision about what to do even though we had already decided to just move down the river.

I saw us struggling down an unrunnable river, rapids halting us at every bend. I envisioned wasting costly time and being forced to turn back at the end of the season without reaching our goal of Angikuni Lake. Despite the northern route's harsh pros-pects, I regretted following the Thlewiaza and scolded myself for such immature decision-making. Why did we change course? Is there a good reason why we're seeing no signs of human passage on this river? Should we turn back again? Will we lose too many days on this route? Is the other way worse?

"We're in over our heads. We're definitely in over our heads on this one," I chanted, aware of how ridiculous I was behaving. But I was unable to stop.

The damp moss soaked through my back while the warm sun in my eyes forced me to close them. The hypnotic roar of the rapid now led me to breathe deeply and listen. Maybe twenty minutes passed when Laurie returned with news of a very faint trail leading up a ridge away from the river. I was composed by then. She knew I went through something but didn't ask, and I didn't tell. I got up and went about the business of moving downstream.

I thought the trail might be an animal path until we discovered a discarded fuel can with graphic designs typical of 1950s marketing. Typically, trash in the wilds would be disheartening. Not today. We loaded packs and started walking.

The trail never really converged to anything obvious; we each followed our own way on the seven trips. The two hours it took to complete the portage allowed me to re-evaluate our situation. We were fine. Just keep moving.

The trail ended in a wet bog so we loaded the boat to search for another site. I reached in my pocket for my knit hat, but it was gone. Although I would be fine without it today, September would not be so forgiving. I retraced what I thought was my last route but ended up somewhere else. A rounded wooden shaft with a crudely carved handle extended from a mossy hummock. I pulled it free and found a rough but beautifully hand-carved paddle, obviously from another time.

Its shape was crafted from local spruce, quite different from the style of paddle I used. The total length was about five feet, half of which was the long, narrow blade that widened to just a couple of inches on either side of the round shaft; it then gently tapered to a long point with a diamond-shaped cross section. From the rough cut, I imagined it was made on the trail. Perhaps it belonged to a Chipewyan. I read somewhere that they used this style of paddle instead of the beaver-tail style popular with white trappers. I carried it back with me and paddled a few hundred yards downstream to our campsite.

The paddle came at just the right time. It was a stimulus that spurred my memory of why we were here. Wasn't this what we had come for? Weren't we looking for real wilderness, unmarked trails, and untraveled waterways? I knew my earlier antics were a gross exaggeration of the problem, but I was venting an accumulated frustration and nervousness about the whole route.

I still worried that we might get caught in freeze-up. Any delays added fuel to my source of worries. But the paddle was a vehicle to times past, and I imagined the life of its creator. What could have occurred to require making a paddle on the trail? Whatever it was, I think the owner met the hardship with seasoned indifference—part of life on the trail.

I hit an emotional low point of the trip that day at that rapid on the Thlewiaza River. We would face more difficult traveling conditions later, but I learned to just keep moving. It took time, but route problems became enjoyable challenges to overcome, like running rapids or traversing windy lakes.

I wrote in my journal:

We really are having a marvelous time. We have the freedom to go in any direction we want. As long as we have food and shelter, we can be very happy up here. This is a very tough route we're following, but we are discovering so much about ourselves, the Far North, and wilderness travel. This is no canoe park; this is real.

I was comfortable with our situation, but I did not abandon all my worries. My journal continued, *"I'm feeling more and more like Hubbard every day. That worries me."*

This wasn't the first time Leonidas Hubbard's canoe journey in 1903 hung in my thoughts. His carelessness with his supplies and discarding of large quantities of food (much like we did), and his route error resulted in plodding progress. An early winter caught the crew depleted of food, wearing torn and tattered clothing, and still attempting to push into unknown lands. They knew they had to turn back. The return journey proved too taxing for the weak and starving Hubbard, and he died alone in a canvas tent while his companions struggled desperately to reach civilization and assistance. I never thought we would suffer the same fate, but the similarities I saw were frightening.

***

With the burden of uncertainty and insecurity lifted, we were free to enjoy a beautiful wilderness river. Cold (maybe forty-five degrees Fahrenheit) but sunny weather kept the bugs tolerable, and the river provided challenging adventures the entire way.

Light-hearted laughter seasoned our conversations as we did the work of moving downstream.

The Thlewiaza River was as expected based my reading of the topographic maps. Small lakes bounded sections of river five to ten miles long that dropped about ten feet per mile, suggesting we would find continuous swift water interrupted with Class I, II, and occasional Class III rapids.

Clear, fast water carried over the bouldery bed. We paddled for steering, rather than propulsion. Swift water turned into small, exciting rapids at every narrows or bend. Large, powerful Class III rapids existed where the map indicated. We ran some, portaged others, and moved through the landscape with the confidence and skill of seasoned travelers. The forest seemed thicker, the trees taller than before. Maybe the joy of experience made everything more grand.

One of the larger rapids sent us to a barely perceptible portage trail without hesitation. We moved swiftly across at our own paces. I gave Laurie a nod and a cheer as I passed her on my first return trip while she struggled under her load. She did the same while I labored under my second.

I caught up to her on my second return trip, exaggerating my stomps for her to hear. She giggled and quickened her pace until I grabbed her waist and pulled her close.

"Mmm, what are you doing?" she murmured. I could see a grin when she turned her head.

The acrid taste of bug dope on her neck gave me pause. Still, I moved my hands in ways that used to inspire passion. But it was less passion than a curious "why not" that led us to lay in the shrubby, mossy ground. It didn't last long. The lumpy ground, the bugs, and the knowledge that neither of us had bathed in weeks combined to create a perfect anti-aphrodisiac. We lay for a time, giggling at the ludicrous situation.

"Maybe tonight," I said.

"Maaaaybe," she replied while putting herself back together.

I lay on my side, head propped up by my hand on my ear, and watched her stride down the path. I was glad nobody joined us on this trip. The deep bond that was growing would have been swamped by the need to include and please others—strangers really, no matter how close they might have been.

"Maybe September," I mused.

I found Laurie at the boat, ready to tackle the next rapid. Of the many skills and techniques employed by the old ones that have been lost to today's paddlers, I am convinced that whitewater paddling is not among them. The standard technique described in old accounts is to maintain a speed faster than the current to maintain steering leverage. No wonder they spoke of the dangers and foolishness of running rapids. That technique in a loaded wilderness canoe invites disaster. With the popularity of whitewater sport and the new indestructible boats, the collective skill level of paddlers has reached a point where some canoeists are confidently paddling rapids previously thought to be the sole domain of rafts and kayaks. I certainly wouldn't paddle such rapids in the wilderness, but the skills can be used to confidently descend rapids that would have sent the old ones to the portage trail.

I prefer to take a slow, cautious approach to rapids. Rather than plunging forward, a combination of back-paddles, draws, and pries can keep the boat moving slowly and ferrying back and forth across the river using the current while still pointing safely downstream. The Thlewiaza River gave us plenty of opportunities to test our skills.

We proceeded downstream with our eyes and ears alert to changing water conditions, counting river bends until the next rapid was near. I would usually hear it first.

"Shh, listen!" Drops of water dripping off our paddles resounded through our ears as we strained to hear; then, the distant rumble of cascading water would cut the silence.

"Ooh, sounds like a big one," I would say in a reverent, almost whispered voice.

We'd drift forward slowly like a hunter stalking prey, inching around the inside of each bend, wondering if the rapid was hidden just beyond. Then, one bend would unleash the roar, muffled no longer by the twisting land, and we would see the telltale sign, a horizon line across the river that dropped over some unseen obstacle. Crests of dancing waves visible over the edge, I would stand to get a better view, then scan the shore for a location to get out and scout. We'd pull over well upstream, crash through the shrubs to reach a vantage point, then evaluate the rapid. After just a glance, one of us would often say, "Not a chance, we're walking this one." We would head back and then begin the laborious unloading process.

Sometimes tempting routes appeared in the frothy whitewater. A series of tongues would connect into a possible path, and one of us would say, "What do you think?" Then we knew we were in for a lengthy discussion on the merits of paddling versus portaging. We'd pick routes, express our preferences, and iterate to a decision on a path to follow.

"Okay, we'll try to stay on river left when approaching that first tongue to avoid that nasty hole there, then we'll follow the chute down the center. When we get even with that pointy rock just above the roundish one, we'll back ferry a bit to use the eddy and run the eddy line past that curly thing there. Then just hold a good brace, keep us straight in the standing waves, and ride it out." I'd take a few confident steps toward the boat, then say as an afterthought, "And if we swim, stay with the boat. It's got all our food."

We'd walk back to the boat, usually in silence, reviewing our choreographed sequence of moves and visualizing our determined landmarks. We went through our pre-rapid rituals like pilots systematically checking their aircraft for takeoff.

"Is everything tied down good?"

"Check."

"Spare paddles accessible?"

"Well, kinda."

"Ah, we won't need them."

"Check."

We'd assume our kneeling positions, tighten the spray cover, and adjust our lifejackets. At the moment of takeoff, when we were about to charge, one of us would say, "Are you sure we should do this?"

"Check!"

I'm confident in whitewater. Still, at the top of each rapid, no matter how minor, my gut tightens and gets tighter as we peel out from the shore eddy, ferry to midstream, spin into the current and drift closer to the slick, black tongue above the drop.

There comes a point when it is too late to turn back, the

nervousness disappears, and autopilot turns on. A smooth, well-conditioned blend of strokes flows out of my arms to the paddle and we weave our way to the bottom of the drop. But sometimes the unexpected lashes up from the rapid, a curling wave knocks us off course, or a hole materializes that we didn't suspect, and we'd scramble to regain composure with whatever strokes the moment demanded. Sometimes our flawed communication system would bring the same result.

"Okay, okay, okay ..." as we bucked through straight standing waves. "Now, draw ... brace ... now power forward through this hole! Now! Whew! That was great!" It usually went smoothly.

As self-appointed captain of the ship, I continually barked commands and often misspoke to Laurie, who had her own ideas of what to do.

"Okay, now draw. Draw! DRAAAW!" I'd yell when a pry was what I wanted, which was usually what she was doing in the first place.

"Why?" she'd scream as she hesitantly obeyed. "What are we doing?"

"Oh, jeez, you know what I mean. PRY!"

But it would be too late and we'd find ourselves off course, scrambling through unscouted waters until we'd squirt through the last bit then breathe a sigh of relief as we floated in the pool below. My chuckles would be cut short by a scowl.

"WHAT were you doing?"

"Sorry, I got a little confused. Just do your thing up there. You know what to do."

I made one of those errors in a fast-water section at the bottom of a rapid with just one boulder left to avoid. Laurie listened to me; we spun sideways and struck the rock midship. Our upstream gunwale bowed low to the water, and we were pinned. Oddly, in that brief but eternal moment when the boat flexed and groaned, I thought about appendicitis, yes, inflammation of the vermiform. In my pre-trip list of potential showstoppers, pinning and appendicitis were the top two. Conjoined scenarios briefly crossed wires in my brain.

"Okay, lean into the rock!"

We leaned hard, struggling to keep water out of the boat. It's an ominous and not uncommon sight on routinely paddled rivers: the remnants of a canoe wrapped around a rock, the insides exposed to the current, the bottom cracked and twisted, bow and stern approaching each other in an unsettling visual. Sometimes bags and boxes dangle in the current; sometimes the boats are stripped clean. Always, witnesses wonder what happened to the paddlers.

We kept the gunwale high; the current eventually grabbed our bow, and slowly we pivoted around the rock, leaning until the boat regained proper vertical and drifted free. No damage.

We devised a better communication system. Instead of commanding strokes, I dictated our moves. "Ferry left, ferry right, slow down, hard forward, let's catch this eddy ..." Laurie figured out her own strokes to execute the moves.

With rehearsed skill and good judgment, we worked our way down the Thlewiaza River. After the trip, I read Downes's opinion of the river. "Both of us agreed over our evening tea and dried meat that this was one of the worst rivers of our experience. What a hellish thing to struggle through if one had a real load!" Downes traveled with just the basic supplies and a small ration of staple foods to be supplemented with wild meat. He didn't even carry a tent. Would he consider our remaining three-month food supply and assorted camping gear a real load?

***

The work was long and hard and kept us traveling late into the evenings to maintain a respectable pace. The portages became easier as our packs became lighter and we stronger. But they were time-consuming. Regardless of portage length, getting our four loads across always took one and a half to two and a half hours. Yet the walks through the forest were pleasant breaks from the boat.

I trotted back from one portage load enjoying the light, free movement along a moderately worn path until our gear pile came into view. From the edges of the pile, a dark, furry mass quickly bolted into the brush and disappeared instantly into the forest, leaving chaotic crashing sounds for a few seconds more. It took a brief moment to process until I realized that the shimmering fur that I saw covered the muscular haunches of a retreating bear. I looked around for others but saw or heard nothing. No cubs or angry mama to contend with, our packs seemed unmolested, and the moment passed.

"What's wrong?" Laurie asked when she saw me standing in the clearing doing nothing.

"I just fought a bear."

"Oh, really? Looks like you did pretty well," she smirked.

"Seriously, I just saw a bear running away from the gear."

She froze for a second, alarmed and focused.

"It's gone."

We both recognized there was nothing we could do, nor anything we could change in our routine except increase our awareness. With a shrug, I shouldered the next load and went on with the portage. Laurie did the same.

On July 19, I wrote:

Nice day ... We have settled into this trip, and it has become our lives. It doesn't feel like we're on a trip. We're just living each day ...

Like life at home, though, sometimes we lived in our own worlds right next to each other. Laurie wrote that same day:

I had a breakdown today ... We just finished portaging over first rapid and I fell for the third time (two w/packs—one on rocks loading boat). I just screamed that I was getting sick of falling six times every day. I can't stand it! Then I sobbed ... I stood against a tree and wailed. Jim stayed back, then he continued to load packs. I was very hurt at the time that he didn't even try to comfort me, but I realize he was just giving me space. That should be breakdown first and last for the season!

Maybe I was giving her space. More likely I just didn't know what to do other than load the boat. Was her outburst her way of telling me she didn't want to be here? Too late for that, so we probably shouldn't talk about it. Keep paddling and everything will be fine.

We woke early on the day when only twelve miles of the Thlewiaza River remained, expecting a full day of portaging around the many marked rapids and constrictions. I stood in the boat when the telltale roar told us we were close to the first drop. It looked runnable! Still, we beached the boat to scout since I couldn't see around the bend.

"Is this whole thing the first marked rapid?" Laurie asked.

"I don't know; maybe they all blend together."

"I think it looks doable."

"I think it looks fun."

We walked along a high ridge on shore and saw that the rapid continued uninterrupted from bend to bend. The whole stretch looked like an enjoyable, technical ride through rock-garden whitewater. We mounted up and ran the rapids while scouting from the boat, working from bend to mysterious bend. The tension of the unknown, the excitement of the moment, and the fear of surprises mounted until we were both physically and mentally exhausted. But the rapid continued mile after mile, and we rose to meet its challenge. We had an exhilarating ride through all four rapids without a portage.

Toward the end, the river shallowed and we scraped more and more until it widened and trickled over a shallow ledge of boulders that extended the entire width. We picked what we thought would be a clean route but soon were forced out of the boat to drag and scrape our way to the bottom. We plopped over the final rocks of the ledge and arrived at Nahill Lake, just one lake before Nueltin.

The physical excitement from the rapids carried us into the lake. But the quick movements and the high energy on the rapids did not belong in this new environment we just entered. An eerie calm settled over the lake; no ripple could be seen across its expanse. Our last several days had been on tumultuous rapids and windy lakes, the silence of the North masked by the thrashing water. This silence was almost disturbing, a sudden change that forced a shocking transition in our mood. We floated motionless to let our racing minds and bodies adjust to the new, gentle world. A storm was brewing in the clouds, but no wind upset the flat surface. Each paddle thump and checked whisper sliced through the oppressive silence and raced across the lake surface into the horizon. A lovely swirl of pastel blues and grays reflected from the sky, and soon, our motions slowed and blended into the new scene.

We pushed directly across the lake toward the distant eastern shore, four miles away, where we expected to find the Thlewiaza River again. Each of our synchronized strokes seemed to push the boat into a perpetual glide over the mirrored water. Our wake spread wide behind us, blurring the once perfect reflections, and the motion of the boat produced a gentle undulation too slight to break the surface of the water we had yet to cross. We passed through a series of islands as a light, warm rain began to fall, and soon we detected the current of the Thlewiaza leaving through a shallow bay.

The current picked up, and we raced over a deep, swift rapid before pulling over a little too close to Nueltin Falls for comfort. A well-used trail brought us to a granite platform extending into a small bay that opened up into the vast expanse of Nueltin Lake.

CHAPTER SEVEN

SLEEPING ISLAND:
GATEWAY TO THE BARREN LANDS

MILE 251-304

"We climbed a hill. What a sight! Islands ... bays ... channels ... islands everywhere, every direction of the compass points, a vast maze as far as the eye could see. What was main shore, lakes, bays, islands, or points was all one endless confusion. Both of us wondered about either getting anywhere or back. It is not easy to paddle and map and get bearings all at the same time."

—Prentice Downes

I thought we might not see anyone the whole time when we were planning the trip. I envisioned telling a story to friends that we were completely alone in the most remote region on the continent for three months. I knew it couldn't really happen, though. Could it? After a week, I thought it might. After two weeks, it seemed likely. After eighteen days, as we approached the end of the southern and most accessible limb of the triangle, I didn't give it a second thought. We hadn't even heard a mechanical noise since Wollaston Lake! Then, at the foot of Nueltin Falls, the tail of a yellow-and-white floatplane jutted out into the lake from a protected cove. The distant drone of an outboard motor slowly overtook the roar of the falls.

We didn't speak for a few moments. It didn't seem real. At least I didn't want it to be. I dropped my paddle across the gunwales, its "clunk" echoed across the water and merged with the sound of the motor as it rose and fell. I felt crowded and wanted to scream with rage.

I recognize that people can enjoy the wilderness however they want, but I loathed those methods we saw that day. We paddled past the base, the shore lined with boats, and dug deep with mighty strokes, feeling as if someone was chasing us, until we made it out of earshot into the subduing calm of the northern evening. I don't know if they saw us. We escaped without any interaction.

My journal entry that night is tough to read with lots of barely coherent ramblings fueled by disappointment, self-pity ... and judgment. Anyone with enough money could hire a plane and see the same thing I had labored for weeks to see. Why learn the ways of the wilderness to see this country if an aircraft can get you here? Proper wilderness clothing, paddling skills, survival skills, woodcraft, weather knowledge, and route finding are relegated to recreational hobbies by the aircraft! I consoled myself by thinking theirs was not a wilderness experience, just a fishing vacation. Do they even know where they were? Why come this far north to pull fish out of a lake?

I pitied them for what they didn't know: that their joyful experience could be even more so if they had gotten there the way we did. How can you understand the land and routes that define the wilderness from ten thousand feet in the air? Yet the nagging awareness that you don't really have to travel by canoe to get north cheapened the experience for me. I even felt a little foolish. At any point in my trip, anybody could drop from the sky and join me for dinner.

Then, another boatload of tourists zipped by to begin their holiday in the wilderness as we crept along the shore, seeking safety from the waves they didn't seem to notice. If they saw us, they might have wondered why we would waste so much time paddling to Nueltin when they could get there with a quick flight. I suppose I am a tourist, too, but for the past nineteen days, I had begun to think of myself as a hardened northern traveler.

I understand that my aversion to seeing people in the wilderness conflicts with my delight from seeing signs of people from the past. But in a way, I guess that's like choosing between graffiti on a rock and an ancient pictograph of a hunter slaying a deer.

***

I expected our arrival at Nueltin Lake to be heralded with screaming winds. The air was motionless that evening. The glassy black water was cut only by the movement of our boat. We cruised at an enjoyable speed until we found a beautiful campsite above a sandy beach on a small island. The numerous islands surrounding our site created a secure feeling. But the terribly exposed Nueltin Lake lay just beyond the islands. The southern portion is so cluttered with islands that it resembles a large network of twisty rivers and streams that break open into occasional smaller lakes and bays. Beyond a narrow corridor, the lake widens into a broad sheet of water virtually free of islands and continues until the Thlewiaza River carries its waters east to Hudson Bay. We were still in the comfortable shelter of the northern forests. Northward, just thirty miles from this night's camp, the forest yields to the enchanting and remote Barren Lands that we had come here to experience. Our arrival at Nueltin Lake inspired a cautious confidence that we might just be able to reach Angikuni Lake.

I spread out some maps on the hull of the overturned red boat that had brought us here. A few new scratches and deep gouges laced the hull. A small chip in the bow must have appeared when Laurie and I miscommunicated in a small rapid. Still, the canoe was holding up pretty well. The boat and our gear were not on my list of concerns. I reviewed the remaining terrain, re-identified the potential problem spots, and re-worried about getting stopped by any of the many unknown sections to come. If conditions worked in our favor, we could be out by September 30—two more months.

We didn't have a map for the southern end of Nueltin Lake. It was just a day or two of paddling, but it would be intimidating nevertheless. I remembered the lake was cluttered with islands so that from water level, it would be impossible to sight the route. The western shoreline is disrupted by deep bays with peninsulas that, from a distance, look like islands, and islands that might be peninsulas. Following the shoreline could add scores of miles, while island-hopping could expose us to the vastness of the main lake. I remembered that the lakeshores converged to a section the width of a large river somewhere to the north. If we held a northern route, we would inevitably end up there. We chose the island-hopping route.

Oberholtzer climbed a hill to scout his way when he was here. I'm sure he felt the fear of uncertainty and wondered if he would make it off the lake before winter closed in. It was already mid-August for him. He and Billy Magee had been traveling for nearly fifty days since The Pas, Manitoba, where they started. I knew about the narrows and the approximate location of our exit point. He didn't even know where the lake ultimately drained to. As far as he knew, his route could have taken him to the Arctic Ocean. He and Magee committed anyway.

Oberholtzer read Tyrrell's expedition account; he must have known about their desperate dash for survival on the remote west coast of Hudson Bay. The image of Tyrrell camped in a blinding blizzard, nearly starved with little hope of making it to the outside world, must have haunted Oberholtzer's dreams.

Undaunted, Oberholtzer and Magee picked their way north and crossed the treeless boundary into the Barren Lands, battling storms, blind bays, and confusing island mazes. On one hilltop, which he named Hawkes Summit, Oberholtzer left a note in a tin can that described their position and the condition of their supplies. Twelve years later, Husky Harris and Windy Smith, prominent traders from the Kasmere Lake region, climbed the same hill and found the note. They didn't know who Oberholtzer was, but Harris was impressed enough to tell Prentice Downes about Oberholtzer when they met in Churchill fourteen years later.

Oberholtzer and Magee reached the salty waters of Hudson Bay after fifteen grueling days on the rapid-choked lower Thlewiaza River. They had reached a state of despair; their supplies were running shockingly low. Winter was approaching swiftly. Facing similar conditions on Hudson Bay that Tyrrell narrowly survived, they had the incredible fortune of meeting an Inuit family living on the coast. They spent some time with them, then bought passage on their small sailing boat to Churchill. If not for this stroke of luck, they would likely have perished on the difficult waters of Hudson Bay.

They rested in the comfort of the Churchill post, but they were still far from home. They faced a long coastal paddle to York Factory, then a four-hundred-mile upstream and overland journey back to Winnipeg. They paddled through cold driving rain, sleet, and heavy snow. Ice froze on their paddles as they struggled up the current of the Hayes River; they wrapped spare clothing around their wet feet to ward off the cold. On November 5, 1912, well into the northern winter, they finally paddled into the frontier civilization of Winnipeg, completing an epic journey of 144 days.

In the years that followed, the region bustled with the activity of those men of the Far North who established the numerous trading posts surrounding Nueltin Lake. The twenty-five years of fur trade brought many transient people through the region, but when Downes set out in 1939 from Brochet, the route was still generally unmapped. Downes's records show that the land had indeed remained the same, but a whole society of wilderness travelers had come and gone. Where Oberholtzer preceded the beginning of an era, Downes saw its end.

Downes saw the lower limb of our triangle when various elements of its history intersected in complex ways. He saw the final days of the Chipewyan living on the land as he sought route information from them. Where Oberholtzer found a camp of Chipewyan in 1912, Downes found only evidence of an old winter camp containing twenty-five graves. He described the place as "a depressing scene of death and abandonment." Still, in 1939, Downes found the Chipewyan holding on to their wilderness lives, although changes were coming to the North. Downes traveled among the last traders, introducing the era of recreational wilderness canoeing. Outboard motors had now found their way to the back of canoes.

Downes and Albrecht traveled up Nueltin Lake and into Windy Bay where they completed their trip at Windy Post, the HBC post that we had hoped to find. There, Downes boarded a floatplane bound for Churchill. Although the floatplane was a recent addition to the North Country, by the 1930s it had already become an essential tool in the work of the North and was becoming a legitimate method for canoeists to enter and exit wilderness rivers. Albrecht, however, paddled alone, three weeks and hundreds of miles upstream and overland, back to Brochet to complete one of the countless unknown yet epic trips in that time when wilderness paddling was a way of life.

Although Downes thought he might be opening up new country, he was excited to learn about Oberholtzer's trip twenty-five years earlier. The two met soon after Downse's trip and congratulated each other on being the only white men to have set a canoe in the waters of Nueltin Lake. We know, of course, that they were not the first. Perhaps it's true that they were the only white recreational canoeists to have set a canoe in Nueltin Lake. But Downes must have known about the two decades of traders and trappers who worked the country between Brochet and Nueltin Lake. He had Keighley's map. Even a Hollywood crew made the arduous trek in the 1920s from Brochet to Nueltin Lake to film the caribou herds for a silent movie. Still, I can't blame Downes for his oversight. He wrote his book when information was less available. I'm guilty of the same thing. I knew a lot about the old explorers, a little about the adventurers like Downes and Oberholtzer, and nothing about modern travelers when I planned our route. Like Downes, I saw myself as following in the wake of those past people of the wilderness.

Fifty-two years after Downes's journey, the land was as remote and rugged as recorded in any old journal. Nueltin Lake still lies hundreds of miles beyond the roadhead. The portages are just as long, the rapids just as raging, and Brochet is still the nearest outpost community. But hidden in the moss, spruce, pine, and granite of this remote wilderness are signs of even greater change than Downes ever saw. Instead of Chipewyan families camping on lakeshores, we found only their old campsites. And the lake that was so elusive even in the 1930s, although still incredibly remote by distance, now hosts a tourist fly-in fish camp. The ways of the Old North cannot be witnessed in the lives of travelers encountered on the trail, but only in the faded pages of forgotten journals. Regardless, we found Nueltin Lake to be a wonderful natural treasure.

***

A slight ripple began to break the calm lake surface as the evening progressed; a steady wind blew from the north when we climbed into our bags. When this happens, it's a good bet that a strong wind will blow through the next day. Our effort to rise early to beat the wind was futile. Large rolling waves crashed against our sandy beach. A flurry of whitecaps laced the ominous lake.

Our route for the day stayed in this cluster of islands for about four miles with little exposure to open water. The wind came directly from the north so most of our paddling was at a safe, direct angle, but it seemed to stop us in our wake from the very first stroke of the day.

We departed our island and headed directly across a mile of water to the next island through the largest waves and most intense wind we had paddled in so far. Each unified stroke, exerted with the effort of doing a pull-up and with seemingly equal forward progress, would get us just over a wave crest, and then Laurie's bow would submarine into the trough of the next wave. There was no glide after each stroke but a halt in forward motion and a quick, feathered paddle recovery before being blown backward.

We inched toward the distant island. It seemed as though we sat halfway across for the better part of the morning, just being tossed around by the waves. The relentless wind created a chaotic symphony of sounds, laying down explosive whips on top of a persistent background hiss, interrupted by the banging of our paddles on the gunwales as we fought to control the canoe. Tremendous gusts would tear across the water, imposing small, rippled waves on top of the large rollers. Spray from the white crests hit us like rain, and we would battle, heads down and muscles tensed, to hold our position. It was a clear, warm morning, but the wind put a clammy chill on any exposed skin.

With hats, gloves, and Gore-Tex suits, it looked like we were on a winter expedition. The trees on the far island gradually took individual shapes as we advanced. The waves grew smaller, the wind a bit quieter, the sun a bit warmer, until we glided into the calming protection of the lee shore. We followed this shore until it angled into the wind and opened to another exhausting crossing.

We were missing several miles of maps for this complex island-and-bay section due to our unplanned route change back on the Thlewiaza River, so we climbed high hills to scout routes. It was thrilling to get a taste of what it must have been like for the early travelers. We only had to round a large peninsula, but several small bays occasionally lured us into their dead-end path, usually requiring a strenuous upwind paddle.

When Downes arrived at this maze of islands on Nueltin Lake, he recorded in his journal:

> We started out after the strong northwest wind moderated a bit. Our course was north and a bit west. We followed the main shore of high sand banks as we had been given to believe that the main west shore was moderately straight. We kept the islands on our right hand. We went along for some hours into a headwind, and at last it became apparent that we had run into a long dead-end bay. This was discouraging as we seemed hemmed in everywhere by points and islands ... This lake had been variously estimated from one hundred and twenty to one hundred and eighty miles long, and

to be hopelessly trapped in the first three hours is not at all a good prospect.

They struggled through the maze until they camped that evening within sight of their previous night's camp. Their frustration and fear of the unknown brought them to the verge of quitting.

We regained our map by midmorning at a large island with a tall hill. After a difficult crossing, we arrived at the island on the lee shore, basked in the warmth of the silent sun, then climbed the hill to get a view. We gained the summit and saw a three-mile crossing running sideways to the wind and waves into very exposed water. We then found a pleasant gravel beach in a small, protected bay on the lee shore and soon were both napping in the warm sun.

The day passed quickly and we spent our time alternately napping, cooking, and just clowning around. The day seemed perfectly calm from our sheltered cove. The warm sun shone through a cloudless sky; the world was silent and relaxed. The conditions seemed prime for paddling, and I would get restless. But the unceasing, violent wind slapped me in the face each time I climbed the hill to scout. Evening came, and we held hope that we might be able to move.

"I think it's a bit calmer now. What do you think?" I asked Laurie, who was perched on a boulder overlooking the lake, her long hair straightened back with the wind.

"What? You have to yell in this wind!"

"Really, it's a bit calmer. Listen, the trees aren't whipping as loudly, and they're not as many whitecaps on the lake."

"I think I'd rather wait a while longer."

We had similar conversations into the evening, alternating roles of the patient and the restless. By 8 p.m., with the sun hanging low in the sky, we both convinced ourselves that the wind had calmed. Unwilling to settle for a four-mile day, we pushed around the island and crossed a small bay to test the waters before committing to the big crossing. That small crossing was just as brutal and wet as the others, and we realized that our impatience had fooled us into false expectations. We sat in the lee of a small bluff before the crossing and debated our situation as a light rain began to fall.

"We should have stayed where we were," Laurie said.

"Well, we're here now. This place doesn't look too hospitable."

"Do you want to go back?"

"Not a chance! It was too much work getting here. I bet we'd be okay if we did the crossing. We don't have to go directly across to the point. We could ferry across, keeping a slight angle to the waves until we get to that shore, then paddle along the shore to the point. It'd be longer, but I think we'll be okay."

"Okay," Laurie reluctantly agreed.

We paddled around the bluff and were immediately confronted by a cold wind that forced us back to the bluff's shelter, then repeated the previous conversation.

"We didn't have the right angle coming into the waves. Let's try it again," I said more to myself or the wind than to Laurie.

After several minutes of indecision, looking for a campsite on this shore, looking over the water to the far shore, and fretting, Laurie finally said out of frustration, "Let's just do it!"

and then dug in hard with her paddle. I followed in the stern, and soon we were making the crossing. We angled our way across, made the far shore with little trouble, and then paddled its length to the distant point. The wind had indeed calmed considerably and the waves reduced to gentle, undulating, easily paddleable breakers. I chided Laurie a bit about her impatient, reckless decision, and the phrase, "Let's just do it!" which soon became a jokey cliché whenever we had a decision to make.

It was 10:30 p.m. in the gray, post-sunset night of the Far North before we finally camped on a small sandy beach just a few yards from the frothing water. I lay in my bag staring at the tent ceiling for hours. I'm not sure if it was the flapping and fluttering of the tent in the increasing wind that kept me awake or the thoughts that were going through my mind. In my map-reading session earlier, I took a closer look at part of our return route and was overwhelmed by the gaping uncertainties we would face. I scolded myself for not thoroughly researching the route and began to consider other options. That point in our trip was still far off, but it dominated my thoughts on that night on Nueltin Lake. The shaking of the tent overtook my thoughts, and I again expected that we might not be able to get far the next day. My random thoughts fused into general tension as I drifted into a fitful sleep.

The wind built back to full intensity by sunrise. Our route for the day closely followed the western shoreline, so we pushed forward. We moved from point to point, resting our arms when we could. On one such break, a collection of well-placed rocks disrupted the randomness of the gravel beach. They spelled out the message, "Canoe Go." Was this a message for us, or had it been here for years? It might have been constructed by a Chipewyan who didn't have full command of the English language, perhaps one of the guides from the fishing base. If it was meant for us, was it a warning telling us to get out as we were told on our arrival at Wollaston Lake, or was it an encouraging cheer? We went with the cheer and welcomed the encouragement.

***

My thoughts relaxed with the fading wind as we crossed bays on the western shore of Nueltin Lake in the rolling aftermath of earlier storms. The landscape was changing. The forested shores of the lakes and rivers we traversed the last few weeks were thinning. High points on islands were treeless clusters of boulders. Distant shorelines were increasingly sparse. We were approaching the northern limit of trees. With each mile we paddled north, the land became more and more barren until we reached the point on our map where green turned to white and we officially crossed the tree line. We recorded our ceremonial crossing with a picture of us standing next to a scraggly tree on a small island hill. The island was forested on the southern side and barren on the northern.

The vegetation pattern of the island was odd, but that wasn't what drew us to its hilltop. A small disruption that looked like a man-made structure broke the contour of the hill. We scaled its height and found a column-like pile of flat, jagged rocks about five feet tall.

"Could this be an inukshuk?" I wondered aloud.

In the language of the Inuit, inukshuk means "something

that resembles a man," or so I've heard. In their vast, feature-less landscape, they erected these inukshuks at various promi-nent points. Sometimes they were built as navigation tools and sometimes as hunting aids to direct caribou into the ambush of awaiting hunters. But they were often constructed simply to mark their land. Perhaps they were built to give companionship in the empty loneliness of the barrens. For us, it was a ceremo-nial gateway to the Barren Lands.

We found an attractive island campsite with just enough trees to provide a comfortable shelter from the intense sun. We napped then lit a fire and made a splendid meal of pizza and barley soup, plus bannock for the next day's lunch. The silence of the North had returned with the disappearance of the wind, a cloudless sky gradually darkened as the setting sun painted the surrounding rocky hills with its golden rays, and a full moon rose through the reddening sky.

"This could be the last fire for a while," I said, leaning back on a red food pack. Laurie slurped a spoonful of hot soup, breathed sharply to cool it in her mouth, then stood and looked at our pile of wood.

"Let's have a fire then!"

There was a thick piece of driftwood I had dragged up from the beach. Laurie pushed the butt-end of it into the fire, and we pushed it further into the fire as it burned into the evening as we wrote in our journals, chatting about the days to come.

We anticipated significant changes in our routine as we entered the barrens. Neither of us had ever camped without the comforting presence of the forest. We spent our honeymoon backpacking in the high mountains of Colorado, but camped below the tree line at night. Ahead of us was a six-week paddle and portage route through the Barren Lands of the Ahiarmiut.

That said, we planned to remain in the sparsely forested land for a few more days. Just before the lake narrows, a few miles from our camp, we mapped out a portage route to take us out of Nueltin Lake and into Windy Lake and the Windy River, which we intended to follow until it re-entered Nueltin about thirty-five miles north.

I gave up on Windy Lake earlier when we abandoned the Putahow portage and followed the Thlewiaza River instead. I didn't want to do it again. Windy's shores were lined with old campsites, traplines, and burial sites that John wanted photographed. A bonus was that the tree line extended a bit farther north on Windy so that we could take advantage of the wood for a few days longer. I later learned that the route I mapped out was the same that Downes had followed to reach Windy Lake and the now-defunct HBC trading post at the mouth of the Windy River.

We woke early to a beautifully calm, breathless day. The canoe seemed to travel on its own as we glided across surprisingly flat water. Within an hour we reached the point where we planned to leave Nueltin Lake.

"Are we portaging out of Nueltin to avoid wind?" Laurie wondered aloud.

"That's the plan."

"Seems pretty not windy."

With barely a word spoken, we changed our plan, abandoned the portage route to Windy Lake, and dug our paddles into the marathon day of flatwater cruising, hoping to make it as far as Smith Bay where the Windy River enters the lake. It was a gamble since we didn't know if the winds would pick up on the other side of the narrows, but the gamble paid off. After the river-like swift-water narrows, we found an almost eerie calm across the massive expanse of Nueltin Lake.

The miles accumulated rapidly, the progress was exhilarating, and by noon we were on track to have our biggest mileage day of the trip. Greedy and drunk on mileage, we paddled hard with the wind at our backs and intentionally cruised right past Smith Bay and the final route to Windy Lake. In that moment, the history that made the region so attractive from my home office was far less inspiring than the miles that fell away behind us and the prospect for more.

I'm a regretter. It's just who I am. I used to believe in the common wisdom that says we shouldn't dwell in the past, that we should just enjoy the present and look to the future. "No rearview mirror if you want to be happy," says every self-help guide on the planet. I don't buy it anymore. When I regret, I linger in the past that gave me so much joy and I imagine how it could have been even better. Those thoughts turn into dreams and visions that inspire me. And I don't live in the moment. I revel in the path that I took to reach each moment; I wonder where other paths might have led; and I delight in anticipating the next moment. My moments encompass all I've experienced and all I hope to become. Why anyone would want to focus on just the here and now is beyond my comprehension.

That evening, after our twenty-eight-mile day on Nueltin Lake, the wind that thankfully stayed away during the day returned as evening slid into night. It occurred to me that if it had been windy that morning, I would have taken the route to Windy Lake and the HBC post. I would have found the remnants of that intersecting culture of Indigenous and new-world explorers and adventurers who lived by the paddle and inspired me to come here in the first place. I sank into a deep pit of regret that I couldn't escape for days. So yes, I'm a regretter. But the inspiration it brings is beyond what I could ever get from living in the moment!

***

Long periods of silence passed as we monotonously pushed our way from point to point on the western shore of Nueltin Lake. A broad, seemingly endless sheet of water stretched before us. We sighted our goals miles away. Landmarks were slow to arrive despite our fast pace. In midafternoon, we were lured into a large and exposed crossing with a gentle breeze beginning to blow. Small waves began to develop, and we soon were tacking back and forth with the growing waves to reach a distant peninsula. We didn't feel threatened but a little discouraged by the slackened pace we were forced into. We were on schedule for our highest mileage day when I heard the unmistakable drone of an outboard motor. I scanned the horizon and spotted a small craft moving swiftly across the water.

It was a boat from the fishing lodge returning from a day's ventures. Immediately, I sank into my well-rehearsed anger and mumbled indecencies at the intrusion on *my* wilderness experience. Four hundred miles from the nearest road and I was feeling crowded. To my disbelief and regret, the boat seemed to change its course and head for us.

"Oh man, is it coming this way? Please go away! Please go away!" I chanted.

"I think it's coming this way," Laurie dryly replied.

The boat pulled alongside us and a friendly voice shouted, "Hello!"

This was our only contact with other humans since we left Wollaston Lake over twenty days earlier. I didn't know it then, but it would be another fifty-two days of wonderful solitude before we sighted any humans again on our return.

The boat held the fish camp manager and two youths. We talked about our route while we floated nervously in the rolling waves and they casually sat in their stable craft.

"Where'd ya come from?" the manager asked.

"Wollaston Lake. We're going to get as far north as possible, then get back to Wollaston just before freeze-up."

"Wow! That's an impressive distance. Freeze-up comes early up here, so be careful. Actually, you're pretty lucky to be paddling now. Last year, a guy came through about this time, maybe a little earlier, and the ice hadn't left the lake yet. He was stuck for a week."

He was aware of just that one paddler last year.

"Hmm. The weather's pretty nice now," I said.

"Yup. Hey, you're in for a treat just ahead. The caribou are coming south already. We saw about five thousand of them coming down the shoreline over that hill up there."

"Really? Isn't it a bit early for them to come south?"

"I don't know. Maybe we're having an early fall. See all those things that look like rocks? Those are the caribou."

"Whoa, this is great! Thanks for the tip."

The boaters motored off, and we immediately forgot about paddling as far as possible. Twenty-eight miles is far enough for a day on Nueltin Lake. Instead, we set our sights on the peninsula.

CHAPTER EIGHT

Tuktu! Encounters with
the Barren Lands Caribou

Mile 304–347

"Wherever there were caribou, that's where we lived
... I lived a poor life; many times we had nothing to eat.
We made our fires with flint stones ... [and] people
walked with snowshoes all day. Once we set up our
tent, a fire was made in it and we cooked whatever we
caught that day ... I lived through it all."

—Dene elder, 1980s

We beached the canoe among the boulders, grabbed the cameras,
and dashed up the barren hill. I saw nothing. The rolling hills
dotted with large rocks seemed lifeless. The silence of the barren
plains filled my ears, and I wondered how five thousand caribou
could disappear in this terribly exposed land. Slowly, my perception of the landscape changed. The distant boulders became
animals—caribou, and hundreds of them!

Across the bay, on the far shoreline a few hundred yards
away, a hillside was alive with the flowing movement of a caribou
herd. What initially appeared to be the undulating distortions of

heatwaves was a dense congregation of caribou rapidly moving up the slope to the ridgetop. The tail end of a herd of several thousand animals extended around the bay to our peninsula. We walked about half a mile to where the main herd had passed and saw the wake of its movement—trampled vegetation, thousands of hoofprints in well-defined trails, and tufts of fur on stunted shrubs marked their passage. Bands of several hundred animals continued to follow the path. We wandered separately, pursuing our sightings in the chaos of roaming animals, snapping photos, visually stalking individuals, and gazing in wonder at the dynamic, undulating landscape.

I approached within fifty feet of about twenty-five animals milling around in a small cluster of trees sheltered in a stream valley before any noticed me. In unison, they lifted their heads from the willows they were feeding on and turned toward me. I froze like the proverbial kid with his hand in the cookie jar. Silent excitement grew as several animals took tentative steps to get a better look at the strange newcomer. We studied each other with seemingly equal curiosity. Somewhere between the size of a white-tail deer and a moose, the caribou supports its barrel-shaped body on spindly legs that flail in all directions when it runs. Their massive frames and rich brown coats radiate strength and power. A long neck supports a head that appears too small for its body. Both males and females sport antlers, although female antlers are twiggy looking compared to the enormous structures males carry. Their thick necks, sometimes white on the underside, taper to their heads, supporting two branches of colossal, symmetrical, velvet racks that arch back from their heads and reach skyward to almost four feet, with nearly equal spreads between the two halves. A third appendage of the rack is a vertical, wind-vane-like plate extending along the ridge of their nose that looks as if it would make them cross-eyed.

These animals looked sick. Ribs showed through sagging skin on most. Maybe they were the old and injured, unable to keep up with the main herd. I expected to see wolves, but none appeared. I read that wolves were constant companions of the herd, trailing the weak for convenient kills. Equally revered and reviled, wolves occupy a strange place in northern culture and folklore with some groups elevating them to almost sacred status while others call for their extermination. I just wanted to see one loping across the tundra.

I sought a good vantage point to be less intrusive. My movement, however, sent the group and several hundred others nearby dashing away in a large arc to get around me and join their companions. They dispersed and joined other bands that also roamed and dispersed.

From a hilltop, I could see maybe five hundred caribou moving around in what seemed random motions but then abrupt formations. Several hundred animals would stand around in a loose pack, seemingly uninterested in travel. Instantly, they would dash off with a clear purpose as if following an invisible leader.

I watched the herd until it looked like the last band had moved over the hill across the bay. The land was once again empty, the silence had returned, and the boulders I saw were rocks. Several times, as I walked back to the canoe looking for Laurie, an old or sick animal left behind would leap from a hiding place in my path and hobble away to catch up with the distant herd. One old, gray buck with a rack far too heavy for him to bear struggled desperately with two crippled legs to escape me. I had come within fifteen feet of his hiding place, perhaps his intended final resting place, as he toiled mightily to stand and flee. His tongue was hanging sickly from his mouth, and I could hear his painful panting clearly until he reached a grove of trees where I think he again lay down to rest.

The reflective silence of my walk back was disrupted as a female caribou approached me and released a noise similar to the baa of a barnyard sheep but without the vibrato. I stopped and turned and saw her staring at me about fifty feet away. She turned to run away, but as I resumed walking, she again ran toward me, bleating. As I continued walking, she repeated this unnerving behavior as if she couldn't decide whether to charge. She never got within threatening distance, but she was distressed by my presence. As I walked away from her, she became more troubled. She ran away until it looked like she had left for good but then came charging back again. She did not appear sick or injured, and it puzzled me why she was not with the main herd. Then I was startled as a small caribou just a few months old jumped from hiding, not five feet from me. The youngster had been injured and could barely walk. The healthy mother had stayed behind with her calf and tried to lure me away with her antics. The young one mustered all its strength to hobble and partially crawl to its calling mother, and soon they were reunited. They slowly wandered away in the direction of the main herd, but they were far behind.

We arrived at our canoe near dusk and decided to set up

camp. This was our first Barren Lands campsite, on the slope of a boulder-strewn ridge rising a hundred feet above the lake. During the day, the trees had faded away behind us and before us lay the vast expanse of the Barren Lands. Infrequently, dwarfed trees appeared in protected gullies, but the first phase of our journey—the forest part of it—was over; we had begun our tundra experience. The task of picking a tent site amused me as there were no boundaries here. Our forest sites had been well-defined with obvious locations—the tent went in the largest clearing and the fire in the safest place. Here we had the odd luxury of unlimited space. No location was particularly advantageous over the next, so we randomly plopped down and staked a claim among the rocks. We took advantage of the driftwood and dead shrubs along the shore and built what we again thought would be our last fire for a month until we returned to the forests.

The blatantly exposed beauty of our surroundings was shocking. Evening approached as the sun hung low over the southwestern horizon, the rolling barren hills painted by golden rays. This was not the flat, gentle tundra I had expected. The soft, moss-covered ground I had envisioned was clearly in some other region of the Barren Lands. Coarse gravel deposits and countless boulders ranging in size from baseballs to Volkswagens covered the land, like a talus slope above the tree line on a high mountain. The unweathered, jagged rocks lay in haphazard piles as if the great ice sheet that covered this land had just recently deposited them. I climbed the gentle hill behind our tent to an exposed igneous ridge, weaving my way through boulders transported from lands far to the north. To the south was the vast panorama of Nueltin Lake where we had paddled. There was no trace of the rich forests where we had camped just the night before.

The sheer space—the wide-open, vast expanse of the barrens—was overwhelming. How could anyone have carved a life out of this stark land? Scarred and bleeding with the waters sprawled across its expanse, this land seemed to offer little to support human existence. Yet, imprinted in the land were clues to the life source for all who lived there. The caribou trails that crossed the land everywhere we traveled were the result of a natural force inherent in the land, like a bed carved by a stream or a dune scoured by the wind. The stream of caribou that flows across the land, at times in trickles and other times in floods, stands as a symbol of steadfastness. Human societies have come and gone, and wolves, hunters, and disease continue to prey upon the herds, but from the time the ice sheet first uncovered the barrens to this day, the stream of resilient rations has continued to flow.

***

Twenty-two days and 329 miles—by both measures we had traveled about three times farther than any canoe trip I had ever been on, and July 24 was a day like none I had ever experienced. Our largest mileage day of the trip occurred on a lake that I feared could halt us, and it wrapped together some bitter disappointments and exhilarating joys. Altogether, July 24 hit most pre-trip goals.

What was one of the most regretful decisions you made? To skip Windy Bay on July 24. What was one of your biggest hopes that went unfulfilled? To go the entire duration without talking to another human, dashed on July 24. What was one of your most anticipated milestones? The day we paddled out of the forest and into the Barren Lands on July 24. What goal seemed the most outrageous? When our first caribou sighting involved a herd of thousands.

I sighted Laurie in the canoe about fifty yards from shore. Her effort to fetch water in the deeper parts of the bay had turned into a peaceful evening paddle. She, too, was lost in the wilderness of her mind, reflecting on our experiences of the day. I got a fire going, ready to cook dinner when she returned with the water.

I rummaged through the packs, collecting ingredients for potato and cheese soup. The cheese cubes were no longer distinct; the wax that encased the individual cubes a few weeks ago melted in the summer heat and fused into an amorphous mass. I ripped off a chunk, picked out what wax I could, and shredded the rest into the soup.

It felt hot sitting on the tundra, brushing away flies as we scooped the cheesy soup with hot cornbread. It rarely reaches eighty degrees Fahrenheit in the Barren Lands of the Northwest Territories, but it felt like it. It was probably more like sixty-five under a bright sun. It surprised me to hear what sounded like light rain on a tarp. The noise grew until my awareness of it transferred from the almost subconscious to the conscious. Laurie heard the noise too and wondered aloud what it was. "I don't know," I said. "Maybe it's the wind blowing our bags around." But when I looked at the bags, they lay as motionless as the rocks around them. The air was completely still, and when we held our faces and hands to the sky to feel the rain that we thought was falling, we felt nothing. Suddenly, with the excitement of a child at Christmas, Laurie pointed over my shoulder and proclaimed, "It's not rain; it's more caribou!"

A caribou's ankle joints are loosely held together by tendons that produce a soft "click" each time they take a step, much like the sound of knuckles popping. The sound is space-filling when thousands of caribou walk in unison, with all four ankles clicking. Sure enough, coming over the hill where I had just been, the front of another wave of caribou following the migration trail ambled toward our tent. With the patience and slyness of the most amateur of wildlife photographers, I grabbed my camera and dashed up the hill.

An incredible sight greeted me. Extending along the main lakeshore to the north, as far as I could see in the fading light of dusk, was a seemingly endless procession of caribou. Our arrival on the hilltop pushed the procession down the opposite slope, but it flowed despite our presence. Five miles to the north, this pear-shaped peninsula on which we were camped connects to the mainland by a quarter-mile-wide piece of land and gradually widens to the south. In their singular focus on heading south, the caribou crossed this piece of land perhaps unaware that they were on a peninsula. They continued along the lakeshore until they reached the end of the peninsula and ran out of land. When we saw them coming over the hill toward our tent, they had turned around and were heading back north to go around the bay as their predecessors earlier in the day had done. But the land across the bay was just another small peninsula. I wished I could have told them it was a false bay and they had to return five miles to the north to get back on track.

We sat on the hilltop and marveled at the spectacle, a large U-shaped parade of caribou following their instinctive yearnings to roam. But this was more than random and purposeless wandering. The line moved rapidly, each animal traveling at a light trot as if they all knew where they were going. I wondered if they did know, or if only the leaders we saw climbing the hill across the bay had a purpose and the others just followed. Were they planning for winter, or were they just following some instinctive urge, confused over their compulsion to travel? Regardless, they were traveling hard and fast.

From the land I'd earlier viewed as lifeless and stark, life in abundance came tumbling out of the north. The rapid appearance of masses of ungulates illustrated the ephemeral quality of life here. This caribou corridor was the secret to survival for northern people who for ages had shaped their lives around great migration routes like this one. The neck of this peninsula, where the herd must pass twice, would have been a fine place to establish a hunting camp.

This was probably the post-calving aggregation of the Kaminuriak herd that the biologist Francis Harper studied in the 1940s when he lived with the Schweder family in that last of the old trading posts in the Nueltin Lake country. Biologists name the various herds that are scattered about the North after the location of their calving grounds. This herd calves in the Kaminuriak Lake region far to the north, near Baker Lake. Each spring, from late March to mid-April, the caribou move out of their winter homes in the forests and head north to their calving grounds in mass movements. This marks the renewal of life on the barrens after the long, bleak winters. Stirred by the lengthening days or the changes in snow cover, the cows, heavy with calves, feel the pressure of spring much greater than the bulls and head north first. They cover over a thousand miles to the same place year after year along the traditional routes from their various wintering grounds to where they were born.

The yearlings that had rarely separated from their mothers typically can't keep up with the demanding pace of the spring migration. They gather in small bands, sharing their new independence. The bulls and infertile cows follow the same paths but at a much more relaxed pace. Traveling is hard at that time of year. The snow is still deep, and food is scarce. But the cows must race to reach the calving grounds in time. Births occur in the first two weeks of June. The time following births is a much-needed resting period for the cows and a critical time for bonding between newborns and mothers. A newborn caribou will follow anything, so the mother must establish her position. Confrontations between mothers and intruders during the first few days after birth can become violent.

It would seem logical that this period after birth would leave the caribou vulnerable to predation, but this is not typically true. The calving grounds were chosen for their safe locations. Wolves, usually the herds' constant companions, stop following them in May to have their pups, and the calving grounds are typically centered in areas unsuitable for wolf denning. Regardless, the cows remain wary.

After just a few days of rest, these gregarious creatures are again seized with the urge to band together and roam. Calves only a few days old are expected to keep pace with the traveling herd. Small groups begin to leave the calving grounds and coalesce. Soon the bucks arrive, and the post-calving aggregations form.

The summer herds are spectacular when all the caribou in a particular region gather and travel as a single force, like water molecules in a river. Animals lose individual identities, and the great herd becomes one overwhelming entity. There are random movements of single animals, but the general motion of the mass always overpowers the individuals. These summer movements are not driven by biological urges like the spring migration but are thought to be attempts to escape the wicked torment of insects. Soon after the new generation of calves are born, a new generation of mosquitoes descends upon the barrens. As if to help each other through a crisis, whole herds band together and aimlessly travel across the tundra, seeking insect relief by traveling into the wind. I assumed we were seeing the final southern migration of the caribou to their wintering grounds in the forest. Could fall be here already? The thought motivated us to travel quickly. Later, I realized they were simply heading into the prevailing southwest wind.

These summer herds once incited mythic legends about enormous populations. Observers seeing the land blanketed with the brown backs of caribou extrapolated their estimations to cover entire regions and came up with numbers in the millions. In the early twentieth century, author and wildlife artist Ernest Thompson Seton estimated that over 30 million caribou graced the Barren Lands. Biologists later noted that accounts like Seton's typically failed to realize that all the caribou in a given region were gathered in a single place while the rest of the area was empty. Regardless, the magnitude of these great herds is overwhelming, with sometimes over a hundred thousand animals traveling together. I had no idea how many animals we were seeing. We tried to estimate and came up with five to twenty thousand, but guessing was pointless.

A typical daily pattern of behavior emerges in the herd during their attempts to escape insect persecution. During the day, they follow windy ridges, constantly traveling and foraging on the move. Occasionally, they are driven into frenzies in desperate attempts to escape their tormentors. During the evening, their pace slackens, and they eventually stop to sleep. Their health gradually declines through the summer, and they become sickly-looking shadows of their magnificent fall physiques. Mosquitoes and black flies constantly surround them during the day, but their greatest fears are the nasal bot and the warble fly. These small but vicious creatures wreak terror in the herds and can send them into stampeding rages. The nasal bot finds its way into the nostrils of unwary caribou and deposits its larvae which can grow to the size of a softball and cause severe breathing problems. The warble fly lays its eggs deep in the protection of caribou fur. When the eggs hatch, the fly burrows through the animal's skin and grows.

The great herds disperse and rest when the bug threat diminishes in late summer. They travel slowly and graze peacefully in small bands, seldom more than a hundred animals, taking full advantage of the fleeting easy life. They regain strength and prepare for the coming winter. When the first snow falls, they band together again and head south. These final southern migrations marked Northern people's most critical time of the year. The animals were at their physical peak: the meat was fat and the hides were thick. Elders would lead their communities to the known crossing places where they would harvest their winter supply. If, for some reason, the caribou changed their migratory behavior or the people failed to meet the herd, a long winter of starvation awaited them.

Late fall is the time of the rut. The bulls have reached magnificent physical peak with tremendous racks extending skyward, and several inches of fat cover their backs. This fat will ensure their survival as they have little time to eat during the violent rut. After weeks of battling, victors emerge and win the right to pass on their genes. Only the most aggressive bulls sire the cows, ensuring the herd stays strong. Winter quickly descends upon the herd when they find themselves sheltered in the forests to wait out the long, dark season before the cycle again comes full circle.

We sat on the hilltop watching the show for about an hour that July 24 evening. The animals continued to come from the north, travel the circumference of the peninsula point, and head around the bay. Soon we saw only silhouettes in the distance as darkness overtook us. We walked back down the hill to our tent. The moon was shining bright, and the clicking of hooves lulled us to sleep.

The morning of July 25 came clear and breezy. We should have left early to beat the wind, but we lingered, enjoying the bug-free morning. I glanced across the bay while eating breakfast and saw that the herd that had passed through the previous night stopped to sleep directly across from our tent. Several thousand animals blanketed the hillside and were rousing like us from their slumber. While I packed, I heard a faint whistle coming from a distance. I looked up the hill behind our tent and saw Laurie, who had disappeared about twenty minutes earlier, standing on the hilltop, waving her hands. "Get your camera!" she yelled.

Laurie looked like a messenger for an Inuit community heralding the long-awaited arrival of Tuktu. I grabbed my camera and raced up the hill once again. I reached the top to see thousands more caribou that had spent the night at the peninsula's point. They were milling about as if in restless anticipation for the sign from a leader to begin their day's traveling. Occasionally, smaller bands of several hundred animals would break away, form lines, and start traveling up the hill toward our hiding place. My camera clicked as constantly as their hooves as they trotted below the rocky outcrop I was seated on.

It was amusing to watch the dynamics of the groups. Large males were always in the lead, but many leaders appeared not to cherish the job. A bull would strike off, and instantly a group would scramble to follow. Often, the bull would travel a wandering path as if trying to lose his tagalongs, but they always followed. One group struck off toward the distant hill where we had seen so many other caribou go, then traveled in a mile-wide circle and got in line behind another group back where they had started. Perhaps the leader lost confidence in his abilities or didn't want the responsibility of finding the path.

A couple of hours passed and the bulk of the herd still had not moved. They wandered, sometimes running aimlessly, obviously wondering who would lead them away. From our high vantage point, it looked like mass confusion, as if we were looking upon a vast open field of people searching for some change they had dropped. Then, as if on cue, a leader emerged, and a constant stream began to flow from the dwindling crowd. Soon an uninterrupted river of caribou stretched from the masses a half-mile across the low valley, around the bay, and over the next hill. I followed the line with my binoculars from the distant hill to its source, marveling at the immensity of this natural event. I followed the shoreline to the north where this herd had come from, and I saw another line stretching as far as I could see coming our way. One of my early desires about this trip was to see a few caribou, but this was getting ridiculous.

I had read about this event in several journals of early northern explorers. Joseph Tyrrell wrote that when he was camped for days, a mile-wide brown river of caribou flowed past his tent. Ernest Thompson Seton described the land as blanketed with the brown backs of caribou so thick that the ground appeared to be moving. They estimated the number of animals by computing the area of land they covered. In my mind I could picture the sights they described, but until now I didn't appreciate the passion with which they expressed their experiences. We were not just seeing a fantastic biologic event; we were getting a glimpse of the very foundation of northern humanity. If physical objects or places have spirits, the spirit of the Far North is embodied in the great masses of caribou. The caribou herd was the sustainer of life, and its movement across the land was blood surging through the veins of a body.

Our conversation ceased, and we both sat in our worlds, captivated by the constant motion in the valley below. My thoughts shifted between the caribou, the striking landscape, and the people whose land it was. I was looking through a window to another time. Actually, time had no bearing on this event. The scene would have been the same had I been on this spot one, ten, or a thousand years ago. This event embodied my northern dreams in a single, comprehensive moment.

Eventually, though, the nagging pressure to travel returned and we walked down the hill to resume our paddle north.

While eating lunch and packing to leave, a young caribou emerged from the water and walked directly toward our camp. He had been with last night's herd but got left behind and was heading for the congregation on the peninsula point. He casually walked through our site, showing no fear, only curiosity. This was the typical behavior that we observed in younger animals. This particular fellow stayed around long enough for me to walk to my camera, load a roll of film, and walk directly at him while he stared. I snapped a photo; then he trotted up the hill.

I don't recall whether the afternoon was sunny and warm or windy and cold, and I don't believe I would have noticed either. My mind was not on the paddling but was still back on our caribou hill. By late afternoon, we reached a large bay requiring a five-mile open-water crossing, forcing us to think about the paddle at hand. The wind blew hard across the bay, sideways to our intended direction. Whitecaps and large rollers moved across the water. Prudence suggested that we wait until evening to make the crossing. A wait in the lee of a small bay turned into an overnight stay as the wind never abated.

***

We ate our first freeze-dried, stove-cooked dinner that day.

Although tasty, stove cooking is less comfortable and rewarding than open-fire cooking. Our small, one-burner allowed only one course to be cooked at a time, and the roaring little flame was not conducive to late-evening fireside chats. Yet, the stove and white gas that had until then been only weight in our packs became useful tools.

To beat the wind, we roused with sunrise at about 3:30 a.m., swiftly broke camp, and began the five-mile crossing of the bay. A light breeze blew from the south as we paddled into the rising sun. The waves were still rolling as an aftershock from the previous day. We crossed the bay quickly to a point where Windy Smith used to have a trading post and soon found ourselves paddling in increasingly heavy winds blowing directly at our backs. We could not let this rare treat pass us by so we rigged up a sail to harness nature's free energy.

It took a bit of comical experimenting to figure out the logistics of sailing a canoe. Our large, green tarp served as the sail; a spare paddle and a camera tripod served as the masts. Laurie sat in the bow facing backward, holding the masts against the wind, braced against a pack in a "V" shape around which the ends of the tarp were wrapped. I sat in the stern and steered. The wind filled the sail behind Laurie and whisked us northward with unprecedented speed. The day flew by as fast as the free miles, and our sailing time was pure delight. The weighty canoe that typically slogged through lakes like a barge with a stubborn resistance to motion seemed spry and lighthearted, ready to travel on its own accord. We cruised at a seemingly unnatural pace for most of the day, creating a slight wake behind the boat. Conversation and laughter flowed freely as we thoroughly enjoyed the easy traveling in the northern sunshine.

Steering must be planned far in advance when sailing a canoe. Sharp turns are impossible. Generally, you can only go in the exact direction of the wind. Tacking is tricky without a keel. I would look ahead to an obstacle or point of land miles in advance and try to keep an appropriate angle to the boat. Inevitably, we would drift much closer to the obstacle than I had planned, then break free into the open again. The wind blew in various intensities but always directly from the south. At times, a surge caught Laurie off guard and sent her toppling backward under the force of the full sail, laughing as she struggled to regain her composure. Other times we sat dead in the water, basking in the intense Arctic summer sun. In these times, I reclined on the stern with my feet propped up on the gunwales, occasionally drifting in and out of sleep as the gentle waves rocked the boat. But when the wind blew hard, I jumped to attention, always cautious of growing waves.

When a powerful surge came from the south, the canoe leapt forward with a burst of energy that rivaled a small outboard motor. The waves slowly grew and traveled slightly faster than our craft, first lifting the stern high above the bow, then breaking under us as the stern fell backward into a trough before riding the next wave. It's easy to forget the dangers of open-lake travel as the canoe under sail swiftly moves over the water. More than once we found ourselves nervously far from shore in heavy water that we would have thought twice about paddling in; each time, we resolved to be more careful. But it isn't easy to turn down the power of the wind when the miles accumulate and the destination grows closer.

We quickly drifted past landmarks and realized we could make it to the end of Nueltin Lake. We raced northward with the increasing wind and struggled to keep control as the rollers broke at the gunwale level. Soon, we turned into the bay that was our exit from Nueltin Lake and broke sail. We made a desperate paddle sideways to an intense wind to the end of the bay where we pulled ashore and made camp.

Nueltin Lake was not the showstopper I had feared. Aside from the occasional wind problems, it was six days of relaxing, portage-free traveling filled with glorious experiences. Every day we would wake, sure that this was the day that Nueltin would stop us, but each day continued to bring good fortune. Twice we tried to follow routes to avoid Nueltin, and twice we were drawn back on its course. The decision to finally paddle its length shaved off three days from the revised itinerary I had planned at the end of the Thlewiaza River. This newfound time put us back on course. We had a chance to complete the entire route. Yet we did not rest. The next phase of travels offered little optimism.

***

We were leaving the familiar, well-known waters of Nueltin Lake and striking off into a country that remained a mystery— the tundra gap. For the next hundred miles to the Kazan River, we were to travel a series of small streams and ponds over three different watersheds—an unknown land unfamiliar with the ways of the canoe. Until Nueltin Lake, we had been traveling through country rich with the traditions of the paddle. Its history was familiar. Although new to us, we followed in the wake of past explorers who had traveled its waters and paved the way for future voyageurs. Routes and methods of travel were established, and the canoe was a familiar component of the land. On July 28, we left traditional canoe country and headed into a raw wilderness that offered no instinctive familiarity.

We studied the topographic maps intently that final evening on Nueltin Lake. I traced routes and almost giggled at the prospect of exploring new country and seeing land few people had seen. I suppose I shouldn't say we were "exploring" new land, as we were following detailed topographic maps, a luxury unheard of by early travelers. Still, those maps were made from aerial photographs, and the land can look quite different when your feet are planted on earth. The excitement, however, diluted into that annoying, ever-present anxiety over what the next challenge would bring. There may be a good reason why the canoe had limited history here.

That evening I climbed a rocky hill rising above the lake-shore and gazed toward our intended travel. I could see a few caribou roaming about the rolling hills, stragglers of the herd we had seen earlier. But there was no obvious waterway leading to our northwest destination. Countless small ponds, many more than our map indicated, dotted the land in every direction. The stream that flowed past our campsite into Nueltin Lake, the one up which we were supposed to travel, seemed to disappear in an endless array of water and rocks.

"Okay, Ernest, I get it. This is thrilling." Maybe I said that out loud. I definitely let a slight grin flush my face at the prospect of taking clues from the landscape to find our way. What was once routine for others was an adventure for us.

But there's no water! How can you canoe without water? Is this where we finally turn around? I stayed on the hilltop until the strong wind that had kept the black flies at bay subsided. The constant pinging of insects on my face and the growing fiery itch on my exposed skin drove me to the tent where we spent an unsettled night wondering about the upcoming days.

The morning was heralded with the rhythmic flapping of our tent fly in the most intense wind we had experienced to date. Nueltin Lake was a raging torment of white that would have kept us landbound had we not finished the lake. This was the notorious wind I had read so much about and feared. This type of wind held canoeing parties captive for days as they paced and diminished their precious food supplies. Fortunately, the wind was a blessing, keeping the sweltering heat and insects away on our overland travels.

We packed the canoe in vain. Thirty yards up the stream my fears were confirmed, and the small waterway to take us out of Nueltin ceased at a rock jam, forcing us to shoulder our load for the first time in seven days. A quarter mile upstream, a small pond maybe fifty yards across offered a bit of a break from the pending portage, but it appeared that the two miles to the source of this stream would be nearly all overland, and the land did not look as though it welcomed travelers. A sea of boulders arranged themselves in a most inconvenient pattern. Small streams too immature to have formed beds trickled through glacial valleys carved from the bedrock, searching for the least resistant path through the jumble of stones.

The first quarter mile of the portage was an agonizing repeat of our early lessons. In seven days, we had forgotten the pain of inefficiency and struggled overland, burdened with excess hand items and poorly loaded packs. I naively thought the packs would have significantly lightened in our portage hiatus but was unpleasantly surprised when the straps dug into my shoulders with a familiar pain. The night before, I had contemplated consolidating our food into three packs. But over the previous month we only reduced the four food packs to manageable weights of about seventy pounds apiece. The painful memories of hundred-pound packs told me to wait awhile longer, so we continued to portage in four loaded trips; each mile of portage progress still required seven miles of walking.

The pond was a welcome break as it allowed us to collect our composure that had been wholly blown in the rambling, stumbling, ankle-twisting venture from our campsite still in view. I climbed a cabin-sized rock to take a compass bearing across the pond to the stream inlet.

The calm, relaxed attitudes we resolved to maintain throughout the rest of the day were thrown overboard during our frustrating traverse of this small, seemingly inconsequential pond. The wind sent Laurie's long red hair straight out from her head and negated all efforts to steer the canoe. Sharp rocks concealed by waves gouged the canoe, but the depths between them were too great to wade. About three-quarters of the way across the pond, the surfaced boulders became too dense to negotiate with the harsh wind and we were forced to drag the loaded boat the remaining distance to what could be considered shore.

There wasn't a shoreline but a zone where the clustered boulders overcame the watery depth and walking became possible. We couldn't tell where the pond officially ended while the stream inlet was lost somewhere in a confusing myriad of wet channels. We spent nearly an hour trying to decipher the maze until we settled on one valley that appeared to have more longevity than the others. According to our map, the stream followed a winding path to a small lake somewhere to the northwest. Since we were confident we couldn't paddle, we abandoned the stream and followed a straight compass bearing overland to the distant lake.

Portaging on the barrens is much different than in the forests. There are no paths to follow or signs that others have taken the route. You don't have the confined, well-traveled routes that let you mindlessly wander along, confident that the path will end at your destination. In the barrens, you simply strike across the vast terrain using land features and compass bearings to guide your way. Our portage route took us through an obstacle course of boulder fields, shrub thickets, high ridges, and open bogs. Ridges composed entirely of loose rock with bedrock cores crossed the land perpendicular to our direction of travel. We searched for low passes when we could but were often forced to scale ridges and peaks with our load. The valleys between the ridges were either wet, boggy areas or dense shrub thickets that tore at our faces while we negotiated the tricky ground hidden below. But our morning portaging had gotten me back into the "whatever-the-conditions" attitude. The powerful sense of wonder at this strange and intriguing land overpowered the pain and sweat of the portage.

I stopped on a ridgetop to lay down my pack and rest. Staring blankly into the void of the barrens, scanning the horizon, and trying to put this land into perspective, I tried somehow to compare what I was seeing to something I had seen before. It was utterly foreign and certainly not conducive to canoe travel. It wasn't like a mountain environment, but the loose rock created the same hazards. There was no tundra, just an endless sea of hard, chiseled boulders. Yet, as unrelenting and harsh as the land was, these words ignore the beauty of the structured relationship between water and rock that dominated the landscape. The cold, rich blue of the countless water bodies contrasted sharply with the warm, earthy tones of stone.

To the southeast, the land descended to Nueltin Lake which seemed to rise to meet the sky at the edge of the world. The chaotic assemblage of water and rock compelled me to gaze aimlessly over the land, searching for a point of focus until my eyes found one particularly large, imposing boulder that must have been the size of a two-story house. It was juxtaposed in an artsy way on top of a much smaller rock, the whole thing leaning precariously over a small, uncharted pond. I was struck by the sheer power of the geologic forces that left such oddities and shaped this fresh, relatively young landscape. The irregular manner of the continental glacier that covered this land some seven thousand years ago—scraping river valleys, sculpting ridges, depositing huge boulders, and stranding water bodies—created an environment so odd and unfamiliar to my mind that I wrote in my journal that night, "I think we paddled to the moon!" And a strange land it is, full of paradoxes with the oldest rocks on the planet exposed in the youngest landscape.

I saw Laurie far ahead trudging through a flat, open meadow toward a distant ridge. She looked so foreign in this remarkably inhuman land. I looked back where we had come from, and amidst the drab colors of the land was a speck of red that was our canoe. How will we transport that and the heavier packs across this land? The ground was far too treacherous and the terrain too rugged to think about carrying the canoe the way we had come. We had to find another route.

Laurie was waiting on another ridge when I caught up to her. From our vantage point, we could see that we were a little over halfway to our desired lake. We made this our first stop and returned for the next load. It was late afternoon and we had only come a little over a mile and a half with three more loads to go. We split up for the return route to scout easier paths. Laurie climbed down to the stream and followed it back to the pond while I stayed high and tried to connect the valleys between the boulder fields. I found a reasonable route and arrived at the canoe first only because Laurie, whose route was much quicker and easier, missed the pond and walked around to its far shore. I saw her trotting along, hopping her way over the boulders over another small ridge about a half-mile away. I blew my whistle to get her attention, but the screaming wind completely muffled any sound and she soon disappeared over the ridge. I set off to catch her, afraid she might find another pond and think it was ours, but she realized her mistake and headed back before I got too far.

Exhausted from the two previous trips, we hoisted the canoe to our shoulders and stepped into the final three-mile leg of this portage that verged on being unbearable. The stream bank offered a smooth path along packed gravel for a while. With limited visibility, however, we followed those short easy paths too far without the more strategic long-distance plan. Soon, we were off any route that either of us had scouted. Lifting the canoe to get a view felt like doing push-ups forced by a coach as a penalty for running laps too slow. Weakened by muscle fatigue, I stopped to rest, lock-kneed, letting the canoe seat drive into the top of my spine because that pain seemed more tolerable than the effort it would have taken to sit down. Laurie's panting breaths muffled hints of crying, but she just waited patiently for me to move again. Unable to lift the canoe with just my arms, I bent my knees, lunged up, and dropped down like a powerlifter, locking my elbows under the weight. I mapped a route in my mind to where I thought our packs were, taking the long view. We'd keep the slope to our left and the stream to our right and just push through whatever obstacle was in the way.

The black flies returned in the dying wind. I let them feast and pushed on through shrub thickets and boulder fields until we reached our valley at eight that evening. With a desperate lunge, we tossed the canoe aside and collapsed on the rocks, relieved until we remembered that our packs from the first trip were still high on a hilltop above our present site. With the steadfast determination of soldiers, we climbed the hill and retrieved our belongings.

The black flies disappeared as the sun dipped below the ridge, and the evening became pleasant. The pain of the portage was soon forgotten and we went about our business as we had for the last twenty-seven days. Strangely enough, we found a dead pine tree among the boulders. We built a fire and cooked a full leisurely meal of chili and bannock.

On a distant hilltop I saw a young male caribou and thought

it was a straggler from the herd we had seen a few days earlier. We saw individuals like this along the portage all day. Laurie spotted several more on another hill. A quick survey of the surrounding land with the binoculars revealed that thousands of caribou were traveling along our portage route toward our site. The swiftness with which they appeared, as if they instantly materialized from the land, was astounding. In minutes, the quiet, eerie calm of the barrens was once again shattered by a crescendo of clicking hooves.

"What are they doing?" I wondered. They looked like they were heading back north.

"Is this the same herd we already saw?" asked Laurie. "They're really close. Do you think we might get stampeded?" she asked half-jokingly.

They marched down the stream valley as we had, then the leaders spied our tent and stopped about a hundred feet away to study the unfamiliar sight. There was a slight traffic jam of milling caribou as they stood for a while, staring, stomping their hooves seemingly in frustration. They darted their heads up and down, trying to figure out the dilemma. We were directly in their line of travel. We stared back, imitating their motions until they decided we were harmless pranksters and walked around us, between our tent and a ridge about thirty yards away to the west. We sat motionless next to our tent for about two hours in the fading light as a constant stream of magnificent bulls passed. Occasionally, a lone animal not paying attention to the direction of the herd would wander with its head down directly toward us until one of us would giggle or whisper, "Look at the size of that beast!" His head would perk up and he would spring backward in shock toward the security of the herd where he would melt into the crowd.

Animals of all sizes streamed past our camp; some looked sideways at the strange intrusion on their trail. Large bucks with enormous racks, cows with small, spindly horns, yearlings, and newborns followed in line. They seemed to be in no hurry, but their direction was clear. If one caribou was startled and ran, they all ran. If one stopped to stare, they all stopped to stare. They came through in waves. First, the bulls, then several hundred cows and calves streamed through, feeding on the brush as they passed. It alternated this way into the Arctic summer night. The sexes travel together during the post-calving aggregations but maintain fairly strict segregation.

When the herd passed us, they didn't continue directly down the stream but climbed the hill to the west and disappeared over the ridge now silhouetted by a fiery orange post-sunset sky. A jostling train of antlers broke the smooth horizon. At about 11:30 p.m., we watched a procession of females pass through into the growing dark before we went inside the tent. We didn't bother packing our kitchen gear or flipping the canoe because we didn't want to startle the herd with the noises.

With us now in the tent, our threat diminished in the eyes of the caribou. The procession shifted toward its original path until our tent was engulfed in the flow of the herd. Caribou brushed by on both sides, unaware of our presence. We would hear the clicking of an animal approaching from behind and soon the tent door would be filled with the magnificent body of a curious caribou. One large bull stopped just ten feet from our mesh door, froze with tension as he knew something was up, turned his massive, racked head our way, let out a disgusting snort, then cautiously walked into the nearby brush to graze. It looked like he was creeping away quietly, trying not to wake us.

We giggled with excitement, burying our faces in the sleeping bag to keep from being heard. Occasionally, the wind blew the tent, or we laughed a bit too loud, and a caribou would realize it was fooled and dash off. One animal lingered behind our tent for about forty-five minutes, snorting, sneezing, and stomping quite intently. Perhaps he was confused by the flapping yellow rock, or he knew we were intruders and was telling us to move or else! I could see five or six animals sticking their noses in our packs, curious about their find.

When it got too dark to travel, the caribou stopped moving and began milling about, making all kinds of noises. "Oh wow, they're stomping out their beds!" I said. "They're going to spend the night with us!" Looking out the tent door, I could see the antlers of hundreds of reclining caribou starting just thirty feet away, and I could hear many more directly behind the tent. I wondered how many Inuit or Dene hunters fantasized about moments like this. I decided I had to try to get a photo, so I got out my flash. Laurie suggested that a flash would not be wise as it might startle the caribou; I reluctantly agreed and went to turn it off. But in the darkness, I missed the power button and accidentally hit the test button.

With the explosion of light, the peaceful valley instantly turned to thunderous chaos. "They're stampeding!" I yelled. Our tent door was filled with the blurred forms of fleeing animals as the ground quaked with the trampling hooves. Gripped by panic, we waited through about thirty seconds, repeating, "What do we do?!" Too dark to see, we heard the rumbles and felt the shakes while the bodies of caribou compressed the tent walls and bent the poles. A small animal crashed into the vestibule then rolled aside, probably trampled by its companions. I reached for the shotgun in its case, but I don't know why.

The rumbling faded until there was just one caribou trotting around, confused. The valley grew silent again. I peered out of the tent and saw the dark emptiness. The caribou were gone; our adrenaline slowly dissipated.

"What did you think you were doing?" Laurie said.

"I'm sorry. It was an accident," I replied.

"Well, it wasn't very smart to try your flash."

"Yeah, well, it's over. They're gone."

"What a bummer. I was looking forward to waking up with them."

"Sorry."

After the initial shock, we couldn't help but laugh at the incident, and the flash became a running joke for us the rest of the trip. We tried to sleep, but we were both too excited, and a little scared, of what might happen next. Within a half hour, we heard another chaotic rush of movement. I looked out and saw hundreds of animals coming back down the western hill into our valley.

"They're coming back!"

"Are they stampeding again?"

"No, I think they're just returning to the beds they made."

Sure enough, several hundred animals crashed through the brush and returned to our campsite to settle for what remained of the night.

A couple of hours later, around 3:30 a.m., I woke to the rising sun. As light pushed back the night, the caribou outside our tent door roused and prepared for travel. I peered under the flap to avoid notice, observing the morning rituals in their private lives. They reminded me of my old dog. He would rise slowly to his feet, arch his back, extend his front legs until adequately stretched, then rock forward, reaching back with his hind legs toward some imaginary object, all in the span of one tremendously long yawn. The older caribou were particularly slow to rise. In time, the entire herd was up and browsing the willow leaves. They chewed and burped and shook the shrubs as they raked the leaves off the branches. Some scraped at the rocks, but lichen is more of a fall/winter diet. These animals clearly wanted willow leaves. Soon after rising and eating, they slowly ambled away in the direction they were headed the previous night. I was envious of their simple, efficient morning procedure.

When the group in front of us was all gone, I slipped out and sat motionless next to the tent while the scores of animals behind us continued to pass within twenty feet. They had to see me as I was completely exposed with my camera clicking, but they paid no heed. The group that filled our small valley eventually left, and I climbed the small hill next to our tent. A few animals were still browsing but soon trotted off to catch up with their companions. One stopped at our packs, nosed around a bit, walked to the tent where Laurie was soundly sleeping, and looked in before ambling away. On the distant hills to the south I could see another large herd coming our way, though they seemed to be following a valley to our east. Satisfied with my morning, I returned to the tent to sleep until the midmorning heat forced me out of the tent, where I slept some more.

A wilderness fantasy day followed. Our preparations to leave were continually interrupted by processions of caribou streaming through our site. Thousands continued to march, unhindered by our presence. I suppressed that annoying urge to travel and allowed myself to rest for the morning, despite the nagging thoughts of freeze-up in the forest gap. But winter was far away on this day, and we could walk around the valley in shorts. We sat by the tent for hours, absorbed by the flow of animals around us. When the movement lapsed midafternoon, we climbed the western hill to get a panoramic view of the valley. Caribou were everywhere. Dispersed processions from three valleys converged in our streambed. They weren't traveling fast in disciplined lines as we saw earlier but came through in waves of several hundred animals just wandering around, seemingly taking advantage of the leisurely day as we were.

On every hilltop we could see small groups resting. Up and down the stream, hundreds of animals drank the water and continued their travels. I was struck by the clumsy, dangerous way these creatures approached streams. They would trot up and crash into the stream without slowing their pace. Inevitably, they would stumble and fall their way across. By midstream, they would realize their situation and become more cautious. Slowly, they would step down from a rock, crash down to their bellies, then up on the next rock until they reached the far shore and trot away. On the other side of the hill, at least a thousand caribou lounged around the hillside, passing away the afternoon; their instinctual wariness seemed to be cast aside for the day. Where were the wolves? I joked later that we found the rock garden of Eden, with animals everywhere, unthreatened and undisturbed.

By 5 p.m., the urge to travel took hold and we packed up to finish the portage to the lake. Within ten minutes, Laurie succumbed to intense abdominal pains that had been building all day. Fears of appendicitis and evacuation forced us to return and stay put for the day. It turned out that last night's chili was a bit too strong for her. Weary, we settled into camp after our shortest travel day of the summer—a hundred yards.

There was no medical emergency, but for an hour we thought there might be. The reality of the situation we put ourselves in suddenly hit us in full. We were in the undefined country between two seldom-visited rivers, lugging a canoe up a dry valley in the most remote region of North America. Families knew we were canoeing in Canada, but not where. Our new Wollaston Lake friends knew we were heading north, but they didn't know who we were. We were as alone as possible on this continent with no way to communicate to the outside. We had the ELT, but in the days before the trip I learned that it only worked if a plane happened to be flying nearby. We hadn't seen or heard a plane for weeks except the floatplane at the fishing lodge on Nueltin Lake.

During the uncertainty of Laurie's situation, I went through the grim mental exercise of planning what I would do if she could not travel. The best option would be to travel back to the south end of Nueltin Lake, which had taken the two of us eight days to cross, and much of it by sail. Would I leave her alone in a tent to travel light and fast? Would I carry her to Nueltin Lake, load her in the boat, and then paddle solo? Those decisions likely would not matter if her potential appendicitis became acute while suffering in this camp. I read somewhere that early explorers sometimes preemptively removed their appendixes to avoid such situations.

Fortunately, Laurie's pain subsided, and we didn't have to implement any desperate plans. But for an hour, the potential medical emergency raised the dark specter that the worst possible scenario during a wilderness expedition—debilitating injury or death—could happen.

***

As evening progressed, a dramatic but tame storm illuminated the surrounding hills with fabulous golden light as evening turned to night. A full double rainbow arched over our Tuktu Valley, our name for this magical place, all while caribou continued to pass through. Thunder rolled across the hills, and a light, refreshing rain fell, each drop illuminated by the brilliant sun breaking through the clouds. The rain was brief but the thunder rolled for about an hour. I read that the Inuit believed that the movements of great numbers of caribou bring thunderstorms. It's perhaps the reverse, where thunderstorms urge the caribou to move. But as I roamed around the hills that evening, a magical presence flowed that tempted me to believe any myth ascribing powers to the great herd.

I walked with my camera through the evening, shirtless in this barren but bug-free valley, dumbfounded and amazed at our almost unbelievable fortune. Toward dusk, a large bull reclined about fifty yards from our tent while dozens of other animals grazed around him. I approached, and all but the reclining one ambled away. It was odd that he was lying with his head down. Usually, they reclined, even slept with their heads up, their huge racks balanced over their bodies. I approached, snapping photos, sure I was as close as possible. But he never moved. I got about twenty feet away when he turned his head toward me. A bloody gouge was below his eye. He attempted to flee but dropped to his chest each time he tried to stand.

This poor creature had been wounded, most likely broken a leg in a fall in the treacherous rocks, and was lying down to a slow death of starvation, dehydration, or predation. He had already eaten all the shrubs around him and could not access the water only thirty feet away. He panted hard, helpless and distressed by my presence.

He was dying. It would be best to intervene and end his suffering. Yet, I felt uneasy about blasting a shotgun in this valley. Hundreds of caribou still surrounded us. We didn't want a repeat of last night's stampede. Introducing a gun to this serene place also seemed out of place, perhaps a bit sacrilegious. I entertained the idea of letting him die naturally. Or even using a knife or spear to end his life. But that would have been silly and naive and definitely beyond my abilities. A peaceful valley, animals living in harmony, is a false fantasy. Life out here is a constant, violent struggle for survival and we are just as natural as anything else. There would have been no wrong or right thing to do. We waited until the next day to see if he might go on his own.

Another herd passed through our site as we rose, but we couldn't afford any more delays and continued with our packing. The dying caribou was still there when we portaged past under our first load. I looked closer on the return trip; his suffering through the night made him look weaker. I dropped my pack nearby on the third trip. It was time to intervene.

I pulled the gun from its soft case for the second time since leaving Wollaston Lake. The first time was to dry it out after leaving it in the bottom of the canoe for a day. The outside of the barrel was somewhat rusted and weathered. I imagined the inside was the same. A gift from Laurie's dad, she felt like we disappointed him with our careless treatment of the weapon. It had become a burden, weighing us down as we portaged our packs. Many times I contemplated leaving it hidden behind a tree or boulder at a portage and walking away from it. But on this day, I was glad to have it.

I unzipped the case and lifted the gun to my shoulder with little delay. It was loaded with alternating slugs and buckshot because a book I read said to do that. I stood about thirty feet away and chambered a round with that cold, metallic two-part sound.

I expected to feel remorse and hesitation, but I was curiously excited and instinctively empowered as I looked down the barrel at the caribou. He stared back, perhaps resigned to his fate. Although no hunter ever had such an easy target, I experienced the buck fever I had heard about. I trembled a bit, and as I pulled the trigger, I lunged forward and sent a slug skidding in the dirt several feet in front of my target. He sat motionless, not even a flinch from the loud blast, and stared at me.

"Is he dead?" asked Laurie, who had to turn her back.

"I missed."

"Oh no!"

I recomposed, breathed, thought, and sent the shot to where his heart would be. He winced and slowly but unwillingly slumped over—a moment of stillness, then extreme and violent thrashing. I grimaced and clenched my teeth, and sent a slug into his heart. Still, he thrashed. I finally put aside the fear of intimacy, approached boldly, placed the barrel to his skull, and pulled the trigger.

His immediate death let me get a close look. His back left leg was broken six inches above the ankle, bones completely separated, his hoof connected to his leg by just a piece of skin. He must have lodged his foot between rocks and fallen forward, something I feared might happen to one of us while portaging challenging terrain. Knowing that wolves and other scavengers would find the remains soon and have their fill eased my conscience as we hoisted the packs and hopped along the rocks toward the lake.

The familiar struggles of the trail reclaimed my attention, and thoughts of the dead caribou faded. They returned that evening as we prepared our light meal after an exhausting day. This time my thoughts were more pragmatic. Why didn't I cut off a steak?

CHAPTER NINE

ACROSS THE TUNDRA GAP

MILE 347–426

"Brooding, immutable, given over to its own essential mood of desolation, it showed so bleak a face to the first white men who came upon its verges that they named it, in awe and fear, the Barrengrounds."

—Farley Mowat

It took just a day into the tundra gap to understand why I couldn't find records of canoe travel across it. It is not canoe country. The Inuit living in the headwaters of the Kazan walked to the trading posts in Nueltin Lake country, and the traders likely returned in winter by dog team. They chose a thirty-five-mile route straight east to west. We chose a hundred-mile route northwest up Tuktu Valley, overland to the Kognak River, then by stream to Hicks Lake. From there, we followed then an overland, pond-hopping route to Dimma Lake on the Kazan River, all of which took eleven exhausting but inspirational days.

Our ascent of the stream in Tuktu Valley to a lake at its headwaters was more like an excessively loaded backpacking trip than a paddling trip. The stream remained as rocky and unforgiving as it was at its mouth. Small ponds on the map were usually watery depressions more tempting than worthy of paddling. Water barely covered the jagged boulders that made up their beds.

Water and rock, seemingly the only components of this simple but striking landscape, weaved their contrasting characteristics over the land. When water overwhelmed rock, we paddled. When the hard, sculpted granite of the Precambrian Shield poked through and choked the waters, we walked. On our first day out of the valley, we spent at most fifteen consecutive minutes in the canoe without stopping at a boulder jam to re-shoulder our load. The difficult access to stable footing enhanced the tedium of the loading and unloading. It was rare when we could approach a shoreline within forty feet through the jumble of boulders that surfaced in the increasingly shallow water. We jammed the boat into the most stable wedge we could find, extracted the packs, and hopped toward the shore, hoping not to send a slipped foot slamming into some unknown underwater crack.

The twisty stream frequently disappeared into wet mazes of glacial debris, forcing us to climb the largest nearby boulder to get our bearings. Several small tributaries trickled into each wet depression or pond from sculpted valleys leaving us to guess our desired path. Fortunately, the treeless barrens enabled sighting over great distances. Our goals were always visible from the nearest ridgetop. We scouted our portage routes from high vantage points like we scouted rapids: "We'll scramble over that ledge until we come to the shrub thicket. It looks passable through there; then we'll angle left across the valley over whatever rock path looks the safest, then we'll just pick our way through the boulders until we come to the huge one on the far hill there. I think we can find the stream just over that ridge. Use caribou paths whenever you can to get through bushes."

Four weary trips would see us across a portage, looking over another sheet of water to the next rock jam. We lost a little of the restrictive respect for the bottom of our canoe and dragged it over many obstacles that would have sent us to shore earlier in the trip. Curly pieces of red plastic floated away from the bottom of our boat at each sharp rock. The price was worth it. The admirable strength of our polyethylene boat served us well, and many times I thought of how much more difficult it must have been in the old wood-and-canvas boats just a few decades earlier or the skin kayaks and birch canoes of earlier times.

The work was rewarding. We remained in high spirits as the rugged landscape captivated us. Occasionally, while sweating and stumbling over loose boulders with the canoe on my shoulders without a trickle of water in sight, I would get a glimpse of some striking component of the landscape, perhaps the rolling boulder ridges over the treeless and scarred terrain, and my thoughts would abandon the driving pain on the back of my neck.

The caribou were as numerous as the boulders. At every break, we'd scan the hills and see the roaming animals, sometimes several hundred together, going about their business of living on the barrens. At times they looked as clumsy in the rocks as we did.

The wind was as ubiquitous as water, rock, and caribou. An incessant, screaming wind that whipped our hair into our eyes, flapped our loose shirts, and battered our tent continued unrelentingly through the days and waned only slightly in the evenings. Even though our paddling was minimal over small, shallow ponds, the wind drove us to frustration as it pinned us to the points of submerged rocks and thwarted our paddling progress. But the abrasive wind provided welcome shelter from two midsummer Barren Lands plagues: the heat and the bugs.

I was surprised at the dramatic increase in temperature we experienced as the season progressed. In the rare times when the wind wasn't blowing, the air felt thick with heat, although it probably only reached the mid-seventies. Still, the physical labor was draining. Occasionally, the wind blew from the north, bringing a blast of Arctic air. But the prevailing wind in summer on the barrens is from the southwest, which brings up the warm southern air. Our attire had changed with the progressing season. I wore just a polypropylene shirt and thin poly-cotton-blend pants. I packed away my tall L.L. Bean boots and wore canvas high-top sneakers over wool socks, making the wading through shallows quite refreshing.

Perhaps we caught a lucky year with the bugs as we found that the supposed plague of black flies that haunted the barrens, able to drive the most disciplined man insane, was no worse than what we experienced in the Adirondacks in May or on my summer paddling trips in Maine. True, there were times when the air would become filled with a fuzzy cloud of raging movement, as though the entire insect population in the Northwest Territories descended upon us at once, but those times were rare. We were rarely forced to wear our head nets on the barrens (black flies slip through the mesh anyway), and we rarely wore repellent. Fortunately, black flies are weak fliers, and the slightest wind sends them seeking shelter. They congregated on the lee side of any object, like Laurie's back while she hunched over the stove cooking dinner. She didn't notice them because they couldn't bite through the thinnest clothing. A simple turn into the wind was enough to scatter the hungry herd.

The key to survival in black fly country is to keep as much of your body covered as the midsummer heat will allow. At the worst times, we tucked our pants in our socks and buttoned our collars tight. Laurie seemed more susceptible to black flies than I. It became a nightly ritual to see how bitten and bloody her neck would be. But we had left the far worse bug problems, the mosquitoes, back in the forests and never again felt as consistently aggravated by flying pests.

We worked well into the night until we reached the small lake at the head of Tuktu Valley. With darkness falling, the stiff wind came to an abrupt halt. Lingering whitecap waves slowly settled to undulating rollers, and the lake took on that mirrored quality of impeccably placid water that eased all the troubles of the day. These times are rare on the barrens, so we continued our paddle into the darkness. The silence, broken only by the gentle splashing of our paddles, brought an eerie contrast to the loud violence of the earlier wind. A waning crescent moon provided just a glimmer of light, and the distant profile of a large hill served as our only visible landmark until we reached its shore. We made a hurried camp in the dark, a few miles before our long portage to the next watershed.

Although the downstream traveling in the tributary of the Kognak River made things easier, the wind and current converged to make weaving through the shallow boulder fields difficult. We had long grown accustomed to this style of travel and tackled obstacles—that earlier would have given us fits—with the benign acceptance of seasoned wilderness travelers. We no longer lingered at portages to delay the work but casually carried on with the same pace as when paddling. The most difficult work was accompanied by light-hearted joking and conversation. Very rarely did our thoughts or conversation drift beyond the confines of our new world, and several times we each commented on how surprised we were that we missed nothing from the outside. Our trip had become a way of life that was entirely fulfilling, leaving us wanting nothing.

The hard work and constant challenges, however, kept us on a sharp edge; attitudes could fall off either side with little prompting. In a rare request, Laurie asked to see the compass and map. I pulled them from under the bungee that held them firmly to the thwart in front of me and carefully handed them to her. I watched her movements. I couldn't see exactly what she was doing, but I imagined her holding the compass to the map, wondering what to do. I waited for a question that never came. Satisfied, she leaned back and stretched to hand me the map in its baggie. Then she put the compass on her paddle blade to serve it to me like she sometimes served bannock sandwiches. But the compass was more slippery than bread. It slid off and plunked into the water. The folding Silva compass with its signal mirror, declination adjustment, and vertical angle needle floated for less than a second before it vanished beneath the surface of the dark water.

My silence, while I scrambled and futilely swirled my arm

in the water, was more of a rebuke than yelling would have been. I stared at the back of her head while she breathed deeply, her back rigid with impatience.

"Sorry," she said after some time.

Agitated, I opened the surplus with more force than needed, searching for a spare compass. I'm not a yeller. Instead, I fumed in silence over this costly mistake, but also because I didn't want to hear about my own mistakes. Like when I let an untethered map blow away in the middle of a stormy lake. Or when I walked away from the portage yokes that I imagined were still sitting at the base of that tree on day three. Or when I let the shotgun that her dad bought for us sit in a puddle of water at the bottom of the boat; in camp, she quietly dried and cleaned that gun with the same demonstrative disdain that I displayed when searching for the spare compass. The rusted patterns on the barrel were as much a reminder of my carelessness as the cheap replacement compass was of hers. I just didn't tell her that I had another good one stashed away somewhere.

***

Among the several corny little games and jokes we developed to help pass the time came two superhero personalities that surfaced during difficult times to save the day. It sounds ridiculous when I think about it, but when you're in the wilderness with just one other person for an extended period, strange behavior creeps up and sometimes overcomes the normal self. Laurie became Tuktalonia, and I became Tuktu Man.

"It's getting rough out here, what ever shall we do?" Laurie mocked.

"Never fear, it's Tuktu Man (spoken with a punctuated emphasis on each syllable and an extended vibrato on man) and Tuktalonia, saviors of the Far North! Not wind nor waves shall keep us from our goal!"

The origins of the name Tuktalonia are a bit odd. I heard Laurie speaking Spanish one day, and she said *pantalones*, meaning pants. I liked the sound of the word, and I began to add *alonia*, my own perverted pronunciation of *-alones*, to every noun I spoke.

"Would you like some bannockalonia?" Or, "Hey, pass me the hot saucealonia." Once, Laurie replied to one of those statements with, "My name's not Alonia!" I thought it was a fun name, and eventually I separated the noun and *alonia* when I spoke to her. "You better tie your shoe ... Alonia."

After a particularly tenacious effort by Laurie to pull the canoe through a shallow narrows, I said something like, "Whoa! You have the energy of a superhero ... Alonia!" I saw a caribou passing by and came up with the name "Tuktalonia." The name stuck, and together we became Tuktu Man and Tuktalonia, defenders of the North, helpers to the weak.

Just before the Kognak River, the stream widened into a large lake dotted with islands so thick that we named it Bazillion Islands Lake. The map indicated scores of large islands, but the water was so shallow that hundreds more surfaced along with countless rocky peninsulas extending from the shores. Islands and shallows blended into one another so that when we did have distant landmarks picked, it was impossible to paddle straight to them. We weaved and scraped about the lake for nearly three hours until we detected a bit of current flowing to the northwest through a maze of glacially abandoned chunks of granite. In time, we squeezed through the last of the rocks and found ourselves in a channel that we correctly suspected to be the Kognak River which flows east into Hudson Bay. We headed west and ascended the river to its headwaters at Hicks Lake. At about fifty feet wide and just a few inches deep, the river demanded the same strategies we had been using for days: paddle when we could, drag when we couldn't.

We saw caribou almost continuously since we left Tuktu Valley, so we weren't noticeably impressed when a calf, probably born earlier in the spring, appeared on a gentle ridgetop along a portage of one of the rapids on the Kognak. He stood and watched us for a while, then let out a bleat and ran down the hill toward us. I have heard that a newborn will follow almost anything if it has not appropriately bonded with its mother or has been abandoned. This young fellow came bounding down the hill as if to say, "Where have you been? I've been waiting for you." He followed us along our path for a while, which was a well-used caribou trail, then trotted away. A traveling herd freshly trampled the entire hillside. Deep ruts were carved in the wet moss, and grasses were slowly springing back to life. I thought the little fellow had been left behind, then a half dozen cows came bounding over the ridge, forded our rapid, and climbed to a raised field across the river. We completed the portage, then paddled across the river to see where the animals went. I climbed the bank to a broad, flat tundra field and was surprised to see several hundred cows and calves lounging and grazing. There were no bucks in sight.

Males and females typically travel together during this time of year. I thought this group had yet to reunite with the main herd after calving, although it was pretty late into the summer for that. These animals were not traveling like all the others we had seen; they seemed to be just passing away the calm afternoon. Mothers grazed and relaxed while their young scrambled about, bumping into them and each other. I looked through my camera at a group of caribou when I heard a rustling in the shrubs behind me. I turned, and out from the shrubs trotted a newborn calf. Startled by my presence, he froze in his tracks. We stared at each other, just twenty feet apart, then he decided that I was no threat and relaxed his posture. With his head down, grazing as he walked, he ambled directly toward me. I snapped the last exposure on my film just before he came five feet from me and dropped to nap.

I sat and studied the napping infant without the camera to distract my attention. At this age, he looked very similar to the white-tailed deer I knew from the American Midwest. His coat was a duller brown, his head a bit more square, and his body slightly larger but supported with the same spindly legs. Large, black eyes bugged out from his head below pointed, seemingly cropped ears. My attention shifted when I heard a thrashing in the shrubs and looked up to see another infant running at a full sprint toward me. I tensed as his pace didn't slacken. Then at just ten feet away he halted, stared me down, and let out a low bleat. Then he sprinted past me, stopped again a few feet away, and dropped to nap.

It seemed unreal to be this close to an unafraid, unthreatened wild animal. The older ones around me weren't as accepting. Several groups closed their distance and the eyes of concerned mothers focused on me. One paced back and forth along a circular path, keeping the same distance, and occasionally turned full front, head low, and stared me down. Each time, she stood tall on her front legs, crouched her back right leg, and extended her back left leg out as if doing a sidestep. I had seen this posture several times before by caribou that we had startled. Initially, I thought it meant they were relieving themselves, but soon figured out that they only did it when they were staring at us. We later figured out that the leg extension was a warning signal to other caribou, much like how a beaver slaps its tail before diving. When a caribou sees another with its leg extended, it knows there is some unknown danger in the direction the signaler faces. The warned one is supposed to warn others or flee.

In this case, nobody seemed interested in fleeing except me. Was the warning sign also an aggressive threat? If so, the threat was short-lived as the herd lost interest and continued to graze. I walked back to the canoe to get Laurie and some more film. Laurie has an unquenchable passion for cute baby animals. We walked around with the herd for about an hour, posing no threat and eliciting little response. Laurie was intent on petting the little ones, but whenever she crept to within a few feet they would rise, move a few more feet away, then plop down again. Eventually, they were irritated enough to walk away and rejoin the herd. We walked, too, then paddled away, elated with the afternoon's experiences.

We continued our ascent of the Kognak. Soon after "Tuktu Field" we came to a swift-water section requiring more energy than we were willing to expend at the end of a long day. We made it to a tiny island in the middle of a widening in the river and made camp. We soon discovered that the island was a nesting site for a large, aggressive flock of gulls. Several gulls circled above soon after our tent was set up. I was looking at one in particular when it dropped into a vertical dive straight toward me. I thought it odd at first, but my apprehension mounted as it looked like he wasn't going to pull out of the dive. It dove with incredible speed and flared its wings to turn just above my head.

"Whoa! Did you see that crazy bird? He almost hit me! Hey, look out!"

Another one did the same to Laurie. We never found any nests, but all evening these gulls made it known that we were not wanted. At first, it was amusing, but in time they grew increasingly aggressive and came so close that we could feel the breeze from their flapping wings on our necks. A bird would break from its flight path high in the sky and slowly circle down to about thirty feet above the ground. It would then casually fly in our direction, bobbing up and down with the flapping of its wings, head tilted to stare us down with one eye. When it came to within twenty feet, it would suddenly drop straight for one of our heads and pull out with a mighty swoosh. My irritation swelled, and occasionally, to no avail, I screamed empty threats with fists raised to the sky. Laurie scolded me for reaching for my paddle with evil intent.

While the gulls swooped, a small herd of caribou traveled along the riverbank. The leaders poked wary hooves into the shallow water. They took a few careful steps, then plunged in and began the quarter-mile swim to the far shore, passing about thirty yards from our island. The remainder of the herd followed in waves through the evening. They were good swimmers, but the young ones were carried downstream before their frantic efforts brought them to safety. One youngster in the last group of the evening plunged in with about ten others, then immediately scrambled back to shore while the others swam away. He paced along the shore, occasionally stepping in, but could not get the courage to cross. The others had reached the far shore and walked over the ridge before he finally braved the current. He let out a bleat and stumbled in the submerged rocks. He was carried downstream as soon as his feet could no longer reach the bottom. When he eventually made it across, he shook off the water like a dog, stared around a bit, then trotted away in the wrong direction. He stopped on a ridgetop, probably to scan the horizon for his companions, but then continued on his own way. I wondered how long he wandered alone before he found another traveling group or perhaps fell prey to wolves.

We woke in the morning to the familiar snuffling and snorting of numerous animals. Our small island, no larger than a half-acre, was filled with dozens of caribou, probably taking a break on their crossing. We watched from our shelter as they plunged, single file, to continue their swim.

***

The third of August was a fabulous reprieve from the difficult traveling we had experienced over the previous several days. We roused early, worked our way up the last few swift-water miles of the Kognak River, and reached Hicks Lake. For the first time in days, we looked north over a large, uninterrupted body of water and grew excited at the prospect of easy traveling. We floated in the gentle waves, enjoying the soothing morning sun before we revived and dug our paddles into the lake. The calm warmth continued throughout the day as we lazily paddled north.

A small aberration appeared on the smoothly contoured top of a distant hill. It was another inukshuk. The Hicks Lake area was one of the last strongholds of the Ahiarmiut, so I expected to see more evidence of Inuit habitation in this region. The island was ringed with an unusual shoreline. Large slabs of granite the size of graveyard headstones were pushed up to form a steep ridge about thirty feet high, and dropped off about ten feet to the island's interior just as steeply so that it looked like a decaying fortress. The size and quantity of slabs were too large and randomly stacked to be artificial. The powerful sheet of ice that gouged this lakebed plucked and scraped the bedrock and shoved these rocks into this formation much like a moraine. The inukshuk was in the center of the island.

We stopped on the granite wall farther up the lake to enjoy a leisurely lunch and bathe in the cold water. The afternoon was so surprisingly warm and bug-free that I could paddle in just shorts, a luxury certainly unexpected in this reputedly harsh land. I waded into the cold lake; the combined air and water temperature seemed warm enough for a total immersion, something I had not yet done thirty days into the trip. Laurie was ahead of me, her naked back muscles ripped from weeks of paddling. She waded in, boldly striding toward the deep like a surfer about to jump on her board. Then she plunged and immediately floundered to stand as quickly as possible. Gasping, the waist-deep water forced her to walk slower than she wanted to as she plowed back to shore.

"Jeez, that's cold!"

I altered my strategy. I waded to my thighs, quickly dropped to my knees, and waited to adjust. I held my breath and dunked my head for maybe two seconds, just long enough to give my hair a cursory scrub. Then I retreated to the mossy shore where I nestled into the shrubs and soft moss. It would have been nice to have a towel. But a thin, small bandana was all I brought, and it was usually saturated with bug dope, sweat, and food scraps. I let the cool breeze and weak sun dry my goose-bumped skin while Laurie did the same somewhere nearby.

I don't need to do that again, I thought. Except for the occasional time I left my hat off in the rain, this was the first and only time my hair felt water. Soon, the instinctual urge to travel overcame the pleasure of the moment. We loaded up and moved on.

The land had changed drastically over the course of the day. The jumbled piles of boulders transitioned to soft tundra with mosses, hummocks, and clumps of grass. Vast, featureless stretches of land reached from the lakeshore into mysterious places. We pulled up to a large island near the middle of the lake to make camp and were ecstatic to find a sandy beach. What a relief to paddle right up to shore without a gauntlet of boulders to scramble over! The sand extended about thirty feet inland before a thin section of shrubs gave way to the endless tundra. A soft, thick layer of moss blanketed the ground; not a single boulder, tree, or other protrusion interrupted the gentle terrain. The living moss covered a substrate of peat, the accumulated remains of thousands of years of dying vegetation. Just a few feet below the surface, the soil remains frozen in permafrost that thrusts and heaves during the warm summer and creates great spidering cracks in the soft surface.

In the distance, the tundra fused into a consistent dark green color that met the blue sky at a distinct, clear horizon. On a macro scale, I wouldn't call the scenery dramatic, but the intricate detail of the groundcover creates its own micro-landscapes. Irregular tussocks of mosses adorned in a plethora of subtle colors roll across the tundra in waves that blend into the exposed terrain. I walked inland from our sandy beach, intent on just looking around. Soon I realized I was walking nowhere because there was no particular place to go. The horizon line was the only distinction evident in my view, and who knows how far away the horizon was? I stopped, lay flat on my back, and gazed at the wispy clouds passing overhead. This moss would make a fine bed. Next to my head and dotted across the ground in a random pattern were the distinctly orange clusters of cloudberries. I picked a handful, stood, stretched, and walked back. When I ran out of cloudberries I picked dead twigs from the shrubs and gathered driftwood to build a small cook fire. Our stove had been performing poorly so we built twiggy fires when we could.

***

A fierce morning wind at our backs pushed us a few miles to the north end of Hicks Lake where we faced a two-mile portage to a twisty tributary of the Kazan River. There were one-liners along the way but I had long since given up the idea that we could paddle those. Sure enough, a stretch of muddy ground existed where the map indicated an inlet stream.

We unloaded our gear as we had done scores of times. The

packs felt light and airy with thirty-three days less food than when we started. At two pounds of food per person per day, we were about 130 pounds lighter—and with the caches that we left, about 170 pounds lighter altogether.

"Let's go on a fourteen-mile tundra hike!" I joked as I easily hoisted a pack. "There are two ponds along the way that we can use as shuttle points."

"Wow! You look like you could carry two packs," Laurie smirked as she adjusted her own.

It occurred to me that I probably could. "Are you feeling strong?" I asked.

"Strong enough, I suppose."

We emptied the contents of the lightest food pack onto the sandy shoreline and organized it into two approximately equal piles which we put into the two other lightest packs. We left the heaviest pack alone so I could carry it, plus the Duluth balanced on top, supported by the tumpline around my forehead. We could get the five packs and hand items across in two trips, then a final third trip carrying the canoe together.

"Let's go on a TEN-mile tundra hike!"

The packs were heavy again, but we were strong. Seasoned. We moved across the landscape with deliberate steps, bearing the weight without complaint. We trudged across the boggy land, accompanied by small bands of caribou the whole way, over the featureless horizon, guided only by my compass until we reached the small, unnamed lake that was our goal sometime in the middle of the afternoon.

The character of the lake forewarned us of the traveling we would face over the next few days. Its rocky shoreline dipped into the shallow waters and surfaced again in a shoal about thirty yards offshore. Over the lake's surface we could see the telltale points of rocks covered occasionally by the violent waves. We paddled north, scraped and dragged when we had to until we arrived at a point of land where the lake turned south into the fierce wind. We intended to camp, but there was a small disruption on the horizon of a hilltop maybe two miles aways. It looked like an inukshuk. Despite Laurie's exhausted protest, we pushed on into the wind and battled our way to a rock-choked narrows at the base of the hill. We were hoping to find evidence of the Ahiarmiut.

CHAPTER TEN

CIRCLES OF STONE

MILE 426-521

"You strangers only see us happy and free of care. But, if you knew the horrors of what we often have to live through, you would understand too why we are so fond of laughing, why we love food and song and dancing. There is not one among us who has not experienced a winter of bad hunting, when many people starved to death around us, and we ourselves only pulled through by accident."

—Knud Rasmussen, interpreting the words
of a Caribou Inuit

Exhausted after dragging the boat ashore, we collapsed in the tundra until cool air and cold feet prompted us to unload. Bits and pieces of weathered caribou bones lay scattered among the rocks that I climbed through to a broad tundra bench about ten feet above the water level. Here I dropped the first red pack. A black raven hopped around picking at something then flew off when Laurie crested the bank. The bowling-ball-sized rocks near the raven's spot seemed unnaturally organized. They were subdued into the gravelly ground and grown over with moss so that it was initially hard to distinguish the circle that they formed which was about twenty feet in diameter. The slow rate of vegetation growth in the Arctic suggested that this ring was very old, likely the anchor stones of an Inuit caribou-skin tent.

The hill rising behind our tent towered two hundred feet over the surrounding land. We hiked to its summit to inspect the possible inukshuk. Along the way, more caribou bones, an old tin mug, and a short piece of rope suggested more recent use. Perhaps this site was still being used as a winter hunting locale. At the hilltop, we discovered not a stone inukshuk but a fifty-five-gallon drum with rocks piled on top. Nearby was another steel drum cut and fashioned into a woodburning stove. Lying around the stove were a few rotted logs that had to have been transported into this treeless land from some great distance. The metal drums disrupted our wilderness experience and, disillusioned, we strolled back down the hill.

I cooked my favorite meal that night, super soup, a hearty stew of barley, lentils, potato buds, powdered milk, dried vegetables, and every spice we had, all topped with heaps of melted cheese. The green dots speckled throughout the cheese mixture looked to be mostly on the wax. I plucked wax while the soup simmered then dumped a couple handfuls into the pot before pulling the bannock from the fire.

Laurie settled next to the twiggy fire to write but the metal drum never left my thoughts. Restless, I walked back to the hilltop, flushed a ptarmigan on the way up, and saw a mother caribou and calf trot over the ridgetop. On the hilltop I saw in one sweeping view the history of the central barrens and its people that culminated in that metal drum.

A dozen more tent rings of various sizes were scattered on the hilltop surrounding the metal drum. The largest was about thirty feet in diameter, the smallest just four feet. Some of the rings looked as old as the one at the base of the hill, while others appeared freshly built, although I knew it had been decades since anyone used skin tents. In a ditch behind one of the rings was the weathered skeleton of a dog, probably used until it had no more strength to haul the provisions of an Inuit family. The reason this place was chosen was apparent: it provided a 360-degree view of the surrounding landscape, a great vantage point for observing the migrating caribou herds. Even today, with the caribou herds greatly reduced, I could see several small bands roaming about the plains below. How many Inuit had sat on this same hilltop doing this same thing?

It's hard to say when these oldest of rings appeared. It could have been just a few decades ago or even centuries. The human history of this land is somewhat uncertain. But it is well known that the last full-time inhabitants of the region left by emergency airlift just over three decades ago. These were the inland Inuit ethnologist Knud Rasmussen called the Caribou Inuit. They inspired Farley Mowat to write about their last days, and me to find their camps. These were the Ahiarmiut who helped inspire the Canadian government to create the new territory of Nunavut, and motivating the Dene to map their own use of the land. Those maps sat buried in a pack since we passed Windy Lake. But this just felt like Inuit country.

However, when Samuel Hearne traversed the region in the 1760s, he was with Chipewyan people the entire time. Yet, 130 years later when Joseph Tyrrell traveled the Kazan, the central Barren Lands were occupied by the Caribou Inuit. Some authors have suggested that the central Barren Lands were originally occupied by Inuit people and that when the Chipewyan in the south acquired guns, they drove the Inuit north and west in order to take control of the central Barren Lands. Others have suggested that this region was originally the homeland of the Chipewyan and the Inuit only moved into the area in the early nineteenth century. The latter is the most logical and accepted idea. Archaeological evidence in the upper Dubawnt River region shows a long history of Chipewyan occupation until the late 1700s. Then there's a break in habitation, probably due to the 1782 smallpox epidemic that decimated the Chipewyan population, followed by a significant influx of the Caribou Inuit. By the 1860s, the interior Barren Lands, once the land of the Chipewyan, became, even in the eyes of the Chipewyan, Inuit land.

Regardless of the confusing pre-history of the central Barren Lands, during the nineteenth century the Caribou Inuit moved down the Kazan River valley. At the same time, the Barren Lands band of the Chipewyan roamed the southern fringes of the tundra. Their homelands significantly overlapped, and despite rumors of hostility, Chipewyan and Inuit had frequent contact in the Kazan River valley. In time, the Chipewyan began to settle around the trading posts of the northern forests and the Inuit established permanent camps farther south up the Kazan.

In 1894, Tyrrell began to encounter Inuit on the upper reaches of the Kazan living prosperous lives just a few days' travel from this hilltop where I stood. These tent rings were likely constructed during that period or before. Caribou-skin kayaks followed Tyrrell's Peterborough canoe and escorted him to shoreline camps.

The Inuit were somewhat nomadic like the Chipewyan, but they set up large camps at places where large caribou migrations were known to cross waterways. Each fall, scouts would stand on hilltops watching the northern horizon for the coming of the deer. Inevitably, the great river of life would come flowing south and hunters would wait at the historic river crossings to make their kills.

I stood on the hilltop in a tent ring fiddling with my camera, imagining I was a hunter patiently waiting for the herald, "Tuktu!" I'd then spring into action. With the other hunters, I'd paddle my kayak to the scouted location where the herd would cross. When the bulk of the caribou were swimming and most vulnerable, we'd appear from our hiding places, paddle amongst the herd, spear the animals, and reap our harvest. The killing would not stop until the herd had passed. Then, the floating carcasses would be gathered, and the celebration of life would begin.

The dizzying flurry of activity in the fall hunt was antici-pated and well prepared for; the survival of the society depended on the hunters' success. The caribou carried the Inuit through the harsh winters until the blessed creatures once again graced the land in the spring. During that long, cold season, fat extracted from the caribou meat lit their igloos, the thick hides floored their shelters and covered their bodies. They lived in close contact with friends and relatives to help pass the season. Drum dances, social visits, and celebrations filled their time when meat was in supply.

If for some reason the fall hunt was unsuccessful, a scramble for survival ensued, often leading to widespread starvation. In bad winters, the people were forced to fish in the lakes for subsistence. Fish, however, was considered a starvation diet as it does not provide enough fat to fend off the cold.

This great dependence on one natural event, the caribou migration, certainly lends credence to the phrase "the land of feast and famine" so often used to describe the fatal fickleness of the barrens. Samuel Hearne first used the phrase when he traveled with the Chipewyan to describe their cyclical eating pattern. When the caribou were abundant, they feasted; when scarce, they met famine.

John Hornby, a famous Barren Lands vagabond in the early 1900s, was moved by his experiences with the Inuit. Their steadfast, unyielding approach to life and death in this harsh land inspired him to begin a book called, *The Land of Feast and Famine*, which went unfinished.

In 1927 in a lonely cabin on the Thelon River, the same year Mallet struggled to reach his cache on the Kazan River, the caribou did not come for Hornby. He, his eighteen-year-old nephew Edgar Christian, and a young family friend, Harold Adlard, intended to reach the cabin in time to catch the fall migration, kill enough caribou for their winter meat supply, then spend the winter hunting and trapping in the Arctic wilderness. It was going to be a grand celebration of Christian's graduation from school. But they moved slowly, discarded food early in their trip, and missed the caribou migration. Edgar Christian documented the gruesome details of his two companions' starvation, then his own. Hornby died first, then Adlard. Then one day in early spring, Christian crawled from his bed to place his journal in the stove for safekeeping. He lay down, crossed his arms over his chest, and died alone some unknown time later. Two years later an RMCP officer found the three bodies.

Helge Ingstad did publish a book by the title, *The Land of Feast and Famine*, in 1931, describing the four exciting years he spent in the Barren Lands. The Caribou Inuit are shown to have lived this life on the edge of feast and famine, and through the generations they acquired the skills and knowledge to persevere. Through good winters and bad, they continued in their traditional ways. They knew where to catch the northbound herd each spring and bring life back into the camps.

Animals were weak and their hides thin after the long arctic winter, so the spring hunt was not as important to the lives of the Ahiarmiut. In addition, caribou could be hunted continually through the summer. Still, the spring hunt provided a much-desired supply of fresh meat.

Summers were relatively relaxing times for the Ahiarmiut. It was a time for preparing weapons, mending clothing, and sampling the other delicacies of the north (the ptarmigan I flushed would not have lasted long). As fall approached, the intensity of activity increased as the hunters once again prepared for the coming of the deer.

A few decades before Tyrrell found them, some Caribou Inuit discovered the most northern outpost in that part of the continent at Brochet. Traders and missionaries told stories of both Inuit and Chipewyan working the waterways of the central Barren Lands and having some knowledge of each other's languages. This is not to say that Chipewyan–Inuit relations were friendly. I believe they simply tolerated each other's presence as stories of conflict transcend centuries to the present day. Even in 1939, Downes's Chipewyan companions displayed fear and resentment when encountering Inuit on Nueltin Lake. Regardless, a trade relationship existed, and from this relationship the inland Inuit had been indirectly introduced to outsiders' trade goods. But the Inuit camps were a long way from Brochet, so little changes had taken place in their world when Tyrrell appeared from a nearly unknown world to the south. Their culture continued into the 1900s as it had for millennia, since the time when humans first arrived on this continent after the great ice sheet retreated, living and dying according to the tempestuous mood of the caribou and the barrens.

The inland Inuit continued to live in their mysterious world until the 1920s when the boom of the fur trade brought traders searching for new, cheap labor. The numerous trading posts that sprang up along the southern fringes of the barrens, the most notable being near the HBC post on Windy River, cut off the long trip to Brochet. White influence on Caribou Inuit culture increased dramatically. The Inuit were enticed to focus their hunting efforts on valuable fur-bearing animals instead of the caribou, and they traded the pelts in exchange for food and supplies that they once procured for themselves. In time, their diet changed from a purely meat to a flour-based one. Like the Chipewyan over a century before, new contact brought new diseases and the inland Inuit population dwindled.

Some elders in the Inuit community began to say that their plight was a direct consequence of turning from their constant source of life, the caribou. They had upset the spirit of the Tuktu, and it had abandoned them. Through the 1920s, the Inuit slowly weaned from dependence on the caribou.

One tragic year after furs became less trendy in New York, the traders did not come. Inuit trappers who had spent their fall catching fox instead of spearing caribou arrived at empty buildings and found nobody to buy their furs. They returned with no food, and found the season too far progressed to cache an adequate supply of caribou meat. That winter on the barrens forced many of the old ones to take their final walks into the Arctic night to reduce the number of mouths to feed, and for the same reason, many infants were left on barren hillsides. Dogs were sacrificed as food, but they had grown thin and provided little nourishment. Treks to neighboring camps and distant trading posts for food turned into death marches. Hurried graves were built on the trail. By the end of that season, the population of inland Inuit was drastically reduced.

Also working against the Inuit was the significant reduction in the caribou herds after the 1920s. The introduction of the rifle to both Chipewyan and Inuit changed their hunting strategies, and overkilling significantly affected the herds. But a far more disastrous force was the trappers who descended upon the barrens with their poisons and unlimited ammunition. A common practice for a trapper was to kill as many caribou as possible, leaving rotting carcasses all along his trapline so that his dogs could have a ready supply of food. One trapper claimed that he alone killed over two hundred caribou in a single season. An average Inuit family needed just over a hundred to survive an entire year. With the advent of the fur trade, the caribou, which was never a commercial fur-bearing animal, diminished on the barrens.

As the herd shrank, the predictable patterns of behavior that the Inuit had learned and depended upon began to change. Many crossing places where hunters waited in ambush never again felt the thundering footprints of the great herds. The entire economic structure of a society was destroyed, and the people were left to fend for themselves in a land that could no longer provide life. The surviving Inuit families faced the fierce Barren Lands winters with no meat in their caches, no oil in their lamps, and inadequate winter clothing. And when spring came, often the caribou could not be found in enough abundance to quench the starvation of the winter. Without dogs, traveling to find the caribou was difficult. Death became commonplace and the Kazan River, called the River of Men in the language of the Inuit, became a river of graves. Through the 1930s, the fur trade experienced cycles of activity as demand for fur waxed and waned, which forced cyclic periods of death on the Inuit. Each time, the Ahiarmiut would change their ways to work for the traders, and each time they would be abandoned and left to retreat to their old ways in a land that became more and more impoverished. By 1940, the Ahiarmiut were entirely forgotten in the depths of the barrens, and the remaining population centered around Hicks Lake (where we found the inukshuk island) tried to rebuild their lives. But their old ways were too far gone, and starvation and disease continued to decimate their numbers. In 1947, the Canadian writer Farley Mowat visited them and found only a small struggling band of survivors of the Ahiarmiut band of the Caribou Inuit. In 1906 their numbers were estimated to be 858. In 1932 it was less than 200. In 1946 it was less than 60.

Mowat flew into the old Windy River trading post and found the Schweder kids living there alone nearly a decade after the post was abandoned, trying to revive the life they had known with their father. Charles, the oldest at nineteen, ran a trapline that extended as far as Angikuni Lake. Fred, sixteen, and Mike, seven, had their own traplines in other parts surrounding the cabin. The life they had seen as children alone in that great wilderness must have been fantastic, adventurous, and frightening. Traveling by dog team in winter, canoe in summer, entirely dependent on the land for survival at such a young age, their real lives paralleled the stuff of wilderness legends. The Schweders had regular visitors from the surviving Ahiarmiut who centered in the Hicks Lake region, known as the land under the Little Hills. The fur industry was just a memory in the North at that time, but the ways of the people had deteriorated to irretrievable levels. Many skills had died with the elders, and those who tried could not extract a living from the once bountiful barrens.

Guns with no shells, tattered trading-post clothing instead of caribou skins, improper diets for the harsh Arctic winters, their lives blended a poor mixture of their old ways with scraps from the new world, and they fell into poverty their people had never known. I imagined the fifty-five-gallon drum on our hilltop was a remnant of this period.

In 1939, Downes helped unload some fuel drums off the plane that picked him up at Windy Post. Perhaps the discarded cans were taken by the Inuit as a new resource from the modern world. On a neighboring hilltop, I saw a real inukshuk through my binoculars. I'm not certain which one represents the more significant phase of their lives, but I know which one is more aesthetically pleasing and less disturbing to see.

I found a piece of a snowmobile belt and the chewed remains of a can of motor oil. Someone visited this place in a recent winter. Perhaps it was a Chipewyan hunting party; my Chipewyan sources had not mentioned having come this far north in decades. I don't know if any Inuit parties continue to hunt in this region but I think not because the nearest settlement in any direction is three hundred miles by air in Churchill.

These tent rings, inukshuks, and graves are nearly the only evidence that a society of people lived on this land. The prehistory of the Ahiarmiut is unclear among anthropologists. Their coastal cousins are descendants of the Thule people who migrated from Alaska around 1,000 years ago and, before that, from northeast Siberia across the Bering Land Bridge around 5,500 years ago. But when the first Inuit occupied the shorelines of these rivers and lakes of the interior Barren Lands is an open question. Their light touch on the landscape, using raw materials that degrade back into the earth, left few lasting landmarks. When they left, however, is very clear. 1959. Just a few years before I was born.

In the 1950s, a few surviving families of the Ahiarmiut did their best to keep what was left of their lives in the barrens, but repeated starvation and disease continued to reduce their population. The Canadian government intervened with well-intended but poorly executed relief programs, including moving them to work at a short-lived commercial fishing venture on Nueltin Lake. Despondent, most soon returned to Ennadai Lake where they survived near a government communication station. Others tried to hang on near Hicks Lake, according to Farley Mowat, perhaps at this very site. In 1959, the last survivors of the Ahiarmiut were forcibly flown out of their final stands in the Barren Lands and placed in shelters in various communities on the west coast of Hudson Bay. Most went to Eskimo Point, now called Arviat, near where the Thlewiaza River finishes its run to the sea, and where in 1912, an Inuit family shared food with Oberholtzer and Magee.

Maybe if we had approached this place from Arviat, ascending the lower Thlewiza River to Nueltin Lake, we might have gathered information about the Tundra Gap from Ahiarmiut elders, like we did in Wollaston Lake with the Chipewyan elders about the Forest Gap. That detailed level of Ahiarmiut history, recorded in their own oral traditions, is stored only in the memories of those last few families who were relocated to Arviat. Did they pass those stories on to anyone? Could we have learned about a better route to the Kazan River from Nueltin Lake? But we didn't meet them. We were alone, finding our way along the most sensible route we could decipher.

Today, no community depends entirely on the caribou for survival, and few people travel these waters in the summer. Nobody struggles year-round to scrape a living from the rocks and tundra of the barrens. The waters below this hilltop will never again feel the wake of a skin kayak, and these ancient rings will never again anchor a skin tent. I looked down the hill and saw the bright yellow and red specks that were our tent and canoe. We were just tourists here, sightseers paddling around in this vast ghost town, carving our own place in the unsettling history of this magnificent place

From the hilltop I could see our route from Hicks Lake to the southeast all the way to the Kazan River to the northwest. The sun hung low in the sky, reflecting on the many small, uncharted ponds and streams between us and our destination. A small, white, fur-bearing animal trotted past me about fifty feet away. It moved swiftly, but not like it was trying to flee. It just looked like it had somewhere to go. The Arctic fox turned its head toward me as it moved along, unalarmed, as if it knew I was no real threat. I watched it dart through the rocks and then perch on top of one. A raven's cackle drew my attention away, and when I looked back, the fox was gone.

I strolled back down the hill; Laurie was already in the sleeping bag. I studied maps in the dim light for about thirty minutes before crawling into our nylon shelter in the rock ring to sleep.

***

The two days following Inuit Hill were much like the previous days of our small-stream travel. Portages at every rock-jammed narrows, sweltering heat during the afternoons, periodic bouts with black flies, and very long days with limited miles of progress. We worked until late in the evening, set up a quick camp, slept a bit, then pushed on for more of the same in the morning. We continued to see tent rings along the shores, and caribou were always with us.

Portaging the canoe over the featureless, trailless tundra was challenging. The soft moss sapped our energy at every step and with no trails to follow, we could only go by distant, vague landmarks to guide our path. With the canoe over our heads, we could only see a few feet in front of us. I usually carried the front end and would periodically thrust the canoe upward to get a view. Inevitably, we would be a little off course and I would overcorrect until I again needed a view. My exaggerated thrusts of the canoe frustrated Laurie because of the uneven weight on her shoulders, and we would continue the portage in tense silence interrupted by painful pants just loud enough for the other person to hear. Once while lugging the canoe over a stretch of tundra at the end of a very long day, we both heard the telltale clicking of a passing herd. We dropped the canoe and for fifteen minutes watched a constant stream of animals appear from a shrub thicket then disappear over a barren hill. The break prompted a well-needed attitude adjustment, and we continued on with the portage.

On August 6, we determined to scrape our way along the stream to the Kazan no matter how long it took. We rebelled at the thought of spending another day on this boat-crunching stream and longed for long stretches of paddleable water. The distance was only ten miles, but we probably walked most of the way. After thirteen hours of struggling down the shallow stream, we arrived at its end, but unfortunately, it wasn't the Kazan River. The stream simply faded away and dispersed into a mass of jumbled boulders and brush about a mile short of the river. True to our resolve, we took a compass bearing, abandoned the streambed, trekked overland with our load to Dimma Lake on the Kazan River, and ended a long, grueling day. As I wrote in my journal, *"Some days you just have to get through."*

When we arrived at our campsite, the hardships of the day

faded and I pulled out my pen and opened my journal:

> *I made an excellent banana bread. Despite the hard day, we had a very pleasant evening. When the work is done and we're sitting around the fire after dinner, all the day's hardships disappear. We could have had the hardest day of the trip, or the easiest, and when evening comes it's all the same. Very nice.*

Dimma Lake was our last safety valve. We could turn upstream and follow Theirry Mallet's return journey and be back on the Cochrane River in a couple of weeks. Or we could drift downstream until it was too late to continue north. The last week of slow traveling gave us reasons for concern and instilled a constant worry. We thought hard about the return route on the unknown Nowleye River and the trip from Kasba Lake to the Cochrane River. Both sections offered the possibility of weeks of travel that could strand us in the Far North and cause us to suffer the wrath of freeze-up. We worried about our dwindling food supply. Perhaps we had hastily discarded too much food so many weeks ago. Several times in the past few days we had made the decision to turn south at Dimma Lake, only to change our minds. On the evening of August 6, it stood that we would indeed turn south on the Kazan and work our way upstream to the eastern lobe of Ennadai Lake, cutting off the Kazan to Angikuni and the entire Nowleye. I wrote in my journal:

> *I think we might be able to make it all the way if we really pushed it, but we've been pushing it for thirty-six days with only one rest day. I think we could use some leisurely days before our grueling route south. Plus, as I've repeatedly*

mentioned, there is a lot of uncertainty in our south route that could give us serious delays. I really don't want to deal with freeze-up. Nowleye would be nice to see, but it may be too risky. I'll probably think differently in the morning.

Morning came and the idea of turning back did not sit well with either of us. We tentatively paddled north "just to see what's up there," intending to turn around at the end of the lake. The end of the lake came into view. We saw the swift current heading north, it grabbed our hearts before it grabbed our bow, and we dug in for the paddle.

The Kazan moves swiftly after Dimma Lake with occasional widenings to slow us down. We still had yet to decide whether to continue all the way to Angikuni, and by late afternoon we came to a small, windswept lake that forced us to shore.

Despite the wind, the day was glorious. Fine paddling, warm weather, striking scenery, and no bugs. We strolled inland, nestled into the soft moss, and napped in the hot sun. The wind was still blowing at 4:30 p.m., so we made an early dinner.

Laurie prepared the meal while I reviewed the maps and I resolved to finally make a decision. Would we turn back or head north? I prepared a new schedule to complete the route that would bring us back by September 30, following what should be a reasonably conservative pace. We had mild weather, so we planned on a late fall. After carefully reviewing and considering all that could happen if we met delays—impassible water on the Nowleye, extended wind delays on the numerous large lakes, injury, and navigation problems in the forest gap—we unanimously exclaimed, "Let's just do it!"

So at 6:30 p.m. in the dying wind, we pushed north to implement our decision. We had a new beginning. The prospect of carrying out our plan, seeing Angikuni Lake and the mystery of what remained, stimulated hard paddling. We paddled until sunset on that gracefully calm lake on the Kazan River before we made our first campsite on its shore.

The following two days on the Kazan were pure delight. The river moved swiftly, occasionally tumbling over exciting but easily paddleable rapids. In short, on these easy days we covered two to three times the distance we had on the brutal days of previous weeks. Shoreline features passed at dizzying speeds. But when we arrived at the wide reaches and small lakes, our pace screeched to a near halt.

The calm stretches seemed to last forever as we stared at distant goals for hours. The air was thick with heat and moisture; no breeze disturbed the silence or the surface. The only sounds were the gentle splashings of our paddles which only got sloppier as the day progressed. We would stop occasionally, far from any shore, and marvel at the absolute stillness of our surroundings. These days of short, easy traveling seemed to last much longer than when we were working hard.

Sometimes the monotony of paddling with nothing else to concentrate on became overwhelming. It's just stroke, lift, feather, repeat ... all day long. It was the same on any calm stretches throughout the trip. That, combined with the unchanging scenery of large lakes, drives you to search your brain for something unique to think about. Of course, the first thing always to pop into mind was our route. I often had to force myself to think about other things or interrupt the long silence and start a conversation about anything. Sometimes I could just concentrate on the repeated motion of paddling, feel the glide over the smooth water, and lose myself in a thoughtless void that would last until the conditions warranted decisive thought.

Those days of mindlessness were rare, though. I usually had some technical problems to consider. The slightest waves made me think about how to approach them or where to head if they grew scary. Intricate lakeshores and rivers kept me tracking our course with the map and compass. Sitting in the bow, Laurie had those trips into the deep recesses of the mind more often, and I always knew when she was slipping. Her head would tilt a bit, her grip hand would barely reach beyond her chest, and her paddle would begin to float with the motion of the boat.

"Hey ... HEY! Where've you been?"

"Sorry, I was just thinking about ... I don't know what I was thinking about."

"You were sleeping."

"That island hasn't gotten any closer!"

We had several sections like that on the Kazan, but the power of the intervening sections snapped us to attention and carried us swiftly along. Plus, the shoreline produced interesting features that continually drew us ashore to investigate. Inukshuks, rock cairns, old campsites, many signs that gave clues to the rich history of the land appeared on most prominent points.

We reached the southwest extreme of Angikuni Lake by noon on August 9. A stiff morning breeze grew into a powerful wind from the southwest. We stopped for lunch in the lee of a high sandy bank. It was a hot day out of the wind, and we enjoyed a refreshing dip in the comfortably cool lake.

Joseph Tyrrell reached this same point in mid-August of 1894, intent on following the Kazan River to Hudson Bay. Although uncertain, he suspected that the Kazan River flowed into Nevill Bay on Hudson Bay, since he and his crew the previous year passed the mouth of a large river there during their desperate paddle south. If in 1893 Tyrrell had paddled along the south shore of Baker Lake instead of the north, he would have noticed the mouth of a large river there. He may then have correctly reasoned that the Kazan River flows to Baker Lake.

Tyrrell encountered the first Inuit community on the Kazan River on August 17 when he came into a camp led by a man named Kopanuak. At one time, his Peterborough canoe was surrounded by twenty-three Inuit "kyacks." Sometimes the Inuit fled from the strange intrusion, but usually Tyrrell was greeted with "shouts of joy." There, without a common word spoken, the Inuit convinced Tyrrell that the Kazan River does indeed flow into Hudson Bay. This delighted the crew and gave them hope that they could complete the mission without the hardships that the previous year's crew endured.

Tyrrell's description of the river from Kopanuak's camp to Angikuni Lake and beyond tells a different story from what we saw. Inuit camps were so common that he used them as mileage markers to describe river features: "Aunah's camp, the river had kept a general course almost due eastward...Below the camp of Ungalluk the river flows with an easy current to a small lake."

Then on August 26, they reached Passamut's camp where they learned that the Kazan River does not flow into Hudson Bay, but it flows north to the south shore of Baker Lake where

Tyrrell passed the year before. He wrote, "To follow the river there would be out of the question, for we would probably reach the Inlet even later than in the previous year, and on the trip down the shore of Hudson Bay, we should be exposed to the same dangers and privations that we had then suffered." They sought an easier return journey.

They learned from the Inuit on Yathkyed Lake that they could portage east into what is now called the Ferguson River and follow it to the sea, thus cutting off several hundred potentially treacherous miles. On September 1, with Inuit aid, they left the Kazan and portaged east for five days to the headwaters of the Ferguson River and then descended the unknown river until they reached its mouth at Hudson Bay on September 18. There, Tyrrell recognized the beach as a place "to which we had walked through the deep snow on September 25th, 1893, when storm-bound on a point a few miles distant at the mouth of Neville's Bay [sic]." But in 1894, their luck held. Although freezing weather gripped the inland waters, the sea remained open, and they raced the weather to Churchill where they arrived on October 1. Although the canoeing was over, they once again made the long trek home by dogsled and snowshoe to complete two truly astounding years of travel.

Three decades later, the traders Thierry Mallet and Del Simmons became the third recorded group of outsiders to see Angikuni Lake. They found the Caribou Inuit camped at the same spot where the river enters the lake. Mallet poignantly wrote about the conditions of the Caribou Inuit and sensed their doom at the hands of his own kind. Just two decades later, Farley Mowat, guided by one of the last surviving Ahiarmiut and whose father had lived in the camps visited by Tyrrell, paddled to Angikuni Lake and found nothing but the tragic remains of a camp that suffered a quick and painful extinction. Hurried graves, bones scattered by wolverines, and abandoned campsites littered the hilltops where Tyrrell, Mallet, and Simmons found Inuit happily living their lives.

Mowat's party camped for several days on Angikuni as a north wind kept them captive. On our day spent where the river entered the lake, a south wind blew strong and urged us to push on and be carried north by its gusty strength. But the rolling green hills stretching back from the shores of the bay tempted us to leave the paddle behind and wander. We crested a rocky ridge on a plateau overlooking the bay's western shore. There, nestled on a large rock platform between the lake and a craggy section of sheared granite that gave way to the sweeping tundra, were the remains of a large encampment. Perhaps thirty tent rings surrounded one large ring with a granite fireplace in its center. Could this be the camp where Tyrrell traded for skin clothing? Or was it the camp that told the tale of tragic death to Mowat? It could have been either, or both. The shores of Angikuni hold many remnants in their far-reaching hills that tell the tale of its people.

Laurie wandered off toward the western horizon where the tundra met the sky. I sat in the center of an ancient circle of stones and let my mind wander. I recalled the path that brought us here and our reasons for coming, then concentrated on the rich land surrounding me. Scattered among the tent rings were the ever-present bits of bone and various scraps of wood that had been fashioned for some useful purpose. Each discovery was a new vehicle to the outer limits of my imagination. But each story I concocted about the early lives of these people always ended with the depressing conclusion illustrated by this empty camp. Across the bay, I detected an inukshuk standing vigil over the empty land. Its purpose was to provide a sign of life, a reassurance against loneliness to the people who passed within view. There was no reassurance for me. I knew the future that its maker could never have known: that those rocks, the artificial man that stood lifeless on that barren hill, would long outlive the people from whom it rose.

I wondered where I would have fit in those days at the turn of the century. Trapper? Trader? Most likely neither. I don't hunt and I'm not a business man. I've spoken of the tragedies that came in their wake, but still, I admire their lives. They were men of the wilderness, seeking means to make a living most efficiently while maintaining a close connection to the northern landscape. Many writers have dumped the burden of blame on the fur trade, but I believe the individual men employed by the trade were just seeking alternative lifestyles, viewing themselves as removed from the society for which they were acting as unwitting agents of change. They may have viewed the industrial world with disdain and sought to make a simpler living in the wilderness, yet they brought change to the very wilderness they cherished. The modern world never physically reached portions of the Far North. But the assimilating spirit of our civilization extracted the life out of the northern wilderness through the hands of the men who disdained the modern world most. It was a complex history for me to understand—to sit there in that cirlce and see the evidence of a people eradicated from their homeland by various faceless perpetrators, none with evil intent.

Who can predict the consequences of their own actions? Would I have been there? I doubt it, not because I would have somehow understood the consequences of what I would have been a part of, but because of the courage, determination, and skill it would have required for such a lifestyle. We were tourists, really, paddling through an extreme wilderness landscape, using the land as an interactive museum.

I left the circle and found Laurie sitting by a small pond. She didn't have to tell me what she was thinking about. We wandered back to the canoe then let the wind and waves toss us north through a narrow section where we paddled into the main body of Angikuni Lake. After forty days and 532 miles of traveling, we had reached our summit, the home of the Caribou Inuit, the shores of Angikuni Kaminyae.

CHAPTER ELEVEN

THE POINT OF RETURN

MILE 521–681

"From the head of Baker Lake we were not to commence a new stage of the journey ... From our camp to the mouth of Chesterfield Inlet on the coast of Hudson Bay measured about 250 miles, and thence down the coast of the Bay to Fort Churchill, a Hudson's Bay Company's post and the nearest habitation of white men, measured 500 more; so that 750 miles was the least distance we had to figure on traveling in canoes before the close of navigation."

—J.W. Tyrrell

A gentle southwest breeze blew through our tent as morning broke on the shores of Angikuni Lake. In the north and east, that vast sheet of water rippled with the signature of a waning wind and stretched toward a horizon where the lake met the sky in a hazy blend of blue and gray. The rolling tundra shorelines, illuminated by a brilliant, low-hanging sun, drifted away into the depths of the inviting north. We would not see that land on this trip; we had reached the northern limit of our travels.

Our path turned west, then south. It was time to begin the long journey home.

The journey home—intimidating, daunting—lay before us and tempered the excitement of our arrival at our summit. For over forty days, we anticipated that moment until we stood rejoicing on the shores of that immense lake. I visualized the return route as we paddled across the early morning calm of Angikuni Lake. Hundreds of upstream miles, countless lakes, and lengthy overland treks through trailless forest lay between us and our new goal—Wollaston Lake. Forty more days. I thought it would take that long to make it back. That number sounded so finite but so very long. The past forty days seemed like my whole life, as though I'd been paddling forever. That meant that we had forever still to paddle. I imagined the possible obstacles ahead—a dry Nowleye River, an impenetrable forest gap, and an early winter. I said to Laurie in a forced tone of optimism, "I think it will only take about forty days to get back. That's not bad, eh?" She didn't respond but continued her smooth strokes. "I know what you mean," I said.

A lengthy silence let my mind return to its natural desire to recalculate our remaining travel time. It occurred to me that we could let the swift current of the Kazan carry us north on a nice downstream cruise a few hundred more miles to Baker Lake, then catch a flight home. But we couldn't. That wasn't our plan, and more importantly, we had no money. We held to our ideals and continued to paddle in the wake of the old ones who had no choice but to paddle home.

Whereas Mallet headed up the Kazan River along the same route he descended, we headed west to the Nowleye River which flows parallel to the Kazan River and which Farley Mowat called the River of Graves. The intrigue was irresistible, although we found no records of anyone traveling the Nowleye River by canoe. Surely, some of those unknown and unrecorded wilderness vagabonds from the early 1900s paddled its length, but had anyone tried to go up it? The appeal of a first ascent up a relatively unknown river was intoxicating during the planning phase. Now, standing where the river enters the lake, I questioned the wisdom of my home-office plans.

We took a brief swim, mostly because we thought people might ask later. It was more like a ceremonial baptism than a swim; the wind and cold did not inspire a leisurely soak. As quick as we could we huddled in the shrubs, letting the weak sun warm us as best it could.

"I'm not ready to go home," Laurie said from her own depression in the shrubs.

"Home is a long way's away. A long time away," I said.

I think she fell asleep. Maybe I did too. For a bit. Soon, miles and rates and travel-time calculations swirled through my thoughts as they always did when my mind wandered.

"Let's get on with it."

***

The Nowleye River runs its final course along a swift, twenty-mile stretch between Nowleye and Angikuni lakes. We turned into its bay off Angikuni and soon felt the exhausting effects of upstream travel. The river was not powerful at this point, just swift enough to take the glide out of our strokes and send us drifting backward at each slight rest. We hugged the shorelines where the current is the slowest. But the river did not maintain this suppressed quality for long. Much of the way to Nowleye Lake was a series of swift-water stretches and boiling rapids that required all our strength and ingenuity to ascend.

The first significant rapid we came to was characteristic of the rest. Shore-fast obstacles created a narrow channel and a smooth, fast tongue that funneled water into a series of standing waves. Shallow, slower water poured over boulder mazes on either side. The river funneled to three-quarters its width and dropped about three feet within thirty yards. A line of standing waves after the initial drop angled toward the center of the river to form a large, powerful "V" of whitewater extending about thirty more yards into the bay where we were floating. Large, boulder-jammed eddies extended into the bay below boulder piles on either side of the initial drop.

We ferried to the inside bend where the current was likely to be slowest. We weaved through the boulders, fighting the current until we came to the ledge where we were forced to enter the main, slick tongue of water. We rested in the eddy of a large rock and readied ourselves for a battle with the current. We looked up the drop from behind our boulder and pushed the bow into the current with powerful thrusts of our paddles. With a quick and powerful draw, Laurie pulled the bow straight into the flow so we wouldn't ferry, and we paddled with all our might to inch our way up the drop. The slightest angle to the boat caught the current and sent us drifting sideways. We pushed and pushed and only succeeded in moving back and forth across the river three times before we ferried back to the shelter of the boulder we had left minutes earlier.

The current was much too powerful for us to paddle, so we clawed our way upstream, grabbing the submerged boulders with our paddles and thrusting forward. Frantic strokes followed until we again found solid ground to give us a boost. We inched our way along until my paddle smacked a boulder amid a wild series of desperate strokes and sent a wave of water into the boat. I saw half the paddle blade floating away. At the costly expense of losing ground, I grabbed the floating wood, threw it and the rest of the paddle into the boat, retrieved my spare paddle, and struggled to a backwater eddy above the rapid. We made it despite the mid-rapid setback.

"That was rough!"

"We got this!" Laurie countered.

Her excitement was contagious, and we attacked the river like the seasoned veterans we had become. We cruised through the calm water faster than I expected for about an hour before we saw the tumbling white of a rapid coming around a bend. There was no sneak route along the side of this one, just the cascading force of the main current over a shallow, rocky drop. The current looked too powerful to paddle, but the channel was braided with several large boulders that created tempting eddies that might be reached by poling.

Poling involves standing in the center or rear of the canoe and pushing off the bottom with a long pole to go upstream, or "snub" off the bottom to travel downstream. With a pole, the skillful traveler could move around stream and river networks with little regard for the direction of the current. Poling has become somewhat of a lost art of wilderness travel since few canoeists travel upstream. It felt like the right time to try it.

I trimmed a pole about ten feet long from a stunted spruce tree that had somehow found its way here from a forest patch somewhere far upstream. I had poled up rapids before, but I was always alone in an empty boat. Laurie sat in the bow with her paddle to guide us into the channel while I stood in the stern and pushed off the bottom with the long pole. Keeping a proper angle so as not to be thrown sideways was difficult with the weight. Tension built between us as we worked up the current. From the shelter of an eddy in the middle of the rapid I said to Laurie, "Okay, you're going to draw us into the current just a bit, then I'll push hard, and you've got to straighten us out as soon as possible so we don't get sideways."

"I know!" she sharply replied.

"Well, let's go."

We pushed forward at an angle far too wide for the powerful current and began to drift sideways.

"Draw! Draw! Come on! What are you doing?"

"I know! I am! You're not getting us forward!"

We lost control, spun sideways, and pinned the boat on a rock. The current threatened to wrap the boat. We pried ourselves free and got on a good course until the pole wedged in a crack and I lost my grip. We spun, got stuck on the same rock, and nearly tipped as the force of the current swept under our hull while Laurie tried to free the pole. I tried to paddle, but after a desperate minute, we dropped downstream to an eddy we had left thirty minutes earlier. Mid-rapid, I switched back to the pole and we spun sideways. We regained control with tremendous effort and finally pushed our way to the top. In one bout of frantic poling, I knocked my strapless sunglasses off my face into the rapid. *We got this,* I thought, one rapid at a time.

We continued up the Nowleye River in this way for seventeen miles until a long, rocky rapid that we could not ascend forced us to portage. We got our last load across at 7:30 p.m. and set up camp. We were ready for a quick meal after an exhausting day.

I lit the stove which had been performing very sporadically. It sputtered and wheezed until it finally gave out. The gasket in the fuel cap had become so dried and cracked that it could no longer hold pressure and finally stopped working. Without a shrub or twig in sight, we built a small fire of moss and boiled up a quick soup. Making fires on the tundra had not been a problem so far, so being two hundred miles north of the tree line without a working stove was not too daunting. It would be inconvenient in bad weather or on particularly barren sites like this one. I often cursed those fuel bottles as I carried them across long portages, but I was reassured by the knowledge that they would someday earn their keep. Now, after just a few uses, the stove and fuel were useless in our packs.

I glued and duct-taped my paddle back together before turning in for an early night. Dull crashes of distant thunder rolled across the tundra soon after we got in our bags. Flashes of lightning accompanied powerful claps of thunder. A hard rain fell through the night for the first time in three weeks. The hypnotic patter helped divert my thoughts from the open-water crossing to come on Nowleye Lake.

We were on the water by 6:30 a.m. to take advantage of the calm after the storm. One final rapid brought us to the flat waters of the lake. Our course due west put us directly sideways to the prevailing winds from the south. The most direct path across the lake involved an eight-mile open crossing with few islands to break up the exposure. We hoped to avoid the several miles that following the shoreline would add. Even the slightest winds can be very frustrating when coming from the side, so we cautiously eased into the lake. The water was beautifully still at this early hour. We paddled directly across the lake, paying close attention to the wind.

We moved swiftly into the open water. The shorelines soon faded into the horizon. We started the crossing like sprinters, but as conditions calmed, our anxiety faded and we settled into the repetitive flat-water routine.

The distant point seemed no closer, and the oppressive silence amplified my thoughts. It seemed as though we sat dead in the water with no landmarks to measure our progress. The only thing that indicated motion was the swirling whirlpools from my paddle that drifted back from the boat. I stared at those patterns for a while, then back to the distant point of land. "That point's not getting any closer! How come we're barely moving?" That point seemed to be the whole purpose of our forty days of traveling. I just wanted to get there.

An Arctic tern flew overhead and broke the silence with its squeaky call. It teased us by swooping low over our heads a few times before flying off toward our distant point and disappearing into the horizon. Incredibly, that bird was probably in Antarctica just a few months earlier. Terns spend their summers fluttering about the tundra lakes, then make a great migration to Antarctica for the winter. Do they ever grow tired of their travels? Do they rise to the task with optimism? Do they even know why they do what they do?

The tern is not the only Barren Lands bird that performs tremendous journeys. The golden plover travels over fifteen thousand miles from its winter home in Argentina to its breeding grounds in the high Arctic islands. Such small birds, it's hard to imagine them undertaking such a journey when we see them hopping around among the tundra hummocks picking at insects. While those great migrations are impressive, perhaps more impressive are the birds that stick it out through winter, like the raven soaring high over the water as we sit on the canoe seats, elbows on thighs, working up the motivation to paddle.

Of course the raven toughs out the winter here. Too often I've spotted the silhouette of a soaring bird and wondered what kind of hawk or eagle it was, then heard the disappointing gurgle gurgle of the raven's ubiquitous call—the same bird I see pulling at roadkill in Michigan, scrounging French fries in a McDonald's parking lot, and tearing apart garbage bags everywhere I've been. But I shouldn't speak too harshly about the raven. The fact that it can winter in the barrens attests to its extreme adaptability. The Athabascans in Alaska long ago recognized the uniqueness of this bird, and the raven became a spiritual symbol.

Of the sixty-six bird species that nest in the Barren Lands, only the raven and four others remain over harsh winters, including rock ptarmigans, willow ptarmigans, snowy owls, and gyrfalcons. I'm not sure which kind of ptarmigan I flushed on the hike up Inuit Hill. It looked like a chicken trying to escape with limited flight skills. Its mottled brown color was a perfect camouflage against the tundra until I nearly stepped on it. Instead of flying south for the winter, they have developed ways of adapting to the cold, white environment. Their plump bodies and thick feathers make them thermally efficient, and their plumage transitions to white to match the winter snow. The transition period can be deadly if they turn white before the season fully changes, exposing themselves to the other two over-winter birds, the snowy owl and gyrfalcon, airborne predators that reign over the winter tundra, sending lemmings hiding under the snow and keeping ptarmigan and Arctic fox looking skyward.

We saw terns and gulls more than any other bird. On portages, smaller birds like thrushes, longspurs, and warblers flitted about. Sandhill cranes amused us with their peculiar mating rituals and once, a pair of trumpeter swans heralded their alarm as we rounded a bend. And the loon, what greater symbol of the North could there be? What northern traveler hasn't been moved by the eerie echoes of a calling loon? Although we didn't see as many as in the forest, the loon was with us on nearly every lake, including Nowleye Lake where we drifted lazily on its surprisingly calm water.

We paddled in the direction of the Arctic tern toward the distant point and moved across the lake for most of the morning, seemingly making no progress on the featureless water. In the forest, trees on distant points gradually take shape as you approach. On Nowleye Lake, with its tundra shores, our goal crept up on us almost without warning. I stood to stretch my legs and gazed across another bay toward another distant point that became our next goal.

We glided along the southern shoreline for eleven more miles under an intense Arctic sun. We completed the lake by midafternoon and settled in for an early camp where the Nowleye River again enters the lake. A late afternoon snack of cinnamon biscuits cooked on a twiggy fire, followed by a hearty meal and an evening stroll in the hills above our camp ended the day.

***

"The middle of nowhere." It's a commonly used phrase spoken whenever anyone tells the story of when they almost ran out of gas on a remote country road. It didn't occur to me when I planned this trip, but if taken literally, the middle of nowhere captures the essence of what I was seeking. I used phrases like "deep wilderness," "land wild by nature, not by law," "land big enough to have a beyond and an inside to it." But nobody really understands deep wilderness unless they've experienced shallow wilderness and longed for more. The middle of nowhere is perfect. We don't know its true boundaries, and its precise location can change with perspective.

Somewhere northwest of Nowleye Lake is the true middle of nowhere by my definition: the farthest spot on the continent from any road or coast. We were close. Maybe fifty miles. I imagine that an Inuit or Dene hunter has been there, but at that time the middle of nowhere was probably farther south. Maybe a trapper or trader wandered through. Who else would leave the main waterways of the Thelon, Dubawnt, and Kazan rivers to cross over a random spot on the tundra near an unnamed lake? It occurred to me to go find it, but the math required to optimize the center of an angular polygon was beyond what I was willing to do with my coarse topographic maps and a pencil.

It's probably best that we didn't go anyway; we had a race against freeze-up to win.

Neither of us slept well that night as we sulked about the task at hand. The work didn't bother us. It was the symbolic nature of turning south. I don't know what I expected to find on the shores of these great lakes, but as we were leaving them, I felt as though I had missed something. We had come to see the homeland of the Ahiarmiut. We found their campsites, stood in their tent rings, and paddled the waters where their kayaks had been. Still, I wanted more than anything else to meet an Inuit hunter, trade some tobacco for fresh caribou meat, and ask what we might find on our ascent of the Nowleye River.

***

The Nowleye River was a mystery to us. According to our coarse-scale maps, the Nowleye and the Kazan rivers both exit Ennadai Lake from different bays and rejoin 110 miles downstream at Angikuni Lake. Why then was there so much information available about the Kazan River and almost nothing about the Nowleye River? Were there unrunnable, unportageable rapids? Were the headwaters too shallow to float a boat? The intrigue was thrilling. We attacked the river with the confidence of the seasoned veterans we had become.

The two-mile section from Nowleye Lake to the next lake is a deep, fast-moving stretch of water mixed with mild to challenging rapids that would make an exciting downstream run. We paddled up eddies when we could and portaged when we had to. We lined with ropes when the rapids were too swift to paddle or pole.

Lining is the method of using ropes to guide your craft upstream. It sounds simple to walk the boat along with ropes, and it can be simple if you have a straight bank free of obstacles. But technical maneuvering is required when rocks, eddies, and rapids obstruct the way. We learned to guide the boat in and out from the bank around obstacles by varying the angle to the current. It's the same principle as ferrying, except using ropes from shore. To move toward the center of the river, the front person gives some slack while the back person pulls in and forward, then the boat ferries out, and you both move forward, hopping along the rocks and in the water if need be. The front person must ensure that the boat does not get too much of an angle or the force of the current may capsize the boat.

My attention slipped and I let the bow drift out so the boat was nearly sideways in a strong current. The rope jerked; I turned to see water pouring over the gunnel. I pulled hard while Laurie loosened up in the stern, and the boat straightened out. It's frightening to stand on the shore and watch your boat with all your belongings come so close to capsizing. I recalled a story of two experienced woodsmen lining up a powerful rapid when they simultaneously let go of their ropes. The canoe drifted away, and they faced survival in the wilderness with nothing but the clothes on their backs. We would shoulder the loads and portage if the rapid was too big and powerful, but as we moved upstream and became more adept, we challenged more and more powerful rapids this way without incident.

On August 13, we traversed a lake so jammed with islands that it resembled a braided river. We paddled up one channel until it became too jammed with rocks to float a boat. Unwilling to retreat, we camped, intending to launch on the other side the next morning. As evening settled in and the wind subsided, the surface of the calm backwater began to ripple with feasting fish. Six weeks into the trip and I had yet to catch a fish. I hadn't tried very much, the only reason I would fish would be for food, and we had plenty of that. Any fish we ate would mean one more day of carrying the food it replaced. But the temptation was too great as the hungry fish continued to roughen the otherwise placid surface. I sat on a rock and cast for about twenty minutes, watching the repeated splunk of metal in water. Laurie strolled down from camp and watched for a couple minutes. It's hard to watch someone fish without wanting to cast. She took the pole, clicked the bail, and threw the lure right where I had just cast. When her second cast was almost reeled in, a dark shadow moved with alarming speed and hit the lure hard. The tip bent and wiggled. Laurie shrieked, "Take this thing!"

Within a few seconds I landed a giant northern pike around twenty-four inches long. With the lure still in its lip, I ended its life with a few strikes with a rock, then went about the business of cleaning it. Anyone around with the slightest experience would have mocked me mercilessly. In my defense, the bones in pike demand special techniques and a sharp knife. I had neither. Still, after fifteen minutes of hacking with a dull multitool, I extracted every piece of meat I could from the carcass, tossed it all in a pan with salt, pepper, and squeeze-bottle margarine, and then enjoyed the sizzling sound of fresh meat being cooked for the first time in six weeks. I intended to save some for breakfast, but after an hour of lounging by the fire, snacking, and enjoying the splendor of the North Country, I entirely consumed the only fish I would catch, or should I say, we would catch, in this wilderness renowned for its excellent fishing.

***

We traveled up the Nowleye River toward Ennadai Lake for nine days. Our travel methods varied with the conditions of the land. Sometimes the banks were too shallow for lining, so we waded and dragged the boat over the rocks. If the water was deep but not too powerful, we could sometimes scrape our way along with our paddles. It was physically demanding, and often wet, regardless of how we traveled. When we weren't in the rapids, we fought intense winds on the lakes, and our progress was slow. The heat had been intense over the previous few days, so we welcomed the cool water. But soon, the weather began to change.

The wind blew with the chaotic force of a changing season. At first it provided relief from the midday heat. Eventually, the nights approached freezing and the days warmed just into the fifties. The transition from summer to fall was as dramatic as the landscape.

We woke one morning to the typical warm temperatures with a southwest wind. During breakfast, however, the wind shifted from the north and within half an hour, the temperature plummeted and icy sleet began to blow across the lake. For nearly a week we experienced the violent weather of transition. One evening a section of our spray cover blew away in the night. This was a frustrating loss as we were at a point in the trip where we needed it most, battling huge waves and cold water. In just a few days, we went from wearing the lightest of our clothes in the intense heat to wearing all of our winter gear to stay comfortable. We huddled behind packs to eat our meals and retreated to the tent during the frequent storms.

Signs of Ahiarmiut life were frequent on the banks of the Nowleye River. On most hilltops, small rocks were positioned in unnatural ways that obviously served as markers. On a hilltop bordering one of the larger lakes along the river, an inukshuk stood silhouetted against the horizon. We saw the inukshuk about two miles away and decided the peninsula it stood on would provide a good break from the wind. The wind continued to blow fiercely from the north, putting a biting chill in the air and tremendous waves on the water. Our path was directly in line with the wind, so we shoved off and raced with the waves. We put no effort into paddling forward as the wind carried us along at a phenomenal velocity. But it took frantic efforts to keep the boat straight in the rollers. We sped along and turned in behind the point to take a break. Two caribou trotted away as we climbed to view the inukshuk.

We pulled behind another peninsula farther down the lakeshore to rest from the wind. A high, inviting hill rose from the lakeshore. The summit seemed like an alpine peak. Rock debris was scattered on the hilltop, and a wind fierce enough to throw me off balance whistled through the rocks. To the south I could see a series of lakes we would soon paddle across. But the route between the lakes was hidden in a maze of islands and channels. The southern end of this lake was cluttered with small islands that obscured passage to the rapid-choked river that flowed from the next upstream lake. We paddled into the maze and set up camp in the lee of a small hump of an island.

My journal entry on August 15 describes our typical conditions over the following few days:

The wind blew through the night, and we awoke to a very chilly morning. Just a couple of days ago we were hoping for colder weather for some relief on the portages. It certainly came quick. Last night was very cold. A few days ago I couldn't believe that freeze-up could occur in late September. Now, I'm a bit nervous. I had heard stories of the nasty weather up here, but we hadn't seen it until now.

The wind blew hard from the southwest all day. I thought maybe it would bring warm weather, but it remained chilly. Gray skies hid the sun all day. We made it through the remaining islands and into the next river section fairly early in the morning. We were able to paddle, track, and drag up most of the way, but had to portage a few times, too. The farther upstream we get, the shallower the water gets. I fear we may run out of water before we reach Ennadai. Most of the narrow sections have to be dragged. We continued wading to make lining easier, although it was not as comfortable as previous days. The water is still warm, but the wind left us with frigid feet while paddling. It was actually a relief to step back in the water.

By midafternoon, a cold rain/sleet started to fall. I remained comfortably warm except for my feet and hands ... The next lake section was again jammed with islands. I knew that many of the channels between the islands would not be passable. It was guesswork trying to find our way, for the maps could not show us which passages to follow. We

*portaged our gear around one rapid between two islands
and lined the canoe up. There was one wave that we just
couldn't trust with our gear. We weaved around the maze
of islands, continually fighting the wind, and encountered
many dead ends. Not only do the islands make a maze, but
the boulders in the passable channels also make a maze. The
waves conceal the jagged tops, and we get stuck frequently.
Many times we could find no passages and would portage
over slippery rock jams.*

*A handful of gorp was all we had for lunch for it was too
cold and rainy to stop and we wanted to get out of the maze.
We pushed on past the last island and toward another river
section before a larger lake. A hard rain fell as we crossed
some open water and the cold hit us hard. We made it to the
last narrows, lined, and dragged up it. I think today's lining
with precarious footing up some large rapids was the most
dangerous thing we've done on the trip. The slippery rocks
make a fall very possible, and this is severe hypothermia
weather. We have no working stove, and a quick fire would
be very difficult in these conditions on the barrens. It's tricky
work finding stable footing.*

A fierce Arctic wind blew our stakes out of the ground that
night and the tent hung limply over our heads on the arched
poles. The morning brought calmer winds, but the air had the
cold that bites at your nose. It warmed up in the afternoon as
the sun came out and alternated that way for the next few days.
The temperature change made us more hesitant with our wet
traveling methods. But we figured we had just a few more days

to get through until we reached Ennadai Lake. Unfortunately, as we moved upstream, the river required us to be in the water more and more. The water became increasingly shallow until it resembled the small streams we experienced while reaching the Kazan River. Rock jams blocked passage at every narrows, and the sections with water held barely enough for the canoe to float, so we were dragging the boat most of the time.

We arrived at the end of one lake and a solid rock jam like a dam three feet high blocked the mouth of the river. We hoisted the boat and found a field of boulders poking out of stagnant water. Slight currents weaved through the rocks, and we pushed along to the next shallow lake. Can this river flow from a lake as large as Ennadai, fifty-two miles long and up to fifteen miles wide? The shallowing water upstream is typical of streams originating from overland flow in the headwaters of a drainage basin, not one that flows from a large lake.

After a couple more days of wading upstream, we reached a stretch of river that was more rock than water. I stood ankle-deep in the cold water, searching upstream for water to wade through, thinking we'd reached the end. I was right. We were thirty miles from Ennadai Lake and the Nowleye River could no longer be called a river. It was just a series of rivulets that dispersed through piles of rock. We were at the head of the navigable river.

The Nowleye River did not flow out of Ennadai Lake as the coarse-scale map indicated. A small height of land separated the two bodies of water. From here, it would be a thirty-mile, pond-hopping overland route to Ennadai Lake. We walked along the river channel when it was good and plotted cross-country routes through the stunted brush when we thought it was shorter.

A tall pile of rocks appeared on a small pond one portage away from Ennadai Lake. Was it an inukshuk? It looked different from the others we had seen. Then I remembered John's map. It had been over a month since we thought about that map, but each stroke south brought us back deeper into Chipewyan territory. The map indicated an old Chipewyan burial site in a large cove downstream of Ennadai Lake. I stood on a distant hilltop, surveyed the land, and confirmed that our pond was what used to be, and probably still is when the water is higher, that cove on the Nowleye. The rock pile may have been a burial marker or a Chipewyan trail marker. In John's transcripts, a Chipewyan elder said, "When people traveled out on the barrens, landmarks were needed. What we did was put piles of rocks on higher land formations. That's how we got around on the barrens. We used to make trips to the copper sites. We knew about these things because we used them."

We were in a transition region that two peoples claimed as their homeland. The open, barren shorelines roll back from the lakes and ponds in undulating waves of mossy hills that harbored some of the last homes of the Ahiarmiut. In their final days on the land, they stayed close to a military communication station built in the northeast lobe of Ennadai Lake. The Chipewyan, too, traveled extensively through this region. Before they moved into communities, many families lived in the forested southern reaches of Ennadai. Perhaps Herbert Hall's short-lived trading post that he built in the first decade of the century brought the two groups into such proximity, in life and death. Another Chipewyan elder in the transcripts said "On Ennadai Lake, I have a couple children buried up there. Up towards the middle of Ennadai Lake. Beside that there are many other graves on that lake ... It's a big lake. I know of Inuit burial sites as well; I've seen them myself. I found one once. I was trapping out on the Barren Lands and I saw a bunch of white foxes around a snowbank. I found out that it contained a grave ... I found the sight contained some small sticks which was useful out on the barrens. I proceeded to remove the sticks and after a while I found it contained some human remains, the hair was still on the skull. I felt bad and put everything back in its place and went on my way."

We finished the portage to the northern tip of Ennadai Lake. A vast sheet of water stretched south where forested shores awaited us. We came within striking distance of the tree line after two days of wind-blown paddling. We intended to find a spot to camp in the trees, but intense winds halted us on a small barren island. The wind had again shifted and was blowing from the southwest. Warmer weather returned, but the paddling was exhausting. The wind on Ennadai Lake was as fierce as any we had previously encountered.

Our early camp, the first before 7 p.m. in over a week, gave us time to catch up on some projects. I sat in the sand and leaned back on the overturned canoe, reconditioning the leather uppers of my boots while Laurie repaired the remaining parts of the battered spray cover. The canoe looked weathered with uncountable scratches, but held up well—unlike our cheese. I hoped to make a pizza, but the waxy cheese blob that I pulled from the bin was too green for any meal where the cheese could be seen. Instead, I made potato and cheese soup and a perfectly baked bannock soaked in squeeze-bottle margarine.

I walked to the top of the island after dinner to take pictures of the lake. A brilliant sunset welcomed a full moon rising in the reddening sky in the south. Tomorrow we would re-enter the forest. I remembered that our last night in the forest back on Nueltin Lake in July was spent under a brilliant full moon. One moon cycle later, we were about to see the forest again.

***

We woke to the familiar sounds of waves lapping on the beach and prepared for another day of battling headwinds. The return of the southwest wind brought milder temperatures and dry weather as we nudged our way into its force. I spotted a large caribou wading knee-deep across a small channel. We paddled closer; he raised his gigantic rack and stared, muscles tense, ready to flee. For a few seconds we were locked eye-to-eye before he trotted up the bank. I said farewell to our last caribou and the tundra, then paddled south toward the forests into a fierce headwind. Landmarks on the shore passed very slowly as we crept along. I glanced back after a long time and saw that our last caribou was still there watching, perhaps feeling the urges of his own southward journey to come.

We rested in the lee of a boulder just offshore. The wind whistled, waves crashed, and explosions of spray vanished in the air. I stood in the jostling canoe and peered over the rock to get a view of our destination. Our barren shoreline stretched to the southwest, as did the opposite shoreline until the two merged at the lake end somewhere on the other side of the horizon. And somewhere along the way, I knew the forests reclaimed the land. We should have stayed put until the wind calmed, but I had an appointment to keep. We were going to meet the forest, and I wasn't going to be late.

We poked our bow around the boulder and greeted the gale with a forward thrust. Traveling point to point all day and into the evening, the distant shoreline emerged on the horizon, and trees began to take shape—tall, healthy pines swaying in the breeze. The wind fought us until the very last when we broke into a sheltered bay and coasted into the sand, shaded by the thick landscape-filling forest.

CHAPTER TWELVE

CLOSING THE CIRCLE

MILE 681–863

"The east wind became stronger with a few drops of rain. While I was waiting in the tent, I read again Mr. Tyrrell's report and realized how serious our position was beginning to look. Bad weather was undoubtedly near and we had no idea how far we were from Churchill. Probably the worst of the Barren Lands was to come, and we were traveling hardly more than five miles a day, and both of us rheumatic."

—Ernest Oberholtzer

The taiga, also known as the boreal forest, is a transitional biome that fringes the northern limit of trees. The underlying geology is similar to the central Barren Lands, with granite uplifts, glacial topography, and displaced boulders strewn about. But shadowing the land is a canopy of tall jack pine, black spruce, and other northern softwoods. Its floor is soft with moss, and its soil is rich with the organics of decaying vegetation.

I wandered the forested shore, climbing the hills, and admiring the tall trees. No more sweeping vistas across the landscape; the most expansive views were across lakes that ended at the forested shores. I stood on the crest of an esker cut by the Kazan River where it enters Ennadai Lake. The location would have been a good resting spot for Chipewyan traveling the Kazan to visit relatives or trade at Herbert Hall's post on the far shore. A few decades of mossy growth and settling obscured the remnants of three old fire rings on a hilltop. A long-dead jack pine with an axe blaze facing upstream stood at the face of the steep bank. It was barely distinguishable from the rest of the weathered tree, but when it was made, the fresh cut would have shown white against the brown bark for the upstream river traveler to see. This was a gathering place. John's map has a cabin marked at this spot.

The upper reaches of the Kazan River begin at Snowbird Lake, flow through Kasba Lake, then tumble thirty miles to Ennadai Lake where we were camped. Our next challenge was to ascend the Kazan River twenty-five miles to Kasba Lake. Every bend in this swift, twisty stretch would be clogged with rapids, and the current in the straights would probably be relentless. The exploratory traders Theirry Mallet and Del Simmons returned from the Barren Lands by this same route in 1926, bound for Brochet. Had I known that they carried an outboard motor with them, I might not have had the confidence to take those first strokes upstream. No matter. We moved along the shore eddies lining, poling, or portaging as the conditions demanded.

On August 24, while lining up a swift-water section, I noticed an orange tint to the tops of trees on the north shore. Within a half-mile, the orange transitioned to black and gray.

The soft moss changed to dusty soot. The forest became a grave-yard of standing skeletons of freshly burned trees. From the top of a high hill, I could see that the forest had burned in all directions—patches of orange-singed trees set against a black backdrop without a hint of green.

We traveled through burned forest for thirteen miles. Any portage trail that might have existed was blocked with fallen, charred trees. Clouds of soot rose around us as we walked. Our packs, hands, and faces were smeared with the grime.

Laurie spotted smoke rising from the western shore of a lake we were crossing. We paddled over and found a small area along the shoreline still smoldering. The fire had stopped within fifty feet of the lake, but the ground cover was still smoldering. We spent about an hour checking out the site. Occasionally, a spot would erupt into flames, then slowly burn out. Several spots were glowing red. Laurie ran around with our small cook pot dumping splashes of water on each burst of flame. This was the dying front of a fire that had consumed perhaps thousands of acres and was moving slowly toward the lake fifty feet away. Still, she tried to save what remained of the vegetation.

Finding a campsite was challenging. What might have been nice clearings were charred beyond use, and unburned spots had smolder lines moving slowly toward them. As we paddled into the evening, unburned areas became more frequent. A sandy esker with a beautiful beach landing provided a safe, clean camp surrounded by a wetland. My journal entry that night of August 24 reads:

The evening was splendid. A beautiful site on a placid lake. I am very fond of the open forests here. The moss-covered ground is soft to walk on, and the trees are spacious enough to permit free roaming. The esker offered a nice beach to land on and plenty of room to camp. Luxury! However, the return to the forest and warm weather brought us back to the mosquitoes. They are swarming but tolerable. It was tough to crawl into the tent tonight. The evening was so peaceful, and the forest provides a cozy comfort I haven't felt in a month. I was captivated by the barrens, but I'm at home in the forest.

***

The power of the river grew as we approached Kasba Lake. The rapids, once separated by flat-water stretches, blended into each other so that we faced continuous whitewater for several miles. We struggled up one long stretch toward an impassable drop that forced us to shore. We planned on a quick portage and then back to work until late in the evening, but a forest of blueberries lured us to camp.

Kasba Lake is a vast body of water; it stretches approximately forty-five miles north to south and is roughly fifteen miles wide. Not counting the Great Lakes, it would be the eighth largest lake in the United States, just a little bit bigger than Lake Champlain. Although smaller than Nueltin Lake, it is not cluttered with islands. Cold winds from the north race uninhibited across the entire length of the lake, whipping up a frenzy of waves.

A light rain enhanced the colors of the forest and cast a

delicate shadow on our surroundings. As soon as we entered the bay, the full force of the wind hit us and sent us racing down the lake. The wind blew sleet horizontally across the lake, whitecaps surged, and our partial spray cover deflected gallons of water. We sighted a distant point that might offer some shelter and pointed our craft downwind.

A worn path led from our sheltered cove up to a small clearing. This trail was the most advanced sign of civilization we'd seen in two months. The path led up to a small trapper's cabin where John's map indicated one should be. It looked like it was constructed a few decades ago, but some litter suggested relatively recent use. It may have served as a winter hunting camp for Chipewyan from Wollaston Lake or Brochet, two hundred miles south. I wanted to resent walking under a roof for the first time in two months, but the relief from the cold rain was a delight. Still, we didn't linger long. The wind would soon make the lake too dangerous to travel.

The wind blew an icy rain down our collars while tossing us down the lake. The whitecaps had grown to ocean-like swells. We'd roll to the crest of a swell and view the immense lake, then dive into a trough where giant walls of water surrounded us. Occasionally, a swell would break and fall on Laurie's lap. The canoe began to take on water through the Velcro seams and cockpits of our spray cover.

These were the most challenging waves we'd faced yet. They would have stopped us two months ago while we were learning about the stability of the craft and honing our skills. Now, they were just another element to manage. The only reason to stop would be fatigue. We slowly crept south, one wave at a time, confident and strong. However, I lost sight of the terrain, and we drifted far out from shore until we found ourselves in a no-mistake situation.

The local landscape and storm path conspired to change the direction of the wind so that it blew with gale force in the opposite direction of the huge waves. With the wind at our bow and waves at our stern, we struggled to find a strategy. If we ran with the waves, swells would roll through and dump gallons of wind-blown spray into our laps. So we tried to surf. We paddled hard and caught a wave; I was lifted to the peak while Laurie sunk three feet to the trough, then we accelerated down the wave, lost the angle, buried Laurie's bow, and struggled to keep from rolling before the next wave swept through. Then it did.

Partially swamped, the next wave knocked us parallel to it despite our best efforts to straighten. (Lake canoeing basics tell us to avoid getting parallel to large waves.) Raised high on a crest, we pivoted to face the waves. With the wind at our backs, we could paddle and brace through the swells and hold steady. Swells gave us a slight break from the panic, but breakers tossed us to random angles. Counterintuitive to my training, staying parallel to the waves felt the most stable. So we tried it again. We let a wave pivot us, then dropped sideways into a trough. We leaned hard into the next wave as the wind pushed us up, then we leaned upwind to descend into the trough. It worked. The waves affected us more than the wind, but we gradually moved toward shore, again focused on one wave at a time.

Thirty minutes with a must-make move every two seconds sapped our strength as the cold water sloshed to mid-thigh as we knelt for extra stability. Nevertheless, we found a rhythm that calmly guided the boat toward shore amidst the chaos of the wind and waves.

The shore was heavily guarded by a collection of boulders the size of small cars that created explosions of froth as the waves alternately exposed and buried them from view. In calm water, it would have taken a lot of twisting and turning to find a way through. In this water, we had no choice but to wet exit. The waves determined our pace, and we approached swiftly. A trough exposed the rocks while we were high on a wave and falling toward them. I jumped and descended with the canoe, intending to land running, then drag the boat through the rocks before the next wave tossed us skyward. The water was deeper than I thought. I moved toward shore as fast as possible, but a return wave halted my momentum. There was a brief moment of peace as I stood waist-deep in the trough before the two opposing waves converged, lifted the boat and myself up, and dropped us down onto a boulder. Successive waves knocked the boat closer to shore each time until it ground into the sand. We dragged the boat a bit further with each wave until only the biggest would lap the stern.

We lay on the beach too tired to move until we got too cold not to move. Shivering wasn't working. I pulled myself up to untie the packs. Laurie was already gone, gathering twigs. Our small cook fire grew to a large, driftwood-fueled beach bonfire that warmed our bodies and filled our souls with awe as stars filled the sky and waves pounded the beach through the night.

Morning brought sunny skies, but the waves were just as violent. We settled in for a day of chores and exploration. Boots needed to be reconditioned, packs had to be repacked for the coming long portages, and our bodies needed rest. We portaged the boat about a quarter mile down the shore to a safer takeoff spot so we could leave as soon as it was safe. The waves became manageable by late afternoon, and we resumed our southern journey. The lake jostled and groaned as it settled for the night, and we landed as darkness fell over placid waters.

***

The temperamental weather of a changing season accompanied us for the next few days as we worked our way south on Kasba Lake. We had been in the forests for nearly a week by the time we reached its southern end, but always on large, exposed waterways where the wind blows fiercely. I looked forward to the more intimate feel of the small lakes, ponds, and creeks we planned to traverse along the pond-hopping route through the forest gap to the Cochrane River. However, my journal entries as early as August 19 indicate I started questioning the wisdom of that route. The long days on Kasba Lake gave me plenty of time to think, rethink, decide, and change my mind. We could stick to the plan or detour southeast along the Little Partridge route to Kasmere Lake.

Joseph Tyrrell reached Kasba Lake on his northward journey by ascending the Little Partridge River from Kasmere Lake and then portaging west to Kasba's southeastern shore. In his records, he mentioned another Native route to the lake over "a long chain of small lakes and portages." We had intended to follow this route straight north from Bigstone Rapids on the Cochrane River to Kasba Lake in early July before we decided to reverse our loop's direction. Now we intended to travel that route south.

Our topographic maps showed a series of ponds connected by one-liners jammed with rapids. Our experience with similar conditions earlier in the trip told us we might walk most of the one hundred miles to the Cochrane River. Depending on the conditions, we envisioned the route taking anywhere from twelve to thirty days. The old Chipewyan we met in Wollaston Lake roughly outlined what he remembered as the route, but he hadn't been there in over twenty years. We would likely wander around, making our own route through the forests from pond to pond. I liked the idea of reopening an old route that had been closed for decades, but the prospect of getting frozen in somewhere in that section was intimidating.

The Little Partridge route would add about fifty miles to our journey, but I reasoned it would be faster. The route would involve at least ten miles of overland pond hopping before reaching Roosevelt Lake at the headwaters of the Little Partridge River. I had not researched this route before the trip, and the maps presented numerous options for reaching Roosevelt. Navigation would be challenging, but it would be only ten miles of wandering instead of one hundred. We knew in our minds which way we would go, but the decision was only confirmed once we reached the point where the two routes split. I recorded in my journal on the evening of August 29:

After a long discussion, we decided that the L.P. route would be quicker, but the pond-hopping route would be more interesting. As I stood in the icy drizzle and the cold stung my toes, I looked about and saw the signs and colors of fall overtaking the bog. We decided our priority at this point in the trip is to find the most expedient way back, so we began our search for the L.P. Perhaps I'll hit the other route on another trip.

Somewhere in that ten-mile span between Kasba Lake and Roosevelt Lake we would cross a slight height of land that separates the Kazan River and Thlewiaza River watersheds. The Little Partridge River offered an attractive thirty-five mile *downstream* run to Kasmere lake, where we had been in July.

The stream we chose to ascend out of Kasba Lake was blocked at its mouth by an unpassable jumble of boulders. We portaged through the brush then paddled and dragged for a mile before the stream faded into the spongy sphagnum of a bog. We made camp on the higher ground and settled in for the cool night.

We slept late and awoke to pleasant temperatures and the promise of clear skies, but soon the sky clouded over and remained gray all day. There was no rain. The temperature, a bit brisk in the morning, stayed nice for portaging; it was cool, almost cold when we weren't moving. The stream bed we were ascending weaved its way through the forests with banks jammed with shrubs. Our destination was the mouth of another stream that flowed into this one about a mile and a half along the stream, or one mile directly overland. We plotted a compass route, loaded our packs, and headed over the hill behind our site through trailless forest. I have described tough portaging days already, so I will just say that August 30 was one of the toughest. We only moved two miles, but they were hard-earned.

With diminishing food, we were able to repack and portage in two trips, so the packs were familiarly heavy again. My first load consisted of the supply pack with the Duluth on top and the camera bag in my hand. The weight of the two packs was probably sixty pounds. My second load was the canoe. I rigged two paddles to act as a harness for my shoulders. The total weight of the canoe with accessories was about ninety pounds. Laurie carried a food pack on each trip and was loaded with excess hand items. Her expressions, her posture, and her pace were reminiscent of those first few portages, but her steadfast strength was inspiring.

We began the portage around 9 a.m., walking through very nice open woodlands over clear sand and gravel. There was no trail to follow; I'm not sure if anybody had ever come this way. On the tundra, trailless walking was not a problem, but in the forests our foresight was restricted to the next cluster of trees or shrubs, and our goals were only visible once we were right upon them.

Accurate compass work was crucial, which required that we knew exactly where we were. We meandered around obstacles, always sure to return the same distance to pick up our original direction. We dropped the packs occasionally to look around. Soon we intersected the stream we were ascending at the point we suspected to find the next stream. From our hilltop vantage, we could see no stream or even a valley that it might follow in wet times. I could identify the hill where we stood on the map, and the first stream was another definite landmark. I triangulated with the map and compass and located where the next stream should be. We forded the first stream to our predicted point and found no trace of water. I walked inland and located a spring, then found a linear patch of vegetation greener than the rest. We assumed that this was our desired stream and prepared for another portage. Our goal this time was a small lake slightly over a mile away at the headwaters of this "stream."

We took a compass bearing from the stream mouth to our desired lake and headed out on what turned out to be one of the more difficult portages of the entire trip. We scrambled up a steep gravel ridge, looked in our intended direction, and saw nothing but the healing chaos of a forest that had been burned a few years back. It was a depressing and gray scene, its desolation heightened by the bleak sky. White skeletons of trees poked skyward. Rolling hills of gravel and rock led to a horizon without a hint of water. A tight latticework of downed trees made access to solid footing difficult, and thick stands of new shrubs filled the gaps. We encountered an impenetrable bog, so we rambled and hacked our way along until we found an acceptable route. We reached a hilltop and down below us saw three small lakes. Our maps only indicated one, but the shape of the middle lake matched our map picture, and we worked our way to its shore. I was concerned about the uncertainties of the land, but I knew if we continued to head east, we would eventually reach the Little Partridge River even if we weren't on the correct route.

We struck off on the second trip, I with the canoe and Laurie with another heavy food pack. The uncertainty of direction on this portage was exaggerated by my limited view with the canoe over my head. I would tilt the canoe back, pick a landmark, then concentrate on the maze of obstacles at my feet. After what seemed far too long, I came to a sand ridge. Puzzled because there was no sand ridge on our first trip across, I rocked the canoe back and saw nothing familiar. I stumbled about, tense, searching for our route. The pain in my shoulders heightened with my frustration. Exhausted, I threw the canoe down at the top of a hill that shouldn't have been there. I looked around and learned I had headed straight south instead of southeast. Our destination was farther away than when I started.

I enjoyed the eerie quiet, huddled against the canoe, warm sun piercing the cold air, expecting to hear Laurie approach from behind. *Maybe she's taking a break*, I thought, as the time got uncomfortably long. I scanned the terrain and saw a red dot moving slowly through the skeleton trees about a half-mile away. Laurie had walked in an equally off but different direction. She was too far away to hear my shouts, so I returned to my own problem. I hoisted the canoe on my shoulders, accepted the pain, and pushed through the jumble until I dropped the canoe among some stumps and logs guarding the lake's shore.

I didn't have a view anymore in the lowland thicket of the lake. I waited, wished I had a snack, and waited some more. We brought three compasses with us but lost one two months earlier and broke another. I kept the third with me at all times. The last time I saw her, maybe an hour earlier, Laurie was headed more east than south. She was slow with the pack, so I thought I could catch her. I moved quickly, hopping logs, using the sun and the terrain to track my route as best I could. I stopped after ten minutes, calmed myself, and let the eerie sensation settle in: we were separated and alone about as far away from anyone else as possible at some random spot in the middle of the northern forest. Laurie has a food pack, I reasoned, she'll be fine if it comes to that.

I went back to the lake where I dropped the canoe. She wasn't there. I walked the route that I should have taken to begin with and didn't see her. I found the spot where we started the portage and sat, contemplating a strategy. I didn't get far before I heard footsteps.

"Where'd you go?" she asked, surprisingly composed.

"To the lake. Where'd you go?" I responded, confused about her nonchalant tone.

"To ... the ... lake," she said, drawing out her words longer than necessary. "I waited for about an hour and thought you were lost."

I just grinned and didn't try to figure it out. We hopped over the route again, amazed that we carried gear over this jumble, until we reached the lake where Laurie's packs sat fifty yards from mine. I pulled out some gorp, Laurie made peanut butter bannock sandwiches, and we chuckled about the what-if scenarios that could have been.

After a very brief paddle to the far shore, we hoped to complete one more mile-and-a-half portage to yet another lake. We loaded up and within thirty yards dropped the packs to search for a passable route. The land was much like on the last portage, wholly jammed with boulders, brush, bogs, and burned fallen trees. For two hours we walked in a maze without our packs, searching for a way through until it was time to camp. An unattractive but clear spot in the blowdown became our home for the night.

The next day, the tough portage kept us working until noon. My two loads seemed even heavier than before. The pack dug into my hips, and the canoe pained my shoulders more than I remembered. Periodic fits of rage flowed through me as I struggled with the canoe through a seemingly inescapable maze of fallen trees and rocks. The canoe caught on overhanging branches, the wind blew me sideways, and the pain grew more and more intense with each staggered step. I caught my toe on a branch, pitched forward, and felt the canoe's momentum drive me to the rocks. I tossed it mid-fall, but the canoe just dropped along my side until the gunwale hit my knee and bent it in a way that knees are not supposed to bend. Otherwise, I landed in a comfortable position, nestled between some rocks. My knee felt fine, but I took advantage of the rest and just breathed for a while. Laurie shuffled by, hunched under her load on her own trail about twenty feet away. If she saw me, she didn't care.

By the time we finished the next four portages, a green, luscious forest returned. My journal reads:

The windless evening created a heavy silence on the small lake where we camped. Every sound we make echoes across the water. It's a joy to paddle on such calm waters. The sleek canoe silently and speedily skims across the water with little effort. Too bad we only paddle a mile at a time.

Laurie wrote:

Today was very hard on shoulders and back. I was in tears carrying olive pack today. It's difficult carrying pack plus ammo boxes. Sometimes I feel like I'm too weak to continue this method of travel. Sometimes I'm angry w/what I have to put my body through. Sometimes proud—as not very many women my size would/could do what I'm doing. Not

many would want to. Had a great dinner of double mac and
cheese and apple cobbler. Bannock, of course, too.

We pond-hopped for six days more before we found any significant stretch of water that could float a canoe. Even the headwaters of the Little Partridge, where I expected to be able to begin paddling, was a familiar jumble of boulders with slight trickles of water weaving through.

The weather was chilly, and rain continued for most of the next week. We stayed mostly warm and dry except for our hands and feet. The effects of cold and wet alternated between numbness and pain for most of each day. Still, the joys of traveling through difficult terrain, competent and confident, let me fantasize that maybe I could have been part of that Old North canoe culture.

The misty atmosphere added an attractive touch to the forests. The small, isolated lakes we traversed were typically calm and silent with pastel reflections of the rumbling sky surrounded by rolling hills covered with the open forests of the taiga.

We settled into a routine of paddling, unloading, portaging, loading ... The walks were usually short and we began to see faint traces of trails. I had a cycle of alternating moods. Sometimes I would be so absorbed by the land that I would hardly notice the struggles of the day. Other times the fears of uncertainty would mount and every little obstacle would cloud my vision. But the evenings, regardless of the day, were always spectacular. When the packs and paddles were laid to rest, the magnificence of the North would sweep in and overwhelm us. My journal is filled with statements like, "I could live like this for a good long time."

Laurie was quiet and contemplative as we worked through camp chores one evening. She gathered wood and sorted through the food pack with deliberate actions while I set up the tarp. I stopped wondering if she was up to this challenge over a month earlier. Now, any doubts I had were as much about me as her. Hell, even after sixty days the physical demands of this section were surprising me. Laurie showed her pain, but rarely voiced it. I waited for outbursts like, "Why did you bring me here!" But they never came. Sometimes I wanted to hear it, perhaps to relieve some guilt for bringing her here without full disclosure. But how could I have explained it to her when I didn't know myself?

On September 4 Laurie wrote:

Jim's really having a hard time controlling emotional expressions. He made me so mad this morning by blowing up and hollering as we were paddling that I said something to him about it. He doesn't yell at me—just at the boat or water or rocks or air. It's a side of him that didn't bother me earlier when it first happened but now annoys me as I experience same frustrations w/no outbursts. My feet hurt.

***

Our evening campfires along the Little Partridge River became an indispensable part of our routine. Earlier, fires were almost always quick and small with just enough wood to cook a meal. When the sun stayed high until long after we went to bed, the fire was confined to its pit, and we didn't need its warmth or light. With the chilly, dark evenings of September, we lingered around the fire tossing twigs into its heart to keep it alive.

When Laurie had the wood-gathering assignment, she started collecting "sock-drying wood," piles of highly flammable pine branches that burned fast but hot. In the warm weather, we'd pull on our wet wool socks in the morning and get on with the day. Neither of us had the fortitude to do that on these frosty mornings. In the evenings we would huddle barefoot in front of the flame with socks dangling from sticks, boot liners propped up on logs, and our leather-topped boots at a safe but warm distance.

After nearly two months of intense personal contact, we should have run out of things to talk about, but most of our time had been spent thinking about the daily needs of wilderness travel and sleeping. With this new sock-drying routine, our conversations turned to light and lively chatter centering on nothing in particular. Even with little words, the shared satisfaction of a warming flame builds intimacy.

The warmth drew us close to its center and cast a light far beyond its pit that defined the limits of our campsite. We huddled close to the fire, under the protection of the tarp that collected heat and warded off the rain. Beyond the light, beyond the silhouettes of the guardian pine and spruce, was a total blackness that, although we saw what was there in daylight, took on an eerie presence in the dark. In the day, the snaps and shuffles of the woods went unnoticed, but when those sounds rested outside the perimeter of light, they blended into the cracks and pops of the fire and added intrigue to the flame. To step out of the light to gather more wood or perform some other duty was to step out of a shelter into a different world.

We sat by the fire until the pile of wood within arm's reach had been burned, then we lingered as the dying coals faded away. Soon, the cold from the bay would creep into our campsite, the spell would be broken, and it would be time to turn in. Laurie would usually hop barefooted into the tent while I remained outside to extinguish the coals. Most times, the fire would have been started before darkness set in, so the night would arrive when the fire would finally be extinguished. Then out of the darkness emerged the magnificent display of stars hidden during the light of summer.

The appearance of stars seemed instantaneous. For weeks it had been too light at night. Then one night along the Little Partridge River I stayed up watching the flames die out, feeling the darkness overtake us. Lying on my back, I was surprised to see a faint star grow brighter, and then another until after an hour or so the entire sky that filled the gap between the forested river banks seemed more white than black. The creamy Milky Way was thick. I looked for the Big Dipper, the only constellation I knew, but couldn't find it among the mess of stars. So I created my own constellations until I drifted off to sleep.

I tried it again the next night but fell asleep before the sky was dark enough. When I was woken by the cold, it wasn't stars that inspired my awe but a spectacular display of the aurora borealis. I had seen the northern lights many times before. In northern Minnesota, a friend and I slept outside every night for two weeks while brilliant displays entertained us until we couldn't stay awake any longer. Another guy who had spent time much farther north in Alaska viewed them with nonchalance.

"I've seen better," he'd say to us. But Ed and I couldn't believe any natural display could be more dramatic. Now, I believe.

Everyone has heard descriptions of the lights in the Far North, and I can only add that the most dramatic description ever spoken is no exaggeration. One night in the headwaters of the Little Partridge River, I stood on a hilltop and witnessed the sky explode in a dazzling array of light and color. From horizon to horizon, shimmering bands of red, green, yellow, and blue flashed across the sky. Trembling and shaking, they ebbed and peaked in varying degrees of intensity. It seemed they had faded away; then they'd burst again with endless moving patterns.

I watched for a while until I was shivering from the night cold then crawled into the tent. Laurie had the tent warmed up and the candle lantern burning. The night was cold enough to force us to bed in knit hats, and the morning had us debating who would get out and start breakfast. A light rain that started sometime during the night showed no signs of abating. This was the start of a rough day.

***

After several days descending the Little Partridge, the river still showed no promise of navigability. We portaged out of camp because the water dispersed through a long stretch of those ubiquitous boulders left by the recently retreated ice sheet. Recent in a geologic sense, it seemed as though those boulders had spent the last eight thousand years since deglaciation just waiting for us. *A nice, narrow, incised channel could carry this amount of water in a floatable depth just fine*, I thought. But Mallet made it up and down this river fifty-five years earlier, and Tyrrell thirty years before that. We'd find enough water to float soon, I mused each time we'd put in, thinking there was water to paddle, only to move a couple hundred yards, then be forced to shore again. We're going downstream, there has to be more water eventually!

After one brief period on the water, the river disappeared into a carpet of boulders as far as we could see. The shoreline was choked with a bog that went inland for about three hundred yards, and the upland forests were thick. My body was done, but we had resolved to push hard every day until we reached water that would float a canoe. We carried through the forests, crossed the shoreline bog, and dropped the packs where it looked like we could paddle for at least a quarter mile. On the return walk, the cold hit me harder than on any other day so far. A bitter wind blew an icy rain into our faces, and I was wet to my knees from traversing the bog. My feet seemingly fractured under each step. I stared at the ground, trying to keep the rain from blowing down my neck. We reached the canoe, and I found it difficult to uncurl my hands to pick up my paddle. I rigged the boat for the carry and looked around for my life jacket. Then I remembered where I had left it. I had set it aside at a portage early in the day and forgot to pick it up.

It was at least three miles back. We had only moved four miles during the whole day and it would be impossible to retrieve it before dark. We left the canoe where it was, set up camp on the other side of the portage, and went back for the life jacket in the morning. We traveled the six miles by midmorning and had a nice, hot breakfast when we returned. On the walk back, a strong wind blew from the north that stung my fingertips.

Clouds began to build and rumble, and the air temperature dropped significantly while we ate. A light snow was falling by the time we were packed. We moved fast and joked about the snow to mask our nervousness. I began to think that the rest of the Little Partridge would be like this, and we might take a week to travel the remaining forty miles. If the weather continued, we might face freeze-up soon. We started moving, expecting a long, arduous, cold trip.

We paddled for about fifty yards before the boulders locked the boat in place. Wedged with just trickles flowing past, we stepped into the cold water and dragged to what looked like one floatable path, then another, until we sat listless on the seats, feet propped on rocks. I snacked on two-month-old caribou jerky; Laurie tightened her collar. The map showed a small lake about a mile downstream. The logical path was to portage the whole way. First, we had to free ourselves from this jam. The water was too shallow to paddle, too deep and cold to walk, and a slight current kept us pinned. We shoved off, but the screaming wind pelted us with snow and blew us into the rocks. After a ten-minute battle, we traveled the twenty yards to shore and prepared to portage. Snowstorms came through in quick waves until the clouds gave way to the sun.

The portage was just part of the day's work—a five-mile hike, three miles under load, warmed our bodies and revived our spirits as we trotted through the trailless damp, green forest accented with hints of autumn. The pains of carrying the canoe were routine and easy to ignore as we followed our route along the creek to our packs at the lake. The warm sun cut through the crisp air, the wind faded, and we glided through the diminishing waves toward where we thought an outlet should be, unsure of what we would find.

We found a legitimate river, deep enough to paddle. A swift current carried us through smooth stretches between minor rapids that required just enough skill to add jolts of adrenaline to the underlying joy of motion. By evening we had cruised a distance that I thought would have taken three days. The miles, our confidence, and the essential beauty of the northern forest made even the returning wind and rain welcome.

A nice clearing with a gravelly beach offered an idyllic spot to camp. I pitched a tarp while Laurie gathered wood. Kneeling, she skillfully tindered a fire at the tarp's edge, blowing on dried moss that she had collected from the underside of a pine branch at a rest stop earlier in the day. Smoke billowed from her cupped hands until a flame emerged. She slipped the burning tinder under her artfully crafted kindling, blowing a steady stream of oxygen into the struggling flames until they burned on their own. She sat back on her heels, hands on thighs, judging whether the flame would survive under the drizzling rain. I propped the grate over the growing flames while she fed them larger and larger sticks until we had a pot of water boiling for tea and dinner.

The biscuity scent of Laurie's bannock collected under the tarp while I studied the map, accompanied by the hissing patter of light rain overhead. She had used the last of the palatable cheese in a delicious although off-color macaroni and cheese a week earlier. It had taken an hour of picking green wax to render just enough cheese for a thick and creamy meal. This night we soaked up the broth of cheese-less mushroom barley soup with our bannock, bowls nestled between our thighs, seated on foam pads, backs resting against packs like we had done sixty-four times before. I tried to conceal a grin while I ate so I could just enjoy this North Country scene without explanation.

"Good news from the map?" she asked.

"This is just ... so nice."

If the Little Partridge River remained paddleable, we would have a simple downstream trip to Kasmere Lake where we had been before. In just forty miles we would complete the forest gap and the last uncertainty that had plagued my thoughts since we first dipped our paddles in Wollaston Lake, which was just 130 miles away. With the burden of uncertainty lifted, we could face the remaining couple of weeks as just another canoe-trip vacation. We sat under that tarp until late into the night, drying socks, retelling stories from earlier in the trip, laughing at minor mishaps. Laurie popped the lid off the baking pan and the scent of apple pie mingled with the smoke and the rain. We were celebrating without really knowing it.

Tyrrell could have camped near here ninety-seven years ago, traveling upstream with Casimir as his guide. Mallet passed through twice while following Casimir's sketch map, once on his way north to find clients among the Inuit, then again on his retreat to Brochet. Maybe somewhere near here was the cache that Mallet had stashed just in case they had to return along this route. If so, he must have felt the reassurance I felt as I studied the maps. This could have been where Prentice Downes turned around when in 1940, while attempting to follow Tyrrell's route, he decided his partner Alfred Peterson, the man who built the Putahow Lake trading post and traveled the North Country by dog team and canoe, was "too domesticated" for the trip. It was challenging for us going downstream; it must have been brutal going upstream in the drought year that they witnessed.

We continued down the Little Partridge paddling numerous small rapids, streams, and lakes. We scraped along a few times but never had to portage. The rapids were well-marked on the map and were typically narrow, boulder-lined channels with very swift water moving over steep drops. There was usually just enough water to skim over the rocks, but occasionally we missed the correct route and jammed up. These rapids were exciting but not powerful enough to give us trouble. We raced along, finished the last marked rapid, and camped just a few miles upstream of Kasmere Lake.

By the time the evening rain started, we were under the tarp with a full stack of wood, drying our socks and chatting about the days to come. By morning, the rain had again turned to snow. A series of small lakes rested before Kasmere and a howling wind greeted us as we paddled into the first.

Whitecaps ripped over the lake across our intended direction of travel, so we plotted a safer route. We planned to paddle to a large island along the far shore, then travel in the protected channel between the two landmasses. A bitter sting swept in with the increasing north wind, and the air smelled of winter. We made it halfway across the lake before a blizzard blew through and blocked all visibility. I could see Laurie and the wave immediately beneath the boat, but that was all. We bucked with the waves for a few minutes, aiming to take each wave as it came and hold our ground since we could not see the shore. The squall disappeared as quickly as it came, and we found ourselves far off course. We redirected ourselves and paddled in the quiet aftermath to an island.

Paddling into a stream channel, we found a spit of land connecting the island to the shore. A short drag through some shrubs brought us to the other side and into a refreshing bit of calm water. A faint trail led up the bank into the woods. What purpose could a trail serve on a small island far from a common travel route? Thin stumps of trees about four feet high lined the path. The clean "V" shapes at their tops told me that they had been cut by a skilled axeman from the old school, and their height indicated that the trees were felled when deep snow covered the ground. The barely discernable trail led to an over-grown clearing where I spotted a rusty pipe, likely the remains of an old stove, standing in some shrubs. Nearby I found a few old bough beds and a cooking pail. I remembered that John's map showed a campsite that the older Chipewyan used in this area. This could have been a winter outpost of one of the trapping cabins in the Kasmere region. It was clear that it hadn't been used in summer for quite some time, but it's tough to say about winter use. Not many people come this far north in winter, but the recently used cabin we saw on Fort Hall Lake back in July was not far from here. It wouldn't be long before the winter hunters made their way north again, I mused, just as another squall drove snow pellets across the lake and down my collar.

The weather continued this way for the rest of the day, alternating periods of snow, hail, and sunshine. Each swiftly moving cloud brought a new storm, but we could usually see beyond it to predict its duration. We timed our crossings with the clear patches of sky. We crossed the last small lake before

Kasmere just as a cloud overtook the sky and the wind gusted violently. We raced toward the channel, our last unknown stretch of water. I wasn't thinking of what might be around the bend as it took all my efforts to keep the boat straight in the violent wind. There were no marked rapids. Even if there were, I would have assumed them to be like the small ones upstream. But I did notice on the map there was a one-meter elevation drop from the lake we just traversed to Kasmere. Maybe a minor rapid; it would have been marked if it was anything significant.

We entered the channel and a swift current seized our bow. The wind had masked any sounds of violent water, and we found ourselves in a tight section of rock-garden whitewater. We followed a tongue around the bend, resolved to catch the next eddy. Instead, a river-wide ledge appeared around a bend just thirty feet from our speeding canoe. In an instant, I conceived and abandoned countless plans as we tried to back-paddle, but the current was too strong. With no chute to drop through and no possibility of ferrying to shore, I purposely disobeyed some basic rules of whitewater paddling. With a hard draw and an upstream lean, I pinned the midsection of the boat to a large rock in a final effort to stop us. I hopped out and grabbed the stern as Laurie's bow teetered over the edge. With a desperate lunge, I dragged the boat onto the rock. Laurie climbed out, and we sat silently as we gazed at our predicament.

To our left, water poured over the six-foot drop in a violent thrashing of white. A powerful hydraulic spanned the length of the channel, followed by a gauntlet of jagged rocks. The river cascaded over a series of tight, jagged ledges to our right. A frothing pool at the bottom led to an undercut rock that sent a huge curling wave into the air. Downstream, the rapid continued for a hundred yards in a series of daunting waves and holes. Now, in the midst of it, we heard the violent thunder of the rapids above all else.

"Was this marked on the map?" Laurie yelled.

"Nope. There's not supposed to be a rapid here," I replied. "I should have been able to tell, though. We should have pulled over earlier."

We let the guise of easy traveling stand in the way of sound judgment and found ourselves in a tight spot. Despite the falling snow, the initial swim would probably have been survivable; although, in another careless act, we both removed our life jackets when we left the windy lake and entered the channel. If we had gone over, we probably would have separated from the boat, all our gear, and each other. Soaked, it would have been the wintery weather that might have been our undoing. I always keep a waterproof lighter in my pocket for emergencies, but while hypothermia destroys the body, it makes the victim think they're not in danger. Arthur Moffatt, a canoeman of renowned skill, suffered such a fate.

In mid-September 1955, Moffatt led a crew attempting to retrace Tyrrell's Dubawnt River route. The route had not been repeated, as far as anyone knew, in the sixty-two years since Tyrrell. There is a lot of controversy and bitterness in the journals and subsequent stories about what led to the accident. But the facts are that on September 15, paddling in a blizzard, two canoes with four men flipped in a rapid. A fifth man fell into the icy water while trying to rescue the others. All five made it to shore where they built a fire. Moffatt was in worse shape than any of them, shivering uncontrollably as his body attempted to generate heat. His companions treated him for mild hypothermia and put him in a tent to warm up. Hours later, they found him dead.

We were much further south, the water was probably warmer, and it was raining instead of snowing. But we were very calculated and cautious for the thirty minutes we spent on that rock making a plan to avoid immersion. Our only choice was to put in on the downstream side of the rock and run the rest of the rapid.

We scouted our route and rehearsed the moves, then dropped the canoe over the ledge into a boiling eddy. I lay on my stomach and held on to the gunwale, feeling the canoe buck like a rodeo bull in the gate.

"Okay, get in!"

Laurie slid down the rock and dropped perfectly into position, on her knees, ready to paddle.

"Ready?"

She just nodded.

The canoe started to move as I slid in, and Laurie drew us into the current while I pulled my paddle from under a cord. She made her moves, I followed with mine, and a wave rolled over the packs onto my thighs. I braced while she got us on line, and we deftly weaved our way through the drop to the calm pool at the end. We then drifted into a bay on Kasmere Lake, whose waters we touched sixty days earlier, and closed the loop.

CHAPTER THIRTEEN

A HISTORY LOST

MILE 863–882

"There is something tragic and forlorn about old, abandoned trading posts. And the two bent and staggering buildings here seemed particularly woeful, left behind to an unkind fate. All the life and bustle and the cheery warmth they had harbored had disappeared. Their old bones creak in the wind. They had done their part, and now deserted and forgotten, they were left to face the bitterness of the north wind and the killing frost alone. Much better than the sturdy, faithful old beams had received a pyrrhic funeral in some warm campfires than neglect and a crumbling, ignominious death before the all-conquering winds they had fought so long."

—Prentice Downes

In July, we left Kasmere Lake from its eastern lobe during the heat of summer, down the Thlewiaza River. On this snowy September day, we entered its northwestern lobe and eagerly paddled toward where we would intersect our previous route. As we approached the bay where the upper Thlewiaza River enters the lake, I remembered a small rocky island where Laurie took a photo of me two months earlier, shirtless under a blue sky, with the green forest in the background. We found the rock and Laurie again took a picture of me, this time dressed in winter gear and the background streaked with falling snow.

The banks closed in as we paddled toward the mouth of the river, mentally preparing for the upstream travel. The individual forms of trees gradually took shape, but they were different. The trees that emerged from the gray skies were black.

A fire had raged through in our absence, leaving complete devastation. The beautiful green shores we had seen two months prior had been altered to somber black and gray with skeletons of once magnificent trees reaching skyward. Stunned, we gazed across the lake and saw the blackened shoreline in all directions. Kasmere Lake had burned.

Laurie thought first of the wildlife. Where would the caribou go in winter? What happened to all the animals: the bears, the rabbits, and the ptarmigan in the forest? I walked inland, and the stretch of black was broken only by the horizon. Explosions of soot erupted with each step as I wandered around. The undergrowth was eliminated, the ground moss burned, and the blackened, defoliated trees shot upward from a smooth layer of ash. But the remains of the fire offered no warmth, and the cold forced us back to the canoe to get moving.

As we paddled up the Thlewiaza River, searching for spots of green along both burned shores, I wondered if we had caused this. Did our campfire start this burn? It was late afternoon and a cold, gray sky threatened more snow. But I wanted to reach our old campsite at the base of Kasmere Falls to ease my conscience. We moved upstream, the river gradually narrowed, and the current moved swiftly. We lined and portaged up a rocky rapid below the falls and reached our campsite as the sun set.

We had thoroughly dismantled our old fire ring. The fire had not started here, or at the other three sites we passed during the next few days of traveling through this extensive burn. I cut some unburned pine boughs from a fallen tree to protect our tent from the blackened ground; then we rested in anticipation of the Kasmere Falls portage.

***

The ancient trail was worn to the gravel and survived the burn. The white, winding path climbed a gentle hill through the monotonous black; Laurie's bright red pack was the only splash of color in the deathly scene. I climbed a high hill to view the land, and the sight confirmed what I had feared. Not a spot of green was anywhere in sight. The forests lay naked below me, extinguished of life from horizon to horizon. The bony skeletons of trees stood tall but looked stripped and beaten like a harvested field of corn. But the river sliced through the destruction as it always had, undaunted, a symbol of defiance against the flames; it held the promise of life.

We whisked across the portage, laughed at the difficulties we faced on this stretch two months prior, and resumed our ascent of the Thlewiaza River. I recognized places we had been and remembered my delight when we paddled through this region rich with the signs of the old ones of the North. Although those characters who enriched the past were long gone when we traveled through in July, the land seemed to suspend their presence in a timeless natural memorial. Today, it was bleak and empty.

I looked for the walls of Fort Hall as we rounded the last bend before Thanout Lake. They weren't there. I scrambled up the bank and saw only the charred remains where the building once was. A few wash basins and some charred caribou bones were scattered among the debris. I kicked around some charred logs and pushed something metal off a timber, exposing an unburned section where I sat. Fort Hall did receive its "pyrrhic funeral," as Prentice Downes lamented that such forts should. But no words of remembrance were uttered.

"We were probably the last people to see Fort Hall," I mused.

"Not much to see now."

I gave a subtle nod but hid my annoyance. Although it was an insignificant building, it still represented something important to me. Like those circles of stones in the Barren Lands, why did those charred timbers around me inspire nostalgia for a place and time I never even saw?

I turned my head to Laurie but didn't speak. She kicked around some boards, fidgeted, clearly not feeling the same loss. She was right, there wasn't much to see even before the fire. It was just a temporary building in a fleeting piece of the past. I propped it up in my mythology as a symbol of a time that I admired for its wilderness canoe culture, conveniently ignoring the complex social layers surrounding it. The fur trade and its impacts on nation-building, Indigenous people, and Canadian culture should temper any glorious visions of the past that Fort

Hall stood for. Still, it would have been nice to get a bowl of soup from the post manager on this cold September day, and maybe stock up on some chocolate since our gorp was running low.

Laurie was standing at the bow, ready to push off by the time I stood up. We cruised along the shoreline and marveled at the stark scene. The standing spikes of charred trees maintained a visual structure, but no foliation filled in the cracks, and the wind whistled through the forest as it did through an abandoned and decaying cabin that lost its chinking.

The sky darkened as we approached the end of the lake. In the distance, we spotted a patch of green, a small island that had been spared. It sat in bold contrast to the black mainland. We beached our canoe as the rain began to fall and set up camp. The green life of the island forest inspired me to shoot a whole roll of film just in case the burn continued to Wollaston Lake. I photographed the trees, the moss, the rain-soaked berries, and all the details I could find that I cherished about the woodlands. The rain fell harder, and the scent of bannock drove me to the tarp.

As we ate our barley soup, the tarp began to hang low under the slush falling from the sky. Our tent was crippled from a pole broken earlier in the trip, and an obtrusive corner in the supposedly arched support weakened its strength. Duct tape and twigs held the pole together, but I worried it wouldn't last under the weight of the melting snow, so I rigged an extra rope support to a tree. We crawled in and went to sleep, wondering what exciting conditions we would rise to in the morning.

The sleet had stopped in the night, but a thin ice crust coated the tent. We packed up, then paddled under a steel-gray sky to the south end of Fort Hall Lake where we found the remains of Peter's cabin that stood here in July. I wondered if he would travel here next month, ready to start a trapping season, and find his cabin and entire trapping area destroyed. I took a few photos of the debris, and we paddled up the stream toward our portage.

A series of ponds brought us to the portage into Blue Lake, the small body of water I found so attractive in July. On this day, it resembled the grim condition that Downes found it in in 1939. He remarked that the forest had burned some time ago, and the trees had not yet grown back. The scene was the same for us, but knowing that the forest had returned to the beauty we had witnessed earlier was encouraging. Fires are part of the natural cycle of the North. They strike with a random fierceness, leave a wake of destruction, and the forest slowly regenerates. This one just seemed so big and so personal. But I found the scene less cold and aesthetically sterile than Downes described it. In between moments mourning the loss of the forest, I admired the land's subtle, sometimes dramatic beauty. The small traces of life that survived the fire, and even the burnt-orange leaves of shrubs, decorated the black land in a chaotic assemblage of stark color. The yellow leaves on the surviving birch trees fluttered in the breeze, and their white trunks stood as oases of light against the charred and chiseled land.

We traveled over two more portages toward the Cochrane River with none of the difficulties we had in July. Our packs were lighter, and our bodies were stronger. The burn ended abruptly on a small lake between the two portages, and the forest came to life. A fine mist hung in the air that enriched the colors of the green forest. The cool, crisp air, the lack of bugs, and the changing season elevated this to my favorite time of year. We made our camp in a small cove on Smith House Lake. In the morning, we completed the final portage of the "Little Lakes," as Downes had called them, and arrived at the north bend in the Cochrane River where we had been nearly two months earlier.

***

"Are you packing a lawyer with you?" one friend joked when we announced we would be alone for three months. Another called canoes divorce boats. We did expect some interpersonal challenges, maybe some resentment, but issues ready to be quickly forgotten along the miles of travel. We prepared for it. But none of that predicted tension occurred when we returned to the Cochrane River. Our wilderness routines had become our normal lives. We slowed down at the prospect of returning to the "real world" with short days, relaxing evenings, and nostalgic campfire chats about earlier parts of the trip. The crisp evenings kept us near the fire until the last stick burned.

The days now felt like a canoeing vacation instead of an expedition. Upstream travel was straining, but there was no reason to hurry. We lined up swift-water sections when the shrubby banks allowed and dug in with our paddles when they didn't. The scenery was more captivating than I remembered it with its mosaic of granite, forest, and water. Each evening I roamed the forest around camp photographing the micro-scenery.

My cinnamon fritters, baked over the fire, inspired Laurie to create another delicious apple pie from our home-dried apples. I melted fruit chews over a custard made from dried milk, powdered eggs, and sugar and put it all in a flour and peanut butter crust to make blackberry custard pie. Over an oatmeal crust, Laurie melted coffee candies to a toffee consistency, covered it with crushed M&M's, and baked it to create chocolate-amaretto fondue.

Although delicious, Laurie's extravagant use of our dwindling M&M's supply was alarming. Addicted to the only sweet item in our food stash, she had been rationing the candy so we could make it to the cache at Bigstone Rapids. The fondue broke the floodgate and we devoured most of the remaining mm-gorp the next day.

Like explorers struggling in the wilderness for a cache of survival rations, we worked toward the Bigstone portage with steadfast determination while our sweets supply dwindled perilously low. We pulled ashore in the bay where we camped two and a half months earlier and attacked the portage with what strength we had left. Our mental markers from July were still there, and I remembered the joy I had when I saw the fungus that meant just two hundred yards to go. We easily trotted across the first mile, retrieved the second load, paddled across the short bay, and then searched for the cache.

My heart sank when I saw the rope blowing in the breeze over a pile of trash. A squeeze margarine bottle was punctured with fang marks and granola-bar wrappers licked clean by critters littered the bushes. A baggie of moldy dried pinto beans was the only thing left. In the rubble were three empty bags of M&M's. We cleaned up the mess and somberly continued the portage, hoping for one last chance on that island eight miles away.

The large eagle nest that towered over our old campsite in July was also gone. A broken tree-top and a large pile of wood debris told its fate. This, and the M&M's tragedy, made the remaining mile long and painful. Knowing this would be our last portage lifted my mood; however, it was both a relief and a disappointment. Just a straight paddle back to the village remained.

We paddled eight miles in the cold and rain to "Gorp Island." There, hanging undisturbed from the tree where we had left it, was the green military surplus bag. I untied the slip knot and felt the cord zing through my hand as the bag dropped to the soft moss. I struggled with the cinch knot until it loosened. There, perched on top of the contents, were three bags of peanut M&M's. Relieved, we sat like bears in a blueberry patch devouring the treats.

A fine mist, not quite rain, fell for the next couple of days as we ascended the Cochrane River. On September 14, we woke to the crashing of thunder and lightning that settled to an eerie calm as the storm rolled in the distance. Silence seemed magnified on these calm, misty days, the way a freshly fallen snow hushes a forest. The ripple of the bow slicing through the water, even the drips off our paddles, seemed to echo across the water. Each stroke propelled the boat into an endless glide. We could have raced across the lake, but the atmosphere seemed to invite slow, graceful motion. The horizon was invisible that day. The water fused into the mist somewhere in the distance. But distant islands were visible so that they appeared to float in the sky. The bright yellow leaves of birches on the shore pierced through the diffuse light and seemed the only splash of color on the lake. But it wasn't a dull scene; subdued brilliance would be the better description.

Sometimes we heard the storms coming. The rain would start somewhere out in the lake then move like a train toward us. As it approached, it sounded like a teapot approaching the boiling point; then, we would hide in the shrubs until the downpour passed. When the mist returned, we continued our glide across the lake. Once, a violent downpour caught us by surprise in the middle of a bay. There was no wind, so the large drops fell with uninterrupted force and exploded on the lake's surface. We could barely see each other through the heavy rain, and the lake appeared to be boiling.

A foreign sound emerged from across the bay as the shower faded. It was mechanical, the first such nose we heard other than the occasional floatplane since we left Nueltin Lake nearly forty days ago.

"That sounds like a generator," I said flatly.

"From where?"

"Well, we're not far from that cabin we found in July."

We floated on the motionless bay and let the impact of what we were hearing settle.

"The trip's over," I said. "We still have fifty miles to go, but it's over."

Laurie just sat and listened. We drifted across the bay; the noise peaked and waned with the breeze.

"I'm not ready to talk to anybody yet," Laurie said.

"Maybe whoever's there will be inside and we can slip by," I said just before I spotted two motorboats crossing the bay, heading toward the green cabin. They looked so fast! A sprinting caribou was the fastest thing I'd seen for nearly two months. We paddled along the shoreline, attempting to slip past the cabin unnoticed. But a cheerful human voice broke my concentration and yelled, "Hello, come on over." The two motorboats holding four men each pulled up to the dock.

"Oh ... sure, thanks!" I said with feigned delight.

"Where'd ya come from?" the youngest of the group asked. He was probably in his mid-thirties.

"We left Wollaston Lake a while ago, paddled north, and now we're headed back," I vaguely explained.

"Oh," he said, not fully comprehending where we came from or even where he was. They had simply been dropped off by a floatplane somewhere in Canada. "So how long ya been rowing?"

"We've been *paddling* a few months."

"I mean on this particular trip. How long ya been out?"

"A few months," I repeated matter-of-factly. "We left Wollaston Lake, just upstream of here, back in early July, paddled north into the tundra, and now we're going back."

"You've been canoeing for two months?"

"Well ... about two and a half I guess."

"No way, really? Jeez, I thought we were roughing it."

We floated for about fifteen minutes, telling stories about our trip. There were eleven men in total. Some walked around with little interest in us, but most were enthralled by our adventure. The youngest was almost giggly with excitement. "Man, I gotta tell my wife about you guys! Maybe I can get her to do something like that," he said.

"Your wife? Ha! Man, you couldn't do it yourself!" another chided.

We told them about the isolation, caribou, Inuit, Chipewyan, and everything we had been experiencing. They repeatedly asked us to come in, but I hesitated to enter a building. I thought it might lead to an overnight invitation, and I wasn't ready to give up the ground for a bed.

"Oh, come on in," an older one persisted. "We've got lots of food. Everything except ice cream. What have you been craving?"

"Well, I really haven't had any cravings. We've been eating pretty good. Actually, ice cream is the only thing I thought might be nice."

"Come on, what about a nice steak?"

I really had no desire for beef.

"Fruit, eggs, beer, doughnuts? Anything at all, we've probably got it. At least come in for some coffee."

In the overheated cabin, we sat at a table for the first time in months, drank brewed coffee, and chatted for about another hour. The human interaction was surprisingly nice. Their excitement over our stories made me feel proud.

"So what's been happening in the world?" I asked.

"Oh, nuclear war. The world is destroyed," one jested.

I chuckled, then repeated the question. "Really, give us some news."

The same joker answered, "There was a coup in the Soviet Union by the hardline commies; they took Gorbachev prisoner, then the people overthrew the commies, and the Soviet Union is disbanding."

I chuckled again and said, "So nothing big has happened, eh?"

"He's telling the truth; the Soviet Union is breaking up," another confirmed.

"Are you serious?" I asked in a way that told them I was tired of being kidded.

"Yeah, really!"

"When?"

"A couple months ago. Man, this is old news!"

"Not for us!"

They viewed us like we were two Rip Van Winkles or soldiers emerging from the forest to discover that the war ended years ago. They answered our questions as best they could. We posed for a few photos and paddled off with a can of peaches and a carton of eggs.

CHAPTER FOURTEEN

HOMECOMING

MILE 882–1012

"We shall not cease from exploration

And the end of all our exploring

Will be to arrive where we started

And know the place for the first time."

—T.S. Eliot

The mist thickened to a steady drizzle as we paddled toward our July 5 campsite. After about an hour from the cabin, I saw the tall tree that we had used to anchor our tarp. At its base were my hand-crafted portage blocks that I lost so long ago.

We ate the peaches from the can and dashed into the tent as another storm brewed. The wind grew stronger through the chilly night; violent waves crashed on our granite shore in the morning. In no hurry, we lingered through the morning, eating omelets made from the fresh eggs, hoping the wind would die. By midmorning, impatient, we paddled into the raging wind and waves. Our confidence in these conditions allowed us to travel swiftly, unlike when we camped here in July when the waves tossed us against the shore and swamped our boat.

We reached Wollaston Lake, chose a direct route through some islands, risked large crossings that had kept us along shore last time, and camped on a lovely island a couple of miles from shore, just twenty-two miles from the village.

Our evening campfire lacked the cheeriness of recent camps, with tense chats about our uncertain future.

"Where do we even drive to when we get to the truck?" I wondered aloud.

"A phone. I need to call my mom."

"You know what I mean. What next?"

"Let's not talk about it."

"Right. Let's just be here. We'll have a final party tomorrow night."

I let the sadness creep in and strolled around the island until the sleet and cold drove me into the tent. Did Tyrrell linger in camp, prolonging his exit? I suppose he did on his first trip when his companions put him in a tent on the ice, near death, and raced to Churchill for help. I imagined Oberholtzer collapsing in a bunk in Churchill, relieved after months of arduous travel. Mallet had a job to do; I imagine his pragmatism, just doing the work to get back to the office and report his findings. Downes was a tourist like us, out there witnessing the fading days of canoe culture in the Far North. He lingered in that trading post on Windy Lake, hunting with the Schweder family, until he boarded a floatplane for Churchill. Maybe he stared at the ceiling in the bunkhouse like I stared at the ceiling in our tent, torn between the fantasy of staying and the reality of leaving.

The wind blew from the north through the following day,

pushing us toward town much faster than I wanted. Motor-boats appeared by midafternoon, carrying fishermen back to the village.

"If we go much farther, we'll be in sight of the village. Maybe we should camp," I said around 3 p.m.

We paddled to an island and discovered the town dump. We found more of the same as we continued along the shore.

"This stinks!" I complained. "We need the perfect final campsite, but this stinks." The sleet continued to fall as we stood in a littered clearing. Chipewyan motored by; I hid as if we were sneaking around on someone else's property. The charm of the wilderness was gone, the cold seemed harder to take, and I wanted desperately to be back north.

"We should have moved slower the last few days," Laurie said.

"Well, we're here now," I snapped. "What do you want to do?"

Laurie didn't answer.

"This is silly," I said. "Last night was a good night. Let's make that one our last and end the trip today."

We drifted toward town, silent as we turned into the bay and saw the buildings. David's canoe was beached alongside his dock. We ground the bow into the sand, hopped out, and pulled the red canoe ashore for the last time. I didn't linger. Laurie fiddled with something on the packs while I bounded to the trailer where David and Paula lived.

***

Paula answered my knock with a curious "Hello?"

"Hi," I said as cheerfully as I could.

She opened the door cautiously, eyebrows furrowed.

"Remember us?"

She stuttered a bit, then looked past me and saw Laurie walking up. "Oh, the canoeists! Of course, come in. I didn't recognize you with the full beard. Wow, you're back! We were getting worried about you. Summer ended over a month ago!"

"Well, it was a long trip."

Her reaction gave me a mental glimpse of myself. Ragged, red beard and long hair curling from under a knit hat. I suddenly remembered that I never repaired the split seam in the back of my pants that extended six inches down from the beltline. My green wool shirt that had doubled as an apron was caked with the dried dough of a dozen bannocks. I wiped it as best I could, exposing my hands, blackened from ashes of eighty campfires. Laurie chatted excitedly with Paula. She wore the grime of the North Country better than I did. Her weathered face under that green felt hat made her eyes and teeth shine, despite the streak of ash across her cheek.

David, my interpreter and town guide, would be away for two days so we accepted Paula's offer to stay. We lingered awkwardly around the house, figuring out what to do with ourselves. There was no tent to set up, no fire to tend, and no dishes to wash. I reluctantly accepted Paula's offer to use their shower since we sat on her furniture. It symbolized the end. I always feel that way at the end of a trip. I like my wilderness clothes; keeping them on makes the trip last a little longer. Laurie had no such hesitations. Seeing her clean glow, I abandoned my reluctance and showered.

My reluctance vanished as the endless supply of warm water flowed over my body. But the brownish-gray water circling the drain was shocking. I borrowed some shampoo from the corner stand and lathered, rinsed, repeated and repeated and repeated until the water flowed clear. Toweling dry, I saw my upper body in the mirror. Each rib was exposed under my chest that looked more defined than when I left. I felt good. Healthy. Laurie saw that I forgot to bring in clothes and laid out my cleanest dirty shirt and spare pants. With just two pairs of socks for the trip, it felt better for Paula's floors to walk barefoot.

That evening we slept in a large, soft bed. I heard the wind raging outside, but the solid walls kept the cold away.

"The tent should be shaking. This feels really weird," I whispered to Laurie.

"We should be cold, too."

"I know; I miss it already."

I slept fitfully that night, uncomfortable with our comfortable environment. For the first time in months, I didn't know whether it was hot or cold, raining, sunny, or snowing outside. I panicked, like I had lost a part of me, and walked to the bay window. A powerful blizzard raged outside. The trees bent in the wind, the bay was tossed in a flurry of white, and I sat comfortably untouched by nature, separated by a thin pane of glass. I suppose that's the mark of civilization—mastery over the elements. But in just one day, I missed the awareness. I spent the rest of the morning reading in the windowsill, watching the snowstorm.

Our moods lightened when David returned and guided us into the lives of the town's people. Evening games, chats, and daytime meetings with locals filled three wonderful days as we told stories of our adventures that already seemed so long ago.

As guests at a town meeting, we laid out the map they gave us in July. The energy in the room was exciting. I described the condition of trails, the cabins, the fire, and anything else we saw that I thought might interest them. I told about campsites and graves, inukshuks and portage trails. I sensed some impatience as I rambled on until a man a little older than me interrupted with, "Did you see the caribou? Where are they?" The room came alive as I told the stories about the vast herds. Some laughed, some nodded. I couldn't understand the conversations that erupted but I felt that they were reminiscing about their own caribou memories.

I caught the eye of the same old man who sketched the route north through the little lakes in July. I'm not sure if he understood my stories, but I think his subtle grin indicated approval. If he was eighty years old, he would have been born about the time Ernest Oberholtzer launched his trip and in his twenties when Prentice Downes traveled through. Maybe he was camped on the Thlewiaza River when Downes sought directions to Nueltin Lake. Perhaps he gave Downes caribou jerky, like I received, in exchange for goods. Regardless, realizing that I was standing in a room directly connected to those early travelers collapsed my sense of time. The old history that drove me north was not as long ago as it seemed. But the changes that these northern people were experiencing have been immense. I was grateful to meet the Edthen Eldeli and have this connection to their past.

We were at the dock the next morning, September 18, when Skipper Jim arrived with the barge.

"Ah, glad to see you made it back. I'm not sure how much longer I'll be making the trips," he said.

"Can we get on this morning?"

"Sure. I've been looking forward to talking with you. We all thought about you a lot."

We retold most of our trip's exciting, well-rehearsed stories for the three hours it took to cross the lake. It was a pleasure to talk to someone who felt the romance of the North. Skipper Jim abruptly halted our chat when he jumped to duty to guide the barge to the ramp. In an unceremonial rush, we unloaded our gear and said goodbye as he scurried off to his next task.

Skipper Jim had parked our truck near the landing for us. We loaded our gear like we did at the end of any other trip, and started the long drove south. David had suggested that we stop down the road to visit his friend Peter who he thought would like to hear our story.

We arrived just before dinner. Peter's son Adam had just shot his first moose and we were there for the celebration. They welcomed us like dignitaries as course after course of North Country food covered the table. We retold the stories of the caribou and the traveling conditions. They laughed at our mishaps and we marveled at their beautiful, rustic home carved out of the forest.

Peter nodded without much expression when I talked about the fire. Then I realized this was the Peter who owned the cabin that burned, and that I had told him about the loss. He took it rather nonchalantly, like I had told him that a fence blew over in the wind. His cabin was gone. Maybe he felt it more deeply than he showed, or maybe this stoic reaction to adversity is what is necessary to thrive in the land of feast and famine.

The silence broke when Peter's wife pulled a large gray mass from a kettle that had been boiling on the stove. She placed it on a tray and Peter sliced off a piece for Adam, then one for me. I waited for Adam to take the first bite of the heart of the moose he had killed the day before. Then, while the family slapped his shoulders, cheered, and raised their glasses to honor the momentous event, I discretely took my bite. Like that night nearly three months earlier when John tossed a bag of dried caribou meat into our canoe, I grinned with each bite, humbled to be welcomed into their lives.

I had a chance to look a little deeper into their lives the next morning when I rode on the back of a four-wheeler with Adam to a nearby pond to help him collect the haul from a fishnet. It didn't feel weighty enough to sustain a family for very long. As we were bringing it in, Adam flashed an embarrassing grin when the haul produced just one fish, then shrugged a happy, "Oh well."

We ran out of gas on the way back. We talked for maybe two minutes of the thirty it took to walk to the house. I asked him something about his life; he asked me about mine. His last question was, "Is it true you can't drink the water down there?" Whether the answer was yes or no, just the question tells how drastically different our worlds were.

We got back to his home, then Laurie and I prepped to

return to ours. With the truck loaded, I waited in the driver's seat of our Ford Ranger. Laurie's green felt hat and blue wool shirt moved swiftly through the woods beyond the dirt driveway as she hurried to join me. Then she stooped to pick some berries that were well past their prime. With the red canoe inverted on the roof, we turned south from the driveway toward one last stop.

John and his family lived in La Ronge, where he worked to protect the rights and culture of the Chipewyan people. By now, we had already refined the stories about our trip. We shared them over dinner and enjoyed a wonderful evening discussing the history and politics of the Dene Nation, their relationship with the Inuit land claim, and a wide range of North Country topics.

He asked why we came and if we found what we sought. I shared my motivation to stand in remote places and repeated my "wild by nature, not by law" trope. I sensed an understanding in him but not a passion. I explained the pure joy of paddling a canoe on still waters, down swift creeks, and through churning rapids. He understood. And then I explained my intense desire to connect to the lost times, to see in the wilderness the record of the cultures that connected through the waterways and portage trails of the North Country. I explained how I desired to connect to that web of the North and paddle a canoe along the waterways of the Caribou Inuit, drift past the camps of the Dene, and follow in the wake of the traders, trappers, vagabonds, and explorers from my own heritage.

That final motivation revealed a deep understanding in John that led him to talk about his own connections to the past and his interest in preserving the stories. The conversation turned to Chief Casimir, the Chipewyan leader who thwarted government census efforts, shunned the treaty money, and led the last band of Chipewyan to live free lives in the forest around Thynara-tueh (now Kasmere Lake). Casimir was reportedly buried standing up, at his request, so he could watch over his people on their search for caribou. John's chest swelled when he retold what he revealed to me months earlier, that Chief Casimir was his great-grandfather.

John nodded when I told him we didn't find Casimir's grave on our way north in July. His jaw dropped and eyes widened when I told him about the burned forest we found there in September. Laurie's face wrinkled with empathy. I sat conflicted, feeling sympathy for John's loss, but gratitude for the opportunity to build our own strand in the web of the North.

EPILOGUE

Change is an inevitable part of anything that has a beginning. We saw change even within the months of our trip, sitting among the ashes of Fort Hall. Soon, if not already, the last forts, cabins, trails, and camps from that time when the Dene, Inuit, explorers, traders, wilderness businessmen, and adventurers shared the trails and waterways will be gone. As the physical icons of any era disappear, their stories survive in the writings and oral traditions of those who were there. And so, we tell our stories and embrace change.

The caribou population in the central Barren Lands is changing. In 1994, three years after we traveled through the migration routes of the Kaminuriak herd, their population was estimated to be about 496,000 animals. In 2008, the herd had declined to 348,000. By 2014 it was down to 265,000, and has reportedly continued a slow decline of about 2 percent yearly. Alarm bells rang over the declining caribou populations as early as the 1950s. While several older studies reported different causes, including wolf predation and overhunting, recent studies point to more complex relationships between land use and climate, including an increasing frequency of mid-winter rain. Rain in the Arctic winter was once rare or even unheard of. Now, most of the Canadian Arctic experiences at least one or two mid-winter rain events each year. Once an ice layer is formed in the snowpack, it typically persists until the spring melt. While caribou can scrape through shallow snow to eat lichen growing on rocks, their hooves are not designed to dig through ice layers caused by the refreezing of rain that falls on snow, limiting foraging and increasing starvation. This, of course, is just one explanation among many describing changes in the complexity of the northern ecosystem.

The changes in governance in the Northwest Territories that we learned about in 1991 continued to completion. In 1999, the Government of Canada enacted the Nunavut Land Claims Agreement and formally separated the new territory of Nunavut from the Northwest Territories. Nunavut is now independently governed by the Inuit people. The vast area is the fifth largest country subdivision in the world. Its boundaries remain the same as what was drawn in the 1993 Nunavut Land Settlement Agreement. I don't know if anything we did on our trip helped the Chipewyan in their efforts to document their use of the land or if anyone even remembers that we passed through. Regardless of Chipewyan participation, the greater good of having such a large territory governed by an Indigenous group is a success. I am happy to have seen the process in action, even if it was just in a town meeting in Wollaston Lake, telling stories that were likely soon forgotten.

The Ahiarmiut culture has likely experienced the most significant change of any characters in this story. In 1991, reflecting on the removal of the last Ahiarmiut families from the landscape felt like I was contemplating an event from the distant past. But it was just thirty-two years before we passed through, the same amount of time between taking the trip and writing about it. Now, the Ahiarmiut culture survives through people like David Serkoak, who was a child when his family was forcibly relocated from Ennadia Lake to Arviat. Since the 1980's to the present day, Serkoak has told the Ahiarmiut story and has fought for justice and redemption. I have not met Serkoak, or any Inuit person for that matter. Writing about them as part of my northern journey seems disingenuous since they survive and tell their own story. In an interview with *Northern Public Affairs* magazine, Serkoak recounts the hardships his family faced. "They never experience[d] salt water before, high tide, low tide. Never seen a seal or taste one before. All these are new to them ... And for us, the younger group, we lost almost one hundred percent of our own dialect and adapt[ed] to coastal dialect in Inuktitut." In 2018, thanks in part to Serkoak's work, the government of Canada issued a formal apology to the Ahiarmiut. The Minister of Crown-Indigenous Relations visited the Ahiarmiut in Arviat and said, "This apology is a tribute to their spirit and their memories. It is an opportunity for all Canadians to learn about and reflect upon a dark chapter in our history. I humbly and sincerely offer these words to all Ahiarmiut past and present. We are sorry." The apology came with a settlement agreement of $5 million.

In the thirty-three years between leaving Wollaston Lake and writing the final version of this book, Laurie and I raised a family, accomplished the bulk of our careers, and completed scores of small, family-oriented trips in the wilderness areas of the American West. Sure, those areas had boundaries, people, and road access, and sometimes, permits were required. But they were magical. We plotted routes using satellite imagery, carried phones and GPS devices, used maps with descriptions of hazards, and even paid for shuttles to take us back to where we started. On each successive trip, I let a little bit more of that wilderness idealism that inspired me to cross the line in 1991 fade. With modern digital maps I even re-located the true "middle of nowhere"—the farthest spot on the continent from any road or coast. As it turns out, Laurie and I missed it by a hundred miles or so. Although my wilderness ethics evolved to suit life's changes, I am grateful to have experienced the North Country in those end times before the information revolution took hold.

We raised three sons on the rivers of the American West. Our methods of travel changed as our family grew. Family-friendly inflatable rafts and kayaks replaced our canoe. I like to think that the wilderness they saw as kids inspired their own adventures and helped build foundations for their lives. While in their late teens and early twenties, we watched our oldest son, Nolan, tramp around New Zealand for six months, our middle son, Spencer, head to Mexico to climb for a season, and our youngest son, Grant, work at a canoe camp in Minnesota. When Nolan was about the age that Laurie and I were when we headed north, he led the five of us and eleven friends on a twenty-one-day rafting trip through the Grand Canyon.

The physical closeness of camping in a narrow canyon and the sharing of stories of our lives for three weeks inspired three significant questions from my family and myself: When was I going to do something about my sleep apnea? When was I going to stop talking and finish the story you're reading now? And would we ever do something like that again?

EPILOGUE

At that last question I grinned a bit, looked at Laurie, then at my sons, and said, "Ever wonder what's really in the middle of nowhere?"

SELECTED BIBLIOGRAPHY

Cockburn, Robert H. "North or Reindeer: The 1940 Trip Journal of Prentice G. Downes." *The Beaver*, Spring 1983, 36-43.

Davidson, James W., and Rugge, J. *Great Heart: The History of a Labrador Adventure*. New York: Kodansha America Inc., 1997.

Downes, Prentice G. *Sleeping Island*. New York: Coward-McCann, 1943.

Grey Owl (Delaney, Archibald). *Grey Owl: Three Complete Unabridged Canadian Classics*. Richmond Hill: Firefly Books, 2001.

Harper, Francis. *The Barren Ground Caribou of Keewatin*. Lawrence: University of Kansas Museum of Natural History, 1955.

Holland, Lynda, and Khailther, Marian A. *The Dene Elders Project Volumes 1 & 2*. Holland-Dalby Educational Consulting, 2002.

Keighley, Sydney A. *Trader, Tripper, Trapper: The Life of a Bay Man*. Winnipeg, Manitoba: Watson and Dwyer Publishing, 1989.

Kesselheim, Alan. *Water and Sky: Reflections of a Northern Year*. Golden: Fulcrum Books, 1989.

Mallet, Captain Thierry. *Glimpses of the Barren Lands*. New York: Revillon Frères, 1930.

Mallet, Captain Thierry. "Exploring the Kazan." *The Beaver*, March 1950, 22-25.

Mason, Bill. *Path of the Paddle*. Minocqua: Northword Press Inc., 1989.

Mowat, Farley. *Tundra: Volume III, The Top of the World Trilogy*. Salt Lake City: Peregrine Smith Books, 1989.

Mowat, Farley. *People of the Deer*. Little, Brown, and Co., 1952.

Norment, Christopher. *In the North of Our Lives: A Year in the Wilderness of Northern Canada*. UNKNO, 1989.

Olson, Sigurd. *Songs of the North: A Sigurd Olson Reader*. New York: Penguin Books, 1987.

Paddock, Joe. *Keeper of the Wild: The Life of Ernest Oberholtzer*. St. Paul: Minnesota Historical Society Press, 2001.

Pelly, David F. *The Old Way North*. St. Paul: Borealis Books, 2008

Pelly, David F. "They will have our words." *Above & Beyond*, March/April 2004, 43-46.

Rasmussen, Knud. *Across Arctic America: Narrative of the Fifth Thule Expedition (Classic Reprint Series)*. Fairbanks: University of Alaska Press, 1999.

Robertson, Heather. *Measuring Mother Earth: How Joe the Kid Became Tyrrell of the North*. Toronto: McClelland and Stewart, 2007.

Rowland, John J. *Cache Lake Country: Life in the North Woods*. New York: W.W. Norton and Company, 1947.

Tyrrell, J.B. *Report of the Doobaunt, Kazan and Ferguson Rivers and the Northwest Coast of Hudson Bay*. Ottawa, Ontario: Annual Report of the Geological Survey, 1898.

Tyrrell, J.W. and Heming, A. *Across the Sub-Arctics of Canada: A Journey of 3,200 Miles by Canoe and Snowshoe Through the Barren Lands*. Toronto: W. Briggs, 1897.

www.ingramcontent.com/pod-product-compliance
Lightning Source LLC
Chambersburg PA
CBHW021701120626
46545CB00004B/1344